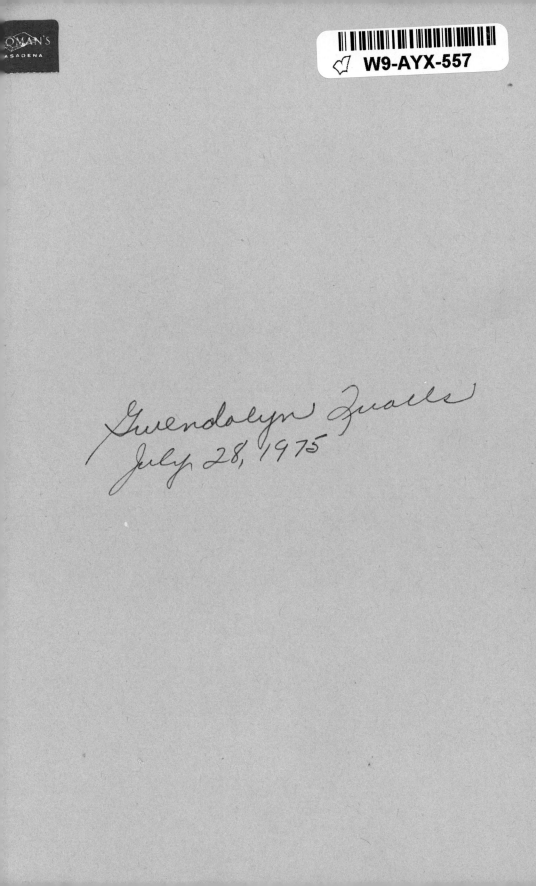

Gwendolyn Qualls
July 28, 1975

PEROFF

By L. H. Whittemore

PEROFF
The Man Who Knew Too Much

by L. H. WHITTEMORE

WILLIAM MORROW AND COMPANY, INC.

NEW YORK   1975

A special thanks to Tom and Kay . . .

Phil Manuel and Bill Gallinaro, of the Senate Permanent
Subcommittee on Investigations, have spent a huge chunk of their
lives on the Peroff story. The author is awed by their work and
grateful for their kind help.

Once again, Marguerite Cannavaro is mentioned here as more than
the best transcriber and typist I know.

John Hawkins and Steve Sheppard have my thanks once more.

I am also indebted to Jim Landis. Readers seldom are allowed to
appreciate the work of a fine editor. Only the author really knows.

Library of Congress Cataloging in Publication Data

Whittemore, L   H
  Peroff : the man who knew too much.

  1. Peroff, Frank. 2. Swindlers and swindling—
Biography. I. Title: The man who knew too much.
HV6248.P415W48   364.1′63′0924   [B]   75-8767
ISBN 0-688-02934-5

Design: H. Roberts

TO GLORIA, EVA AND LORNA

To the Reader

All characters in this book are real. All events did take place as described, to the best of my knowledge and research. U. S. Government documents verify most, if not all, of the details. Frank Peroff is a real person, now using a new name.

On the other hand, many names of characters, including their exact titles, are fictitious.

The real names are: Vernon Acree, Mr. Andrews, Michael Armstrong, John Bartels, Carl Bornstein, Conrad Bouchard, George Brosan, J. Fred Buzhardt, Frank Cotroni, Pepe Cotroni, Vic Cotroni, Paul Curran, Bill Gallinaro, Peter Grant, Lou Greco, Senator Henry Jackson, Norman LeBlanc, Phil Manuel, Mr. Meyers, John Mitchell, Richard Nixon, Mr. Phelps, Maurice Stans, Robert Vesco and John Wing.

L.H.W.

The two men left Canada with half a million dollars' worth of counterfeit money. The bills were printed as United States currency, all hundreds and fifties, tightly packed inside a suitcase. The men boarded a plane in Montreal and flew directly to Amsterdam, where they put seventy-two thousand dollars' worth of the bogus money into a hashish deal. Then they took a flight to Rome.

The balance of the counterfeit bills, exactly $428,000 worth, was scheduled to be placed in the hands of a global crook named Frank Peroff, who could put the bad paper into various bank swindles in Europe and turn it into large sums of real cash. But Peroff had other ideas. Wanting no part of the shipment, he reached out for help instead.

That decision was the biggest mistake of his life. It plunged him from the heights of worldwide criminal success into a nightmare of undercover agentry and never-ending blackmail. Over the course of less than a year, he would find himself in constant danger, with no more careful control over his own decisions, bankrupt, his family uprooted, his surroundings like a hall of mirrors in which the faces of the underworld and the government became indistinguishable one from the other. Even Peroff, the master con man, would be unable to tell which were the good guys . . . and which were the bad.

I

One morning in early January, 1973, a large, well-dressed man named Frank Peroff was strolling up the Via Veneto, the so-called American street in Rome, thinking that at the age of thirty-seven he had arrived at a major turning point in his life. Years of criminal activity, including a string of minor arrests but no major convictions or time in jail, were behind him. He had achieved rare heights of international wheeling and dealing as a "paper man" specializing in stolen stocks and counterfeit money, his schemes having reached into nearly fifty countries of the world. Yet there was still time to legitimize, go straight, make a new future as an honest businessman.

Everything, this morning, seemed to be going well. He had just concluded a meeting at the Hotel Excelsior in Rome with an ex-diplomat from Panama who had been part of one of his operations. Their conversation had focused upon Peroff's ongoing scheme involving the currency of Zambia, the small African nation, and he was hopeful of winding up with a pile of cash before it ended. Aside from that venture, all of his other projects were on the level and growing.

Many of his current deals had been started with phony certificates of credit and stock, but they were, in fact, reputable enterprises. There was a hospital project here in Rome, high on Peroff's list of major investments. Another venture involved negotiations to purchase an entire shipyard in Italy. He had sunk cash into a leather factory and had just begun a deal having to do with olive oil. Also he had interest in several hotels, in Gambia and England and

France, the latter on the Riviera. All of these projects required careful nurturing. Peroff's gradual movement away from crime had been steady but painful, the withdrawal agony equal to that suffered by any addict trying to kick his habit. But it was working.

He was on his way up the Via Veneto, heading toward the spot where he had parked his black Mercedes. Peroff's appearance was striking. He stood over six feet and weighed more than two-fifty, and he wore expensive clothing that was finely tailored to fit his large frame. Today he wore a checked sports jacket over an open-collar shirt, a heavy gold medallion hanging down on his chest. He wore dark glasses and puffed on a long, thin cigar. He was Jewish, from the Bronx in New York City, but he had earned his reputation as an underworld figure in Florida, where he'd been given the nickname Miami Frank.

Since leaving Florida not quite two years before he had risen dramatically in his profession, such as it was, acting almost as a one-man crime syndicate, a loner who had private jets at his disposal and key contacts all over Europe. But it was difficult to place him in any of the normal categories associated with criminals. As a paper man he dealt with hot stocks and bonds, counterfeit money, stolen credit cards, forged traveler's checks, certificates of stock, time deposits, insurance papers, passports and immigration documents. He had passed or placed millions of dollars' worth of bad paper—passing it on to other crooks, for a fee, or placing it into deals and schemes of his own. He was a con artist, scam expert, bank swindler, wheeler-dealer, manipulator, gold smuggler, money-washer, pilot for mob figures—a businessman with an adventurous spirit and a larcenous mind. Through it all, he had maintained an extraordinary degree of privacy and personal control over his dealings, always remaining a step removed, acting as the invisible but necessary link, the coordinator who set the rules and created the plots but who never surfaced. It was this privacy and control which were about to be lost.

It was near noon in the northern sector of Rome when Peroff heard his name being called. A short man in a modern-style blue suit was waving his arms at him and yelling, "Frank! Frank! How're you doing?" Peroff had no idea who the fellow was, and he nearly laughed out loud at the sight of the man's flamboyant

4

costume draped over his dumpy body and balding head. The stranger looked completely out of place, a combination of a wealthy hippie and a cowboy, with his straw hat and colorful neckerchief and fancy suit and even platform shoes. The man was speaking in French.

Peroff stared at him, trying to recall who he might be. The man had switched to Italian, which Peroff understood. But the stranger gestured frantically, beginning all over again in English. Before Peroff could do anything more than squint through his dark glasses, the man shouted, "Conrad is my boss! Conrad? Conrad!" At which point it all came clear and Peroff stood there in amazement. Without warning he had bumped into a representative of the Canadian Mafia, right in the midst of a crowded street in Rome, four thousand miles from Montreal.

"You remember me, Frank? I'm Angie! I met you when you came to see Conrad, right?"

Peroff knew. Conrad Bouchard, age forty-one, the highest-ranking Frenchman connected to the Canadian mob. An ex-nightclub singer, Bouchard was almost handsome, his voice having a quality similar to that of Vic Damone, although Connie Bouchard sang in French and was strictly a local talent in Montreal, where he'd been born and raised. To look at him, Peroff recalled, one would never guess the range and depth of the man's crimes or his capability for violence.

"You remember me, Frank?"

Sure, he thought, nodding and glancing at his watch. It was now exactly noon. He had a hundred calls to make. Impatient to get going, he said nothing, remembering that he had seen Angie only once, in Canada, when he had first met Bouchard. Angie was on the underworld leader's payroll, one of his many hit men. At that time, Angie had worn a wrinkled suit under an old tan raincoat —and no wonder, Peroff thought, that I didn't recognize him at first.

"I've been looking all over Europe for you, Frank! Conrad sent me to find you! He wants to speak to you!"

"Bullshit," Peroff muttered, looking around, over his shoulder, to see if he was being watched. For Chrissake, he thought, I'm

5

standing here with the mob! Suddenly annoyed, he removed his sunglasses and glared down at Angie and said, "Connie is in the can. He ain't looking for nobody."

It was almost exactly a year ago when Bouchard had been arrested in Montreal and thrown into prison for having masterminded a ten-million-dollar heroin-smuggling scheme. Peroff had dealt with him only during the six months prior to that, using him as a supplier of counterfeit money and, mostly, stolen securities. All of his business with Bouchard had involved bad paper.

The relationship had begun in the summer of 1971, when Peroff was still living in Florida but transferring all his crooked activities over to Europe. A mutual friend had called to say that Bouchard wanted a meeting, so Peroff had flown up to Montreal, where he'd been ushered around the underworld in the manner of a visiting dignitary. Bouchard had given him what amounted to a personal demonstration of his prestige and power, taking him to the best nightclubs and introducing him to various members of the mob. On the surface the French-Canadian was generous and outgoing, warm and polite, throwing money around and buying meals and drinks for whole crowds, and at one point he showed Peroff a suitcase jammed with $800,000 of real American cash.

On that trip, Peroff had been impressed by Bouchard's capacity to survive as a criminal. The man's prior convictions stretched back twenty years, forming a spectacular record involving robbery, violence and fraud. As a mob member, Bouchard could get his hands on huge amounts of stolen stocks and other negotiable paper. He had printers who could turn out millions of dollars' worth of counterfeit money in both Canadian and American bills. He ran a credit-card ring composed of postmen who stole the cards from their mailbags. His education had stopped somewhere around the third grade, but he was shrewd and inventive as a crook.

When Peroff sat down with him to talk business, Bouchard announced that he had become the world's leading producer of counterfeit traveler's checks. Peroff saw some samples, which had all the earmarks of the real ones, down to the smallest details of the printing. Impressed, Peroff put in an order for three million dollars' worth of hundred-dollar checks. He would pay Bouchard 4 percent and pass them to another paper man in Europe for 10 percent, earning a profit of $180,000 just to make the transfer. But the traveler's checks never were delivered. Apparently they had been diverted to mob figures in New York who had peddled them to a U. S. Army general in South Vietnam.

So Peroff had reordered a shipment of checks and, meanwhile, had begun doing business with Bouchard in other areas of the bad-paper field. Within a period of several weeks in late 1971 he received from Bouchard about two million dollars in counterfeit money and nearly eight million dollars' worth of hot stocks and bonds stolen from airports and brokerage houses. Peroff allegedly flew into New York to receive the shipments from a supplier in the Manhattan Hotel; and from there he was able to place the paper in crooked deals in Switzerland, Germany and England, turning it into sizable sums of good cash for himself. It was a two-way street, Bouchard being the supplier of the goods and Peroff providing the outlet for them.

All during that time, however, Conrad Bouchard had been at the peak of his heroin business. In fact, his paper deals with Peroff had been done primarily to finance new narcotics-smuggling schemes originating in Mexico and France. Within four years, Bouchard himself had estimated that he had directed the smuggling of nearly a ton of heroin into Canada and the United States, traveling frequently to Acapulco and Paris to put together one deal after another.

But then came his arrest in January of 1972, exactly one year before, on conspiracy charges in Montreal. One of Bouchard's henchmen was seized with the narcotics while Bouchard himself was arrested on conspiracy charges at the Bonaventure Hotel.

Peroff didn't find out until three months later, in April, when he called Canada to inquire about his shipment of bogus traveler's checks. At once he vowed to forget that he even knew the name of Conrad Bouchard. That was the end of the brief relationship, as far as he was concerned. The news of the arrest had come as a shock, but not totally. Bouchard had violated one of Peroff's most sacred credos as a criminal: Never do something that will get the world mad at you; go against institutions, not individuals. Peroff had hurt large banks and corporations, governments and countries, the Mafia and even the Vatican, but he had never dealt in violence or narcotics. Heroin was a dirty, sordid business that directly affected individuals —killed them, in fact—and he had avoided it at all costs. If you got caught smuggling narcotics, the way Bouchard had gotten nabbed, the world became so angry that there was no chance of survival. It was the same as kidnapping or rape or murder, possibly worse, and no way was Connie Bouchard going to see the street again.

Shortly after hearing of Bouchard's arrest, Peroff moved his family from Spain to Rome. He unloaded dozens of boxes full of the French-Canadian's hot stocks and bonds and bogus money, and he held a huge bonfire with it on the grounds of his lavish villa. It took him three days to burn it all and it became a kind of symbolic break with the Canadian Mafia, a cleansing of his hands.

Since then he had forced Bouchard out of his mind, preferring to deal with European suppliers of bad paper and, more important, beginning his gradual transformation into an honest businessman. And now, ten months later, standing on this crowded street in Rome, he was taken aback by Angie's next words:

"No, Frank, you're wrong! Conrad got out on bail! He's out, he's free—and he's looking for you!"

"What do you mean?" he asked. "Connie got caught with junk! On a ten-million-dollar drug rap! I thought his ass was locked up for good."

"No, no. Conrad spent six months in the can, but his trial was delayed, so back in June they let him put up bond! We've been trying to find you ever since!"

Peroff puffed on his cigar, letting Angie's words sink in. "Where is he?"

"In Montreal! Listen, we gotta go call him right away. He'll be very glad to hear from you, Frank. Come on, we'll get to a phone, let's go."

Peroff shrugged, disgusted at the thought of possibly being seen with someone of Angie's background. While he had worked for the mob, he had done so at a distance, seldom socializing with its members. Before he knew it, though, they had walked into the Hotel Excelsior where, in the lobby, Angie was already placing a long-distance collect call to his boss in Canada.

"Conrad? Listen, I'm in Rome! I'm with Frank Peroff . . . Yeah, right, I found him!"

Angie handed him the phone and Peroff listened to the faraway voice on the line, instantly recognizing Bouchard's distinct French accent and broken English. "Frank?" the voice was saying. "How are ya? What are ya doing, eh? Where've you been?"

Peroff felt a leap of curiosity. True, Bouchard was the worst sort of criminal; he was a liar and a cheat and, without question, a vicious animal; but he was also a fountain of information about the underworld. It might even be fun to hear the latest news.

"Hi, Connie."

"You son of a bitch," Bouchard said with affection. "I'm free, you know? I've been trying to get in touch with you!"

"I *just heard* that you got out of the can. I didn't know!"

"Yeah, I'm out, but the bail restrictions, eh? I got a lot of problems, you see?"

"Right, Connie."

"Listen, we should talk, yes?"

"Sure," Peroff said, suppressing a slight concern. The last thing he wanted or needed was to resume business dealings with Bouchard.

"But Frank, I don't want to talk on this phone right now, eh? I'll go out to another number. Let me give you a safe one where you can call me back."

Peroff jotted down the new number in Montreal. "Call me there in four hours," Bouchard was saying. "We can catch up on old times, right?"

"Yeah."

When he hung up, Peroff's mind turned back to the many calls and appointments he had scheduled for the rest of the afternoon.

"Frank," said Angie, "let's you and I do the town tonight, eh?"

Peroff looked around the lobby again. "I may have to leave Rome on a trip," he lied. "But give me the number where you're staying. Maybe I'll buzz you later."

He broke free and hurried outside, walking quickly to his car at the top of the Via Veneto. Behind the wheel of the black Mercedes, driving through the countryside, he crumpled up the paper on which Angie had written his number and tossed it out the window.

He lived in splendid isolation in a hilltop villa overlooking all of Rome. From his office on the third floor, he could gaze out the window and see St. Peter's and the Seven Hills in the distance.

His whole future seemed as limitless as the view from up here; he would simply call Bouchard and trade gossip with him and nothing more would come of it.

At four o'clock that day he relaxed in the easy chair by the phone. Ruth, his wife, was downstairs fixing dinner. Peroff glanced out the window again, at the fields that sloped away from the house. There were flocks of grazing sheep on them, and, closer to the house, he could see the vineyard and the swimming pool. On the opposite side, the rear yard ended at a cliff that dropped three hundred feet. For a while Peroff stared down at the grounds in front of the villa, at the huge iron gate near the main road, at the large circular driveway with the statue and rose gardens in the center, and he saw his three children playing.

The children. There were two girls, the oldest aged twelve, and the third child was a boy, six, whose looks seemed almost angelic. Underneath, pervading Peroff's whole existence, had been his family. Ruth and the kids had been the most precious aspect of life, and it was for them that he had taken such care to remain anonymous and untouchable, for them that he had been trying to "legitimize" his activities.

It had become increasingly difficult to explain to them about his world. The oldest girl, Janet, was particularly bright and curious. Her questions were daily becoming sharper, more astute, and at times he had found it impossible to look her directly in the eyes.

He thought again of Ruth, the woman who had been his wife and confidant over thirteen years. He remembered promising her, back in their Florida days, to do what he could to change. Well, he thought, it's been up and down. One adventure, a search for gold in the Tonga Islands, had ended even before they had left the States. But the past year in Europe, first in Spain and now in Italy, had been a kind of roller-coaster ride, filled with honest ventures but taking him over the gamut of paper crimes, at a much higher level than before. There had been a long European banking caper, a complicated swindle which reportedly had grossed nearly a million dollars in cash after eight months. There was also the money-washing scheme in Zambia, involving both real and counterfeit currency, and that adventure still had not yet ended. There had been too many alluring propositions which he had been unable to resist, although now he was nearing the final period of transition. The prospects for legitimizing were brighter than ever.

The villa had sixteen phones and two separate lines, so Peroff could avoid asking a caller to wait on "hold" while he spoke to a second party. Telephones and airplanes were natural tools for Peroff; they made the world a tiny place, as if it were his own chess board. He could put enormous, complex deals into motion by just using the phone, and he could bring people together with private planes so they could meet and travel in secret.

But as he dialed Bouchard's number, he told himself that this was one call which meant absolutely nothing. It was a courtesy, no more. He leaned back and decided to simply enjoy the conversation and to avoid all talk of business.

"Hallo?"

"Connie? What's new?"

As Bouchard began talking amiably, Peroff found himself lapping up the tidbits about who was in jail and what mobsters were in trouble—all the fights, rumors and gossip within the underworld. Bouchard told about his arrest a year ago, stressing that the charge was "conspiracy" to smuggle heroin.

"How was life in the can?" Peroff asked.

"Ah, well, I took over the place."

"Yeah?" Peroff replied, laughing.

"Sure, I was king of the jail."

"How the hell did you get out?"

Bouchard explained that he had been granted $25,000 cash bail because his trial had been delayed so long. The prosecutor had objected strongly, arguing that "the public is entitled to safety" and calling the case "one of the most important in the annals of the Montreal judicial district." But the judge had no choice but to let Bouchard go, though under stringent bail restrictions. His Canadian passport was taken away and he was ordered not to leave the city limits of Montreal and to be home each night by nine o'clock. Still, he was walking free.

It was amazing how much difficulty the authorities had trying to put someone like Bouchard away for good. Here was the top Frenchman in the Montreal mob, yet all they could catch him on was fifteen kilos out of nearly a thousand. Even then they only had him on circumstantial evidence, so that with enough legal help it was possible that he could beat the charges at his trial in the future.

"I got a million expenses," Bouchard was saying. "Not only this trial, you know, but the others."

The others, Peroff knew, involved the counterfeit traveler's checks and also bogus postage stamps and assorted other schemes in which he'd been caught. They were minor charges compared to the heroin case, but obviously the legal fees were high.

"I'm paying lawyers all over the map," Bouchard went on. "And they tap my phone about twice a day," he added, referring to the fact that the Royal Canadian Mounted Police had him under surveillance. "I gotta be home every night and it's just a bad deal, you know? The bail, the lawyers, they're all sucking the bread away."

Peroff shifted uneasily in his chair. Was Bouchard leading up to something? This was not the same man he had known. He had never heard the Canadian's voice sound so bitter and desperate. But why? After all, Connie Bouchard was the right arm for the legendary Lou Greco, whose credit was good for any amount of narcotics that could be ordered. Greco was known as the "junk man" for his volume of heroin smuggling into the North American Continent. He was the direct representative in Canada for the powerful Magaddino crime family of Buffalo, and Bouchard, his main link to the Marseilles heroin labs, lived on the top floor of Greco's house. With such a powerful, direct source of Mafia power, how could he be in so much financial trouble?

"How's Lou?" Peroff asked.

"Greco?"

"Yeah. How's he doing?"

"You mean, Frank, you don't *know?* You didn't hear?"

"Hear what?"

"Lou Greco's dead! He died last month!"

"Connie, I really didn't know," Peroff said, and by now he was sitting upright, gripping the phone tightly, the consequences of this news just beginning to sink in. He listened, fascinated, as Bouchard recounted the details of Greco's violent but apparently accidental death, back in December, at Gino's Pizzeria in Montreal.

Greco had owned a network of Italian restaurants which he had used as his legitimate means of making a living. The pizza parlors were a front for his widespread underworld activity, primarily involving narcotics, and they were also used as meeting places for the mob as well as "drop spots" for heroin smuggled in from Europe. On the morning of his death a month ago, Greco walked into Gino's and discovered that four workers were trying to wash some grease off the floor. The Mafia boss took charge with characteristic flair. He fetched a can of gasoline, overlooking the fact that the pizza ovens were going full blast, making the air in the room stagnant and hot. He dumped out the gasoline and at that moment the entire restaurant burst into flames. Greco caught the full brunt of it, yet he managed to help the others outside to safety before collapsing. Three days later the underworld boss was dead.

When Bouchard finished describing it, Peroff could not rid himself of the vision of the flames bursting into Greco's face.

"You should've seen his funeral," Bouchard added, telling how thousands of people had attended the service, mostly mob members and their relatives, not to mention plainclothes Mounties, but no one had been more grief-stricken than Conrad Bouchard himself. "I sang *Ave Maria*," he said.

"Really?"

"Yeah, for the whole crowd. What a thing."

"Son of a bitch, Connie. I didn't know."

"First I go to the jail, eh? Then I come out and I'm facing all this crap, you know? And then the guy goes and gets himself killed."

"Where are you living, Connie?"

"Same place—in Lou's house. The top floor. But his wife is trying to sell it, so I might have to move soon. You know, it couldn't be a worse time, Frank. All these lawyers and trials. . . ."

Peroff was barely listening suddenly, because it was all becoming clear and he knew why Bouchard sounded so bitter and cynical. With Greco gone, his entire situation had changed. No longer having the full backing of organized crime to finance his heroin-smuggling deals, Bouchard was undoubtedly being forced to reach out more impulsively, take more risks, even lie to other members of the mob to get what he needed. On the one hand he was trying to keep from going back into prison and, on the other, scrambling to put together dangerous deals for quick money.

"Let me have your number there," he heard Bouchard say. Peroff hesitated, pondering his choices. He was about to make up some excuse but then, unable to think of one, he found himself giving out his phone number. "Listen," Bouchard went on, "a couple of friends of mine might be going over there."

"Where?"

"To Rome. I'll tell 'em to look you up."

"What for?"

"Just a visit."

Peroff rubbed his forehead, saying nothing into the phone, waiting for more of an explanation.

"They just might come to see you, but then they'll leave."

Bouchard remained cryptic until the end. When Peroff hung up, he lit a cigar and consoled himself with the thought that he could always turn down any propositions that Bouchard's friends might offer. At dinner that night he sat at the head of the table, thinking that his current life, and certainly his future, had no place for Conrad Bouchard in it. Right now he was on another path, leading directly away from Montreal. Life here in Rome was suiting him just fine. In addition to this villa he had a house on the Costa del Sol in Spain and penthouse suites all over Europe. He had three cars, including a Cadillac, and a forty-two-foot cabin cruiser at the Port of Fumicino. There were servants and a score of shaky but growing financial assets. He and the family had taken a two-month yachting trip, not long ago, through the islands of the Mediterranean. If there was such a thing as being "successful" in crime, Peroff figured he could apply the term to himself. In order not to worry Ruth, he would tell her nothing until Bouchard's "friends" had come and gone.

Bouchard called the villa once a day over the following week, repeatedly warning, "Listen, Frank, when these guys get there, don't mess with 'em. You know? I mean, just see 'em and then you and I will talk about it. Right?" Peroff agreed, but exactly why the emissaries were coming all the way from Canada was a mystery, and, besides, this entire renewal of relations with Bouchard already seemed like a growing, invisible cyst. Here I am, he thought, at the very peak of my life, at a turning point; and Bouchard is over there in the exact opposite situation, down at the bottom, a desperate rat trying to stay out of prison. I don't want him to touch me.

The phone rang again one evening and it was Bouchard again on the line, delivering a brief message in his French accent: "I want you to talk to somebody. A friend of mine." There was a silence and Peroff waited until a low, gruff voice, right out of some bad gangster movie, growled into his ear:

"Hi, Frank. This is Herman."

Peroff made no reply, nearly laughing out loud at the absurdity of the introduction.

"I'm coming over," Herman added. "I just wanted you to hear my voice, so when you hear it again you'll know it's me."

I'll know, Peroff thought. The voice had seemed like a caricature of someone's notion of a hoodlum.

The next night there was another call from "Herman," who spoke in the same raspy voice: "Hello, Frank, it's me. I'm in Amsterdam. Hold on a minute. Here's my partner."

Peroff waited with the phone to his ear, expecting a similar growling tone, but this time it was a man with a heavy foreign accent who said, "Frank? My name is Irv! We're coming in tomorrow!" With that, the man burst into giggles.

Herman got back on the line and asked Peroff to arrange rooms for them at the Cavalieri Hilton in Rome. That was where Peroff maintained a message service for himself and a luxurious penthouse apartment for business meetings. He was paying almost $8,000 per month for the setup, which included spacious bedrooms, large salons, a kitchen and a dining room. He was too well known at the Hilton. It was better if Bouchard's crazy-sounding friends didn't go near that hotel. So after he hung up, Peroff reserved rooms at the Excelsior instead.

The two men from Canada were spending the night in Amsterdam. In the morning, Peroff checked the incoming flights and guessed that it would be a midafternoon arrival. He sent one of his helpers, a young Italian named Stefano, out to the airport to greet them and take them into town to the hotel.

That evening, at about six o'clock, Peroff parked his Cadillac near the Vio Veneto and walked slowly toward the Excelsior. The two visitors were up on the fourth floor, waiting for him. He came to the door of one of their rooms and knocked softly.

When the door opened he found himself staring at a well-dressed, gray-haired man with a horrible frown on his face. The corners of the man's mouth were turned downward in the manner of a tragedy mask or a grotesque, sorrowful clown's face. Peroff nearly turned full circle on his heels to walk in the opposite direction, thinking that maybe he had come to the wrong room.

"Hello," the man said. "Come on in. Glad to meet you, Frank. I'm Irv Spellman."

When Spellman reached out to shake hands he inexplicably burst into the same high-pitched giggles that Peroff had heard on the phone. Up went the corners of Irv Spellman's mouth while he temporarily lapsed into what seemed like hysteria. But then, just as abruptly, the giggling ended and the tragic mask returned. Peroff followed him into the hotel room without saying a word, wondering what the man might do next.

"Herman will be right out," Spellman said. "He's taking a crap," he added, his voice spiraling upward again into the high-octave range of nervous laughter. "Have a drink, Frank?"

"No. But thanks."

"Herman and I are both from Czechoslovakia. Originally, that is. We've been in Canada for fifteen years."

"I see."

"We own restaurants in Montreal."

Just then the second man emerged from the bathroom. Peroff thought it was an apparition. The man was short, no taller than five-seven, but he had to weigh at least three hundred pounds. His robe was unable to close over the massive flab of his belly. The man had arms that were like flanks of beef, and his hands seemed the size of catchers' mitts.

"Hello, Frank," came the gruff voice. "Glad to know you. I'm Herman Savotok."

Spellman and Savotok! Comedy act of the year! Peroff's hand was nearly crushed inside Savotok's as they shook, but he hardly felt it now because, to his amazement, he saw that Herman Savotok had some sort of artificial or disfigured eye. And while the bad eye veered off one way, Savotok spoke in his gruff, deep tone of voice from the opposite side of his mouth! He was about forty years old and Spellman was in his midfifties, Peroff judged.

"I'm starving," Savotok growled. "Where can we go get something to eat?"

"Well," Peroff said. "there's a nice restaurant not far from this hotel. The Piccolo Mondo."

"Good. I'll get dressed. I got something I want to show you, but not here in the room."

Peroff said as little as possible while Savotok dressed and Spellman drank, frowned, giggled and produced several brand-new, stolen credit cards.

"Conrad gave me these," he said. "Dinner is on me tonight, gentlemen!"

Savotok asked, "Frank, you ever been in the can?"

"No," Peroff replied.

"You're smart, eh?"

Yeah, Peroff thought, but how the hell am I going to get out of this mess? What have they brought with them? What has Bouchard promised them?

"Let's go eat," Savotok said.

The Piccolo Mondo (Small World) restaurant was only three blocks from the Excelsior. When they were outside, Peroff led the way down a side street, thankful that it was already dark in downtown Rome.

"Stop," Savotok said.

"What is it?"

"Here, Frank. I want to show you something."

Peroff saw him reach into his jacket. Savotok glanced furtively around, pulled out two bills and thrust them at Peroff. The three men resumed their walk down the side street. Peroff now held a bill in each hand, and just by feeling them between thumbs and forefingers he could tell they were counterfeit. One was a fifty-dollar bill, the other a hundred-dollar bill, American money, just average printing jobs, not even engraved from plates. The numbers on the fifty-dollar bill had been put on terribly.

He put the phony bills into his pocket, leading Savotok and Spellman around a dark corner. A maroon car came from behind, cruised slowly past, now stopping at the end of the block where they were heading. Peroff slowed his pace, squinting in the darkness to see if anyone had gotten out of the car, which was finally turning. It disappeared.

In front of a small hotel up ahead, a man in an overcoat stood holding a newspaper. The typical image of a cop trying to look inconspicuous. They walked past him on the opposite side of the street. The man looked up from his newspaper and Peroff quickened his pace. At the door of the restaurant, he opened it for Savotok and Spellman to pass through. He quickly gave a glance backward and followed them inside.

He sat near the corner with the two men on either side of him, his elbows on the table and his hands partially covering his face. Earlier, when they were led to their table, Savotok had asked Peroff to accompany him into the washroom. Alongside the urinals, he had unveiled two packets of fifty-dollar and hundred-dollar bills, wrapped in tissue paper, totaling $28,000 in counterfeit American money.

"We left the rest in Amsterdam," Savotok had said.

"How much more?"

"Four hundred grand."

Peroff had put the two sample packages into his own jacket before they returned to join Spellman at the table. Peroff had been unwilling to order a full meal, only prosciutto and melon, so now he was waiting, feeling miserable, while the two men attacked course after course of food.

The pair explained how they had transported the counterfeit money from Canada to Amsterdam. At Dorval Airport in Montreal, they had checked the hot suitcase with their other bags, as luggage. In the waiting area, they split up and sat apart from each other until it was time to board the plane. Savotok went first, finding a seat near the front. Spellman followed a few minutes later, walking past him inside the plane and sitting toward the rear, next to a nice elderly gentleman. All during the flight, Spellman complained that he was feeling sick, pretending to get dizzy spells, and several times he excused himself and went to the bathroom. When the plane landed in Amsterdam, Spellman staged a final "attack" and pretended to faint in the aisle. Then he stood up, holding a hand over his heart, and whispered to his elderly companion, "Will you do me a favor and get my luggage for me? Here are my tickets for the bags. I think I'm going to be sick again." The kind old man readily agreed. Spellman watched from behind a pillar in the airport as his unwitting accomplice picked up the bags, including the suitcase crammed full with counterfeit money, and walked them past the Customs desk. Had there been any problem, Spellman would have disappeared while the innocent gentleman would have been detained and possibly arrested.

"But then we had another problem," Savotok was saying, while Spellman still giggled over the story. "We're not familiar with the customs procedures here in Rome. So we took the samples and left the suitcase behind. We need your help, Frank, to get it in here."

Peroff shuddered. "You want me to go to Amsterdam and bring it in here *for* you?"

"Sure," Savotok replied. "You're a pilot, right?"

"Connie told you?"

"He said you can move Fort Knox in a plane."

"I'm not flying right now."

"But you know how to bring stuff into Italy, right?"

"I don't act as anybody's courier. Let's get that clear."

Savotok glared at him with his good eye. Spellman's frown seemed worse than usual. The first to speak was Savotok. "Let's discuss what you can get for the stuff."

"Who says I'm doing *anything* with it? What is this? I don't need your crap. If I did have a need, I can get a lot better stuff than *you've* brought. Tell Connie to forget it."

"Maybe you don't understand," Savotok said. "Bouchard's got nothing to do with this paper. And we don't work for him, either! He owes us money!"

Savotok went on to explain that a month ago, after Lou Greco's death, Bouchard had come to him with a proposition: if he, Savotok, could come up with $40,000, Bouchard would offer the right contacts in Paris. The money could be used to purchase ten kilograms of pure heroin, which was worth a quarter of a million dollars on the initial resale to mobs in North America. (For his services as a middleman, Bouchard would get a small but lucrative percentage.) Savotok went to a financier who put up the $40,000 in cash. Then he and Spellman went over to Paris and paid Bouchard's suppliers—but the Frenchmen ran off and disappeared! Savotok and Spellman were left stranded in Europe with neither the money nor the drugs, and they went back to Canada ready to murder Bouchard if he didn't make it up to them.

"Okay," Peroff said at last. "So Bouchard owes you guys a lot of bread. That's not *my* problem."

19

Savotok seemed to be trembling with suppressed anger. Breathing heavily, he said, "Connie and you made a deal."

"We did? What kind of deal?"

"He said you'll place the counterfeit for us. He *guaranteed* your help. You're already *committed*. If you don't want to perform, well, there's gonna be trouble. Not only for Bouchard, but for you, too."

Peroff was stunned. So *that* was it. Bouchard pays his debt by guaranteeing *my services*. Without even telling me! He must have given them a big story that I was all set to help them! And if I refuse, I get into the midst of a war!

Sweating as he lit a cigar, Peroff realized it was too late just to flatly refuse. These men are here because they expect my services, period. Bouchard is *counting* on the fact that I can't say no. To save his own skin, he put my neck on the line with his! Better stall, buy time, until I find a way out.

"Now," Savotok was saying, "let's talk business."

Peroff pretended to give in. "Okay," he said.

"You'll help us get the rest of it from Amsterdam, right?"

"Sure. No problem."

"And how much can you turn this counterfeit into?"

"Half a million? Well, that depends. Up to sixty percent, according to how it's done."

Savotok was pleased. "Irv, here, will be coming with you to help."

"Yeah," Spellman said. "I'll do anything you like, Frank. I'll be the courier, the front man, the patsy—anything you want."

While Spellman's giggling tapered off, Peroff wondered how to discourage him from his offer of help. If there was going to be any way out, he couldn't have him looking over his shoulder.

"Well," he said, "there's only certain places where I can fool with the stuff right now. I just got through doing a counterfeit deal in Sweden. But my man there is unavailable for the next couple of months. Maybe we'll take a trip down to Africa."

"Africa!" Spellman exclaimed.

"Yeah. There's some bad places, you know, where I can do some things. We can do some gold and diamond deals. Only thing is, we gotta go into the mines."

"Like where?"

"Well, like South Africa. Or Zambia, or the Ivory Coast. Maybe

Rhodesia. I know some people in Niger. I got a contact who knows his way around. But when we deal down there with something like this, it has to be right with the uneducated people. Right at the mines."

Spellman giggled out of nervousness. "The jungle?"

"Look, it wouldn't be a big city or anything like that. It means trips into the bush. And Irv, you can't mess around with your credit cards and all that business. Not down there, baby, because I'm telling you, we'll never make the jails. They'd kill us first."

"Why?"

"What d'ya mean, why? Who's gonna protect us? And if we *do* make the jails, they ain't like no other jail *you* ever been in. It's no joke. Down there, you got black people, African black, you know? And we're white. So if you're gonna go down there looking to jam us up, forget it."

"All right," Spellman said.

"So we work our way to the diamond mines, where I know a foreman. That would take a couple of weeks. Then, from Africa, we'd go to Hong Kong. My guy over there will actually take us across, and we'll go into Communist China."

By now, Spellman's grostesque frown had deepened, and his face had begun to twitch.

"Listen," Savotok interjected, switching the subject, "it's my idea that whatever you get, we split the take down the middle."

"No, no," Peroff replied, adding that he never got less than 60 percent of whatever he earned from the sale or placement of counterfeit money. He and Savotok continued to negotiate while Spellman, apparently still panicked over the thought of traveling into the African jungles and Red China, said nothing.

"So we got a deal," Savotok concluded.

"Yeah," Peroff lied.

Later that night, Peroff went home and showed Ruth the $28,000 in counterfeit hundreds and fifties. He dumped the packets on the kitchen table and said, "Look at this, will ya? These are just samples. They got the rest of it in Amsterdam, altogether more than four hundred grand. It's all crap. See how bad it's printed? The numbers aren't even on straight."

"What will you do?"

"I'm not dealing with it, that's for sure. You should see these two guys. There'd be nothing but trouble and aggravation. And besides, there's heat all around. I think we were being followed the whole damn night!"

On impulse he placed an angry call to Bouchard in Montreal, hoping there was still a chance to back out of the situation in an easy manner. By talking in tough language and appealing to Bouchard on his own terms, perhaps he could erase this unexpected intrusion from his life and cancel it at the source.

"Hallo?"

"Connie, it's me. It's Frank."

"Oh, yeah. How are you?"

"Listen, you son of a bitch, what is this? How come you send these guys with such shit? The quality stinks!"

"Oh, you can handle that, Frank."

"Who are *you* to tell *me* what I can handle? Connie, I really don't have any market for this stuff, not here in Europe. I've checked out all my sources," he lied, "and they're just dead. I can't do anything with it."

"Come on, Frank."

"It's true, Connie. My sources have dried up, and—"

"Frank, I know you better than that."

"Look, it's the truth!" Peroff shouted, but he realized that this line of attack was faltering. He switched abruptly to another argument. "Anyway, Connie, this Savotok tells me the stuff ain't even yours! He says he don't work for you! He says you owe him money! He told me you don't get any part of it!"

"Wait a minute, Frank! When you turn that stuff, don't give 'em a thing! I'll settle with Savotok—that's between me and him. You don't give him a nickel!"

"This whole situation stinks, Connie. You lied to them! And you lied to me, too! First you give 'em a line about us having a deal. Well, we didn't have any deal! You didn't tell me nothing about this crap! So I'm just not going through with it. I'm bowing out. Forget it!"

"You can't bow out."

"Connie, I make my own decisions. If you're so worried, I'll get the rest of the paper from them and send it all back to you."

22

"No, Frank. You can't do that."

"Why not?"

"Because it's too late, Frank."

"What do you mean?"

"Just what I said. It's too late. It's out of my hands. For you to say you don't want any part of this deal, well, you'd start a war, you know? A real war, Frank. Listen, that Savotok is a funny guy, you know?"

Peroff knew. Funny meant unpredictable, dangerous.

"Do your best, Frank. Okay?"

"Yeah," he said, the words "too late" still ringing in his mind as he hung up.

The next day, Peroff and his wife discussed all the options while the two visitors waited at the Excelsior. If he could not refuse to perform, what other choice was there but to go ahead? Yet if he *did* try to place the counterfeit money, the delicate balance of his current business deals could be tipped the wrong way. There was the prospect of more and more involvement with Bouchard, all over again, just when Peroff was directing his energies along legitimate lines.

Pondering his choices, he wondered what would happen if he *pretended* to go ahead with the counterfeit deal. What if he went along with the whole thing and then, abruptly, announced that the bills had been grabbed? What if he turned around and told Bouchard that a courier had been arrested with the bad money in his possession? What then? Perhaps he could say to Bouchard and the others, "Okay, look—the cops caught my man with the stuff. Now I'm really hot. They're after me, now, and I've lost all ability to work any more deals. You'd better stay away from me." And that would be the end of everything!

It seemed the simplest way to dispose of the whole problem. It would cost Peroff almost nothing in terms of time and effort. But there was still one hitch. In order for Bouchard to believe that the counterfeit bills had been seized by the law, he would want to see something about it in the newspaper. He would demand some evidence or proof. The question was, how did Peroff get a phony story into the news?

The only way was to have the U. S. Government do it. The Secret Service, whose headquarters for Europe was in Paris, often boasted about its confiscation of counterfeit bills. Wouldn't the agents be pleased and eager to have $428,000 worth of the stuff thrown into their laps? Surely in return they would put out a press release with the all-important cover story.

It is not often that a white-collar criminal will reach out to the authorities. Usually it means that the crook is on the verge of being caught and therefore wants to make the first move. Peroff wavered, realizing that calling the Secret Service represented only the last resort after all other options had been explored. But that afternoon his mind was made up for him.

From the top floor of his villa, he could see a black Fiat parked under some trees off the roadway. He remembered that same car from the day before, when he had driven into Rome and back. Was it possible that he, too, had fallen under surveillance? Maybe whoever had been tailing Savotok and Spellman was following him, now, as well. Either that or, by sheer coincidence, he had picked up his own heat from elsewhere. He had noticed a number of strange cars and faces over the past few days, but had been unable to come up with an explanation.

He watched the black Fiat through binoculars. The driver was facing the roadway as if ready to spring out from his hiding place. A little fat guy in the car. Well, Peroff thought, let's get it over with. He walked downstairs, grabbed a gun from a desk drawer and said to Stefano, his helper, "Come on." They went outside to the Cadillac. Peroff took the wheel and drove slowly down the driveway, through the iron gate to the road. He crept up to the black Fiat and swerved without warning to the side, facing the car, head on, partially blocking its escape route.

"Okay," he told Stefano. "Stick with me."

He hopped from the Cadillac and ran over to the driver of the Fiat, waving his gun.

"Who are you?" he yelled. "Why are you following me?"

The driver pleaded in Italian that he couldn't understand English, gesturing wildly, and Stefano repeated the questions in Italian. Peroff opened the car door and grabbed the man by his shoulder, pulling him out and tossing him to the ground. The man picked himself up, shaking, and said in Italian, "I don't know who you are! I don't know what you're talking about! It's a mistake! I'm looking at land, real estate, and—"

Peroff moved toward him. The man suddenly fled, jumping back into the Fiat and slamming the door shut behind him. He locked it, started up the engine and jammed his foot down on the gas pedal. Peroff stood watching as the Fiat's tires squealed and then took hold. The car roared past the Cadillac to the road and sped away.

There was still no explanation, but Peroff knew that he had to act soon. The Italian police could burst in unannounced and find the counterfeit bills. Police in Italy had no need of search warrants, and they could make someone leave the country within an hour. In one minute, he could lose all his possessions and assets in Europe and find himself in trouble with the U. S. Government as well. All for something he had not even initiated; all because of Conrad Bouchard and his desperate need to make money.

In the early evening, Peroff placed a call to the Secret Service headquarters in Paris. When the switchboard operator answered, he asked to speak to the boss, Tom Glazer. He knew that Glazer was the man in charge of the Service for all of Europe and Africa.

"Hello," came a new voice. "Mr. Glazer is away from the office. This is his assistant. Can I help you?"

"No. I only want to speak to Glazer."

"He's in Scotland right now. He's testifying in a trial there."

"When will he be back in Paris?"

"I'm not sure."

Cursing silently but almost relieved, Peroff gave his name and phone number and added, "Tell Glazer it's important that I talk to him soon."

"What about?"

"Never mind," Peroff said, hanging up. Now at least he was on record as having tried to make contact. There was still time to think about the move and, perhaps, back away.

The first step was to pretend to go along with Savotok and Spellman. When they called, he agreed to help them retrieve the suitcase from Amsterdam. He sent Stefano to accompany Savotok on a

25

flight to the Netherlands and back, and they brought the hot bills into the Rome airport as part of their luggage, with no problem whatsoever. Apparently Savotok had given a portion of the counterfeit money to a friend in Amsterdam, because now the suitcase contained $400,000 worth.

Peroff took Spellman out to the airport to greet the arriving flight from Amsterdam. They locked the suitcase in the trunk of the Cadillac and drove to Peroff's villa. The task was to keep pretending and, at the same time, stalling and buying time. Eventually Tom Glazer would call and Peroff would find a way to dump the bogus bills into his lap. Then, the Secret Service would issue a press release with the cover story.

Peroff was bringing the pair to his home for a specific reason, part of the plan to stall them. He would have to persuade them that several weeks were needed to perform his services. Otherwise they might just stay in Rome, looking over his shoulder the whole time. So he would take them into the house and demonstrate, personally, just how much work had to be done.

When they walked into the villa, Peroff's three children stared in awe at the sight of Savotok's massive figure and his bad eye, not to mention Spellman's ugly frown. These men were not their father's ordinary house guests. Ruth ushered the children into her husband's private office and locked the door.

Peroff was startled by the commotion, almost laughing as he led his two visitors up to the photography lab on the third floor. "In here," he told them, "I play with paper. It's just a hobby of mine—I get a kick out of it. But I've never *passed* a counterfeit bill in my life. Place it, yeah. Anyhow, I can do some very involved things in here."

Aware of how ignorant they were on the subject of counterfeit printing, he set down the suitcase on a table, next to the original stacks of hundreds and fifties that they had given him.

"You know, of course," he said, "that these bills haven't even been printed with plates."

"No," Savotok said. "What does that mean?"

"Look, this is really bad money. Even in Africa, it's gonna give us problems. Wherever we go, it's *so* bad that unless we do something to it, we're not gonna get away with anything. The paper is awful. The printing is shit. I'm gonna have to treat the whole batch."

Savotok heaved his huge bulk, breathing heavily from impatience. "What d'ya mean?" he asked. "Treat them how?"

"Well, just look at the stuff!"

Spellman took an eyeglass from his pocket and leaned over to examine the counterfeit money. The ass, Peroff thought. He doesn't even know what he's looking at.

"They're just terrible," Peroff went on. "We gotta do something to make 'em look old, so you can't see the printing as well."

"That fucking Bouchard," Savotok muttered.

"With this equipment here," Peroff said casually, "I can turn around and make every bill look different."

Savotok grumbled, "How?"

"Well, it's a long, tedious process of dunking each bill in various degrees of strength of coffee. And—"

"Coffee," Spellman exclaimed, giggling.

"Right. Then you wash the bill in a certain way, and you dry it on a print dryer and do it over again. You can take a hundred bills and make every one look different. Some older, some less wrinkled. See, you get them wrinkled when you soak and dunk them. It's a complex, difficult process. Basically I can do it right up here, the whole bit. And, as I said, this particular stuff is absolutely no good. It's *all* got to be treated. These bills are too fresh. To do the whole job, I'll need some time."

"Jesus," Savotok complained. "Bouchard said these were the best!"

"Connie's a crook, too."

"Well, how long will it take to fix 'em up?"

"At least a month."

"A month!"

"Yeah, because, see, afterwards you also have to take a wax candle and put the *feel* to it."

"Hunh?"

"But don't worry," Peroff went on, aware of Savotok's complete confusion. "It won't have the shine of the wax, if that's your concern. It just makes the paper look older. And it gets stronger, too."

Fortunately these bills were, in fact, poor in quality. On the

27

other hand, Savotok and Spellman were such novices that Peroff probably could have made them believe anything. They stood there with expressions of awe while he continued to lecture them on the fine art of counterfeit printing. That night he even treated some of the bills and, the following morning, went to their hotel to show them the difference. They were amazed. Cursing Bouchard, Savotok growled that he and Spellman would wait until all the bills had been treated in the same manner. The ploy had worked.

They were still in Savotok's hotel room at the Excelsior, admiring Peroff's "treatment" of the counterfeit samples, when the pair announced new plans.

"I'm going to fly to Paris soon," Savotok said. "But Irv, here, will stay behind to help you. As I promised, he'll be your front man, Frank. He'll be the courier or whatever you need to carry out our deal."

"Good," Peroff lied.

"Wait a minute," Spellman said. "Do you still think Africa's the best place?"

"Well," Peroff bluffed, "we could try first in Niger or over in Kenya. We could go in there armed, in case nothing works out. I mean, we might pull a couple of robberies in the diamond mines."

"What?"

"Only if we have to," Peroff went on, aware that he was being anything but subtle. The idea was to talk with enough recklessness so that Spellman would be frightened off, but to make sense at the same time. "The route," he explained, "will be Africa first. We'll work a deal for diamonds with some of the bad paper. Then we go to the Far East. We use, say, a third more of the stuff with my man in Hong Kong."

"Listen," Savotok said abruptly, "before I leave Rome, I want to buy some jewelry first. I got a girl friend in Paris."

"What kind of jewels?"

"Just some good stuff. And maybe paintings, too. You got any sources?"

Peroff thought a moment. This might be a chance to frighten Spellman even further. "Well," he said, "down in Naples I got one of the biggest sources for hot jewelry that exists. These guys, they're the young Mafioso—the new generation—you know? You just tell them what you want and they go rob it for you."

The next morning they were in the Cadillac, with Stefano driving, on their way to Naples.

"They're young guys," Peroff was saying. "But they're tough sons of bitches. They'd kill anybody on the spot. Their leader is about nineteen. He's in a little section not far from the black market. The cops don't even go there. In fact, they're not allowed."

Savotok asked, "What kind of prices?"

"Well, you get the jewelry for about a third. As I say, it's all hot stuff. You can get whatever the hell you want. And wait'll you see this kid. His name is Chino. He's got a whole gang working for him. They got broads, you know, to hustle the servicemen. And they got marijuana, guns, whatever you want."

Peroff remembered that the first time he'd gone down to see this gang of young boys, he had taken the precaution of carrying a gun. The section was run strictly by local orders of the Italian Mafia, with its own laws and its own way of policing itself. An individual in that area was guaranteed none of the customary protections of society.

"I've done business with Chino several times," he went on. "We made some deals with jewelry and religious articles. A couple of hundred grand worth. And some arms deals, too."

When they reached Naples, Peroff told Stefano to drive directly into the black market area. Soon the car came to a stop near an alley that was too narrow, so Peroff jumped out and walked the rest of the way. About a dozen gang members greeted him and Chino appeared. Peroff explained that he had brought two men who wanted to buy some jewelry.

Chino asked, "You're sure they're not cops?"

Peroff laughed. "No, man, they're anything *but* cops, believe me."

"All right. Come back tonight at eleven-thirty."

The rest of the evening was chaotic, with Peroff only half involved, part of himself always watching Savotok and Spellman from a distance, with growing distaste and contempt. Since they had four or five hours until the appointment with Chino, he took them over to the NATO base in Naples, using some fake credentials at the gate. Spellman giggled hysterically and Savotok growled with amazement as they walked right into the Officers' Club and sat down for drinks. Later they checked into a small hotel and went out for dinner, which turned into a twelve-course feast with separate plates of lobster, fish and meat. Savotok gorged himself while Spellman kept getting up from the table to offer morsels of food and bottles of champagne to other diners in the restaurant. "Would you like a taste of my herring?" he would ask a stranger, his loud laughter causing all eyes to stare. Peroff merely winked at Stefano, who was enjoying himself immensely. At the end of the meal, Spellman paid for it with a freshly stolen American Express card, a gold one which Conrad Bouchard had given him in Montreal. As he'd done at lunch, Spellman wrote in a generous tip with a flourish, apparently taking great pride in his ability as a low-grade flimflammer.

When they walked into the black market area near midnight, Peroff entertained the fantasy that both men would end up stabbed in the back. It would certainly eliminate much of his own problem. And, in fact, the fantasy almost came true. At least fifty members of the gang were surrounding them once they had reached a tiny butcher shop. Young men approached silently from doorways and alleys, glaring, and Chino appeared in their midst with a handful of glittering diamonds and gold rings. Spellman immediately examined them with his eyeglass, but then he actually dropped a ring into his pocket! Peroff stood there in disbelief as Chino quickly pushed Spellman into the butcher shop and hurled him against a large slab of beef. Spellman frantically protested, "I'm not *stealing* it, I'm *buying* it," and Chino, completely calm, asked to see his money. Terrified, Spellman purchased the ring and a gun as well.

Later, when they had reached safety again, Peroff warned Spellman that he'd better not act that way in the African bush country. "This was nothing compared to that scene," he added. "You pull that in the jungle, man, and you'll *never* get out alive."

"Never mind," Spellman moaned.

"You're chickening out?"

"Look, I'm feeling sick and I have to go to Paris with Herman. Call me there, when you're ready."

So the trip had been worth it. They *both* would be leaving Rome

30

soon and Peroff would have the freedom to dispose of the counterfeit money.

Their stay in Rome was prolonged by one more day when Spellman announced that he had to buy some "gifts" with his stolen credit card. With Stefano's help, he went to a luggage shop and purchased a single suitcase. Then he went from store to store, buying everything from clothing to perfume to gold pens to jewelry and watches. When the suitcase was filled, he went into another luggage store and purchased a new bag. From there he continued down the streets of Rome, buying an expensive chess set, some toys and dolls, and more clothing. This went on and on, even the luggage itself being purchased with the stolen card, until Spellman wound up with twelve suitcases filled with merchandise for which he would never pay.

Stefano was intrigued by Spellman's method of using the stolen card for profit. Along with the goods, which were worth $20,000 or more, Spellman picked up a three-hundred-dollar suit for Stefano plus some shirts, earning Peroff's utter contempt. In the first place, he was worried about the young man's being led astray. But more important was the fact that Stefano might learn the wrong rules. A man with any brains never, never went out on the street to pass bad paper. You could sell stolen cards to other swindlers, but you never dirtied your own hands by *using* the cards.

Peroff nearly collapsed with relief when Savotok and Spellman scheduled seats on a plane bound for Paris. He offered to have Stefano drive them to the Rome airport and see them off. They said they would stay briefly in Paris and return to Canada, with plans to come back to Rome in about a month. Spellman continued to promise that he would be "available" as a courier, once Peroff was ready for him.

Now the decision still hung in the air as to whether he should call the Secret Service again. But that night the phone rang and it was Tom Glazer, the European boss.

"I hear you've been trying to get in touch with me."

Peroff gave him some details and added, "I just don't want anything to do with it. I didn't order the stuff—it was brought here, period. All I want to do is get rid of it without being killed."

"What do you want from us?"

"Look, I just want a cover story, you know? If you could fix an article in the papers, about some courier getting grabbed with the stuff."

"Well, that wouldn't be any problem."

"See, I really have to make these guys believe it. If I say their stuff was confiscated, I gotta have a few clippings to back it up."

"I understand," Glazer said.

"Can you make it a guarantee?"

"Sure."

"Remember, I'm coming to *you* on this. Not the other way around."

"I know."

"So we have an agreement?"

"Yep."

"Because if you say no, that's okay, too. Just tell me the truth."

"Frank, you have my word."

Peroff believed him. Glazer was the very top man here in Europe for the U. S. Secret Service and could deliver.

"Thanks," Peroff said.

"Listen, Frank, I'm calling you from Scotland. I'm still over here on other matters. But I'll have our Customs attaché get in touch with you. He's at the American Embassy there in Rome. He'll see you on behalf of the Service, until I get back to Paris."

"Will you come here, then?"

"Yeah. Meanwhile, you can trust the attaché there. His name is Nunzio Galli. I'll tell him to call you. I'd like him to see the counterfeit stuff and count it. And let him take it off your hands."

"No, no," Peroff said. "First we work out the cover story."

"All right, fine."

So it was settled.

II

Nunzio Galli of U.S. Customs called from the Embassy in Rome and came out to the villa. The attaché was a middle-aged former policeman from New York City who had served the Government for many years. His demeanor was one of relaxation and candor, making Peroff feel genuinely at ease.

Peroff brought him up to his private office and dumped out the counterfeit bills. Galli whistled in awe at the sheer bulk of the bogus money, then set about the task of counting it. He took a sample hundred and said he would frame it for his office wall.

The two men met several times over the following week, usually at a small hotel about five miles from the villa, near the top of a hill with a splendid view of the countryside. Perhaps surprisingly the two men found that they had a great deal in common. Both had been born and raised in New York City and had grown up in tough ethnic neighborhoods. Peroff himself had come out of the South Bronx, where he had roamed with gangs of Irish and German and Italian youngsters; but even then he had been a loner. At age fourteen, for example, he worked after school in a defense plant, translating blueprints for German workers and earning a hundred dollars per week. Not that he could speak or read German; rather, he had bluffed his way into the job by using Yiddish that, somehow, the workers understood.

For Peroff, life was a kind of survival game requiring constant ingenuity. When he enrolled in the High School of Music and Art in Manhattan, he learned to play the trumpet and soon worked in bands all over the city. To make more money, however, he also sold mimeographed copies of stolen examinations at ten dollars apiece.

"It's a thin line," Nunzio Galli observed. "We came from similar backgrounds, but some of us became cops and others wound up in your line."

Peroff mentioned how he had joined the Navy at seventeen and how, when he returned to New York at twenty, his father and mother had moved to Florida. He no longer had any real roots, so he fell into a circle of friends who, like himself, lacked the patience to accept a "normal" sort of life.

"The world was moving too slow for me," Peroff explained. "I turned around and analyzed things, and I found that nothing was big enough or complicated enough to stop me from doing anything I wanted."

His friendships spread from Manhattan to Miami and Las Vegas, and Peroff moved among a chaotic blend of women and fast money and illicit dreams. He spent his time with people who ran the nightclubs, with the show-business crowd, with men connected to the mob. His friends were bookies and gamblers and fences and loan sharks.

"All you had to do," he said, "was learn the rules of the game and play like hell."

A tailor's son, Frank Peroff preferred being in business for himself. He and Ruth got married when he was twenty-three, and his first decision was to open a string of beauty shops in upstate New York—selling homemade cosmetics in famous-name packages. Later, in Miami, Peroff created a million-dollar clothing store—financing it almost completely with bank loans, some obtained on false pretenses. In less than two years he was charged on five counts of bankruptcy fraud. It was his first federal charge—he was acquitted—and his last.

He and Ruth moved their growing family to the suburbs of Washington, D.C., where Peroff started selling kitchen cabinets and bathroom vanities for new homes and apartments—often sabotaging his competitors' products in order to make his own seem more desirable.

During that same period, in the mid-1960s, Peroff also opened a string of retail boutiques and became involved in three car washes in Washington, D.C. He dabbled in actual construction, too, which soon became his "passport" into the world of white-collar crime. In the building profession, Peroff's eyes were opened to the endless possibilities of mortgage juggling and not-quite-legal financing. He learned that in a real sense the modern world is built on a foundation of paper, and that the higher you go the less important actual cash becomes.

"The building trade," he would tell friends later on, "is where I got my real education in paper. It's not something that happened overnight. What you need is the inclination and the talent, and then you gotta find a person who can become a bridge between you and the bad guys. And I found my bridge."

His so-called "bridge to the bad guys" was a man named Marcus Jones, and the two soon became closer than most brothers. Jones was involved in construction and real estate and had even formed his own bank in Maryland. He was a minor slumlord in Washington, D.C., and had interests in several hotels, but his main asset was his link to members of organized crime. Through the mob, Jones had unlimited sources for securities which had been stolen from airports and brokerage houses. And Peroff, who was just beginning his education, learned how to use Jones as his own source and, in turn, to sell the hot stocks to various builders.

A major builder would obtain, say, 80 percent financing for a new construction project. He might even throw in money from his own pocket, but wind up without the final 10 percent needed to complete his building. If the project cost two million dollars, that meant a shortage of $200,000—and at this point, Frank Peroff would step in to help. He would sell the builder a batch of stolen or even counterfeit stock to use as collateral for a loan from a private lender. As soon as the builder completed his project and began making money, he would buy back the collateral before it had a chance to surface; in which case, no one ever got hurt.

Peroff soon realized that a large amount of hotel and motel construction in the United States was being financed in whole or in part by stolen securities in such a manner. There was also a huge market in foreign countries. The ongoing building-construction boom in Spain, for example, was being financed by tremendous amounts of hot stock from the States. Eventually Peroff himself would dispose of at least twenty million dollars' worth of the bad paper, all around the world, not only with private lenders but in banks of every size.

When Marcus Jones decided to move down to the Bahamas, it seemed natural for Peroff to do the same. He spent time in a house in Freeport with Jones and moved his own family to Orlando, Florida, where he soon outgrew his teacher and reversed the relationship, finding his own sources for bad paper and becoming the supplier himself. He soon developed a reputation as "the end of the line"—someone who could dispose of any kind of document, for cash in return.

"Stolen stock is worth nothing," he would say, "except what you can do with it."

What he did with it varied and grew over the next five years. The possibilities for intrigue and adventure were so enormous that Peroff was never idle, always scheming and developing new plans. If the world was, in fact, made of paper, then a paper man like himself could hardly have a boring moment.

On the most basic level, Peroff would simply take orders for stock and then go get it from his sources. A man would come to him and say, "Frank, I need some assets. I was told that you could help me."

"What kind of assets?" Peroff would ask.

When the man's needs were established, Peroff would go to his own suppliers—other swindlers in Florida, sometimes mob figures—and put through his specific request. Most of the time, the transfer of phony or hot stocks was made without his having to see or touch the goods himself.

He developed a growing reputation, cultivating crooked bankers around the world, and soon it was a natural extension of his activities to get involved with airplanes. Almost any kind of plane was valuable, not only for quick and easy transportation but as a public-relations tool. If he wanted to do business with someone, it was most impressive to show up in his own plane and offer its services. At first he bought a single-engine plane merely to hop from one part of Florida to another. By this time he had a new string of car washes spread across the country, and also, he had begun traveling frequently to the Bahamas, where Marcus Jones was in-

36

volved with vending machines, real estate, car rentals and other businesses in which Peroff became a partner.

The possibilities, with the paper and now the planes, were mind-boggling to Peroff. He had flown as a pilot since his late teens and loved to take the controls as a form of relaxation, but soon he hired pilots and began buying and leasing more planes, juggling the financial arrangements so that he seldom paid anything aside from the operating costs.

It didn't take long for the word to go out that "Miami Frank" was willing and able to fly anyone or anything—except narcotics— to anywhere, for a healthy price. His fleet of eight planes became a kind of unofficial charter service for mob figures who wanted to go places without being followed or traced. He had learned how to take someone out of the United States and back into the country without having to go through the normal Customs procedures, sometimes landing entirely undetected. One of his steady customers, in fact, was Lou Greco from Montreal.

At the time, Peroff knew Greco's reputation as "the junk man" but made it clear that no drugs of any kind were allowed on his planes. He personally flew Greco to the Bahamas many times, and his pilots took the mob leader to Mexico on several occasions. Once Greco directly propositioned him to fly heroin, saying, "We could do some big business together." Peroff shook his head and smiled, but Greco went on, "You don't even have to see it, touch it, or smell it," but he dropped the conversation when it was clear that it was leading nowhere.

It was in 1970, in the Bahamas, when Peroff first laid eyes on Greco's so-called "French connection," Connie Bouchard, although he was not to meet him face to face until a year later. On that first occasion, Peroff did not even allow the French Canadian to notice him. Peroff was dividing his time between the two homes in Orlando and Freeport. He flew into the Bahamas one day when Marcus Jones was gone on a trip, and he went alone to the house. The front door was unlocked, so he walked in cautiously and went toward the back. On the rear patio, next to the swimming pool, were at least ten people, men and women, one of them with long hair and a bushy mustache and sunglasses. Peroff knew it was Bouchard, who apparently was trying to disguise his facial features.

The underworld figure from Montreal was there with his hench-men and his women, drinking and carrying on, so Peroff immediately backed out of the house and left.

Bouchard was there, he knew, at the request of his friend Jones, who had given him free run of the house. Jones had hired the mobster to come down to the Bahamas to plan and carry out a large-scale assassination, and to provide underworld protection afterward. Jones had become involved with some Bahamian officials, but the experience had gone sour. As a result, Jones wanted revenge. He had summoned Bouchard from Canada to come down with his professional hit men to kill half a dozen people. He had even spoken to Bouchard about having his partner Frank Peroff fly the mobsters off the island once the assassination was over.

Peroff wanted no part of Bouchard or his hit men. He left the house that day and later persuaded Jones to abandon his act of revenge. He told him, "You go to this guy Bouchard and let him know that I'm not flying him anywhere. I'll fly most anything, but I'm not gonna do it with any Air Force chasing us."

Bouchard had put a price tag of exactly one million dollars on the entire package of murder and protection. After Jones told him to forget the whole idea, the French Canadian and his people remained in Freeport for a month, living it up at the house at Jones' expense, before returning to Montreal. A year later, in 1971, Bouchard would become Peroff's main supplier of stolen stocks and bonds for crooked deals in Europe.

Peroff's distaste for narcotics and violence had grown out of the general philosophical framework within which he had begun to operate as a scammer or swindler. It wasn't just "not getting the world mad at you" but also "balancing the profit against the risk." Attached to the word "risk" was the question, "Am I equal to the task? Is it something within my capabilities? Can I minimize the danger so that the profit is worth it?"

The formula worked well with the airplanes. The risk involved in flying, say, smuggled diamonds from Freeport to Florida was far less than that involved in flying a planeload of mobsters who had just assassinated a deputy prime minister.

So Peroff got involved in flying his planes to South America, moving money in and out of Argentine banks and even smuggling currency from Chile and Peru. The Government of Chile had restricted all of its currency from leaving the country, but you could buy Chilean money down there at a cheap rate and, in the States, sell it for much more.

To balance his equation of risk and profit, it was necessary to invest in a jet and send an emissary down to Chile beforehand. The emissary would buy enough Chilean money to fill an entire trunk. Peroff would fly into Chile with the jet, land, go down to the far end of the runway as if he were going to taxi around and park, and have the emissary run out of the woods with the trunkful of money. Before the Army came running, the partner would hurl the trunk up to the plane and jump aboard as it was heading back for immediate takeoff.

Peroff achieved success with his bold strategy about a dozen times, but on the last occasion the Chilean Army was ready for him with machine guns set up at the terminal building in Santiago. Peroff landed and, as usual, kept rolling to a remote section of the airfield. When his partner ran from the woods, the machine guns opened fire. Peroff pulled up the trunk, but his partner then ran away. With bullets peppering all around him, Peroff shouted to his pilot to make the turn and take off. The plane got off the ground with its door still hanging down and then a squadron of Argentine planes gave chase at Chile's request. They went a hundred and fifty miles until the Argentine planes turned back, and Peroff eventually flew into Florida, at a low altitude to avoid radar, landing on a desolate field that he knew was a blind spot. A few weeks later he converted the Chilean money into American cash, but the formula had almost been upset.

In the space of a few years, Peroff's planes carried "skim money" from Bahamian casinos into the States and also stolen diamonds from Europe and emeralds from the Colombian black market. Once there was a storm, and a fire started in the cockpit of a small plane, so he had to land on the ocean. He and his crew were rescued, but two and a half million dollars' worth of hot diamonds sank to the bottom in a black bag.

When he left Florida for good, bringing his family first to Spain and then to Rome, Frank Peroff turned his back on what he estimated to be ten million dollars' worth of "deals in the works." The projects were varied, to say the least, including a "fake farm" in the Bahamas that was to be a huge "scam" from beginning to end. It involved a complicated illegal conspiracy between the Bahamian Government itself and mob figures from the United States. Five thousand acres of abandoned farmland with its own airfield would be transformed into a bustling enterprise—although the farming itself would be done minimally, with crops grown for the sake of appearance only. In actuality, vegetables and beef would be supplied by organized crime in Florida and brought over in secret, on planes and barges, with no taxes paid at either end. Once the commodities were in the Bahamas, they would be sold as if they had come out of the farm; and all major hotels on the island would be forced by the Government to buy the food. Peroff himself was planning to operate the "farm" and actually live there. And, as a side project, he was going to establish a new airline for the Bahamas.

Another venture was an attempt by Peroff and other swindlers to take control of a Hollywood film-production company. The plot involved $1,600,000 worth of phony escrow certificates, which would be used as collateral for the bulk of the purchase price, until such time as Peroff's organization could liquidate all the remaining assets that the company held. Peroff, in charge of the swindle, ultimately came to feel that he was "too far out in front" and in danger of being caught, so he backed off.

He backed away from it all, in fact, because of growing heat from the law in central Florida. At one point in 1971, when Peroff was already extending his reach into Europe and was away on a trip, the District Attorney came to his Orlando home and asked Ruth if she would be willing "to make a statement about your husband's underworld activities." When the D.A. left, she packed up and took the children to the airport and left for Spain.

Even before then, Ruth had urged her husband to make a clean break with his past. True, they had a nice home and cars and lots of money to spend, but the undercurrent of fear was catching up.

"He's still in Scotland," Nunzio Galli said over the telephone, referring to Tom Glazer of the Secret Service. It was mid-January, 1973, a week after Galli and Peroff had first met at the villa. "They're having a long trial over there, but Tom should be back in Paris by the end of this month."

"And he'll come here to Rome?"

"Oh, yeah, he's planning to make the trip. Listen, Frank, while we're waiting, could we have another meeting?"

"What for?"

"I was thinking that maybe you could do me some favors."

"Well, sure," Peroff said. "Just remember, though—I'm not anybody's informer."

"No, no, it's nothing like that."

The two men met again the next day at the nearby hotel.

"Well," Galli said, "about those favors. We have some problems with immigration, and I'd like you to get me some passports. So I can prove to my people at the Embassy just how easily a guy like you can get them."

"What specifically do you want?"

"A couple of Panamanian passports and some Italian immigration passes. Also about ten Canadian passports, if you can."

"Easy," Peroff said.

Through crooked diplomats and other friends, Peroff could buy, illegally, all sorts of documents such as driver's licenses, passports, credit cards, whatever kind of paper anyone needed. Within the next three days he was able to pick up the Panamanian passports, including the validation stamps, right there in Rome.

One morning the following week he sneaked into the American Embassy in Rome, crouching down in the back seat of Galli's car as they rode through the gate. Inside the building he was shown a number of photographs from which he identified Conrad Bouchard, Herman Savotok and Irving Spellman.

"By the way," Galli said, "we've been having inquiries about you from the Zambian government. What the hell have you got to do with them?"

So *that's* where the heat came from, Peroff thought. It was the Zambian situation, not Bouchard, that was causing him to be followed and harassed.

"I can't be arrested for it," Peroff said, "but I know I could get shot."

It was Peroff's last big scam, an attempt to blackmail the Zambian Government by using tremendous sums of both real *and* counterfeit Zambian currency. At one point, Peroff himself owned about half of the bogus currency plus nearly eight million dollars of real money in various European bank accounts. The impression received by the Zambian Government was that Peroff and his partners were almost able to bankrupt the republic. It was as good a motive for assassination as any, so the recent evidence of surveillance was understandable.

"What'll I tell them?" Galli asked, referring to the Zambian officials who had inquired about Peroff.

"Well, say that I'm willing to talk to 'em sometime. I'll sit down with 'em once this thing with Bouchard is over."

The trouble was, it would never be over.

Galli's request for ten Canadian passports required Peroff to plan a trip to England, to see the man who had taken Bouchard's place as Peroff's main supplier of counterfeit money. He left Rome on a commercial flight with Stefano, his young Italian helper, and they checked into the Skyline Hotel at Heathrow Airport in London. According to Nunzio Galli, Tom Glazer of the Secret Service would be returning to Paris soon and the cover story would be issued within weeks.

The next day there was a message from Galli in Rome. Peroff returned the call from his hotel room and said, "I got what you wanted. Ten new Canadian passports will be sent to me in Rome."

"That's great," Galli said. "Listen, Frank, I also need some driver's licenses."

"Yeah? What kind?"

"Canadian again."

Suddenly Peroff felt weary. "Jeez," he muttered, "I'd have to send my kid to Montreal! I'd have to send him directly to Bouchard for those!"

"But can you do it, Frank? Listen, have him also pick up some credit cards."

"Okay," Peroff mumbled. "I'll send my kid over to Canada."

"Wonderful, Frank. Listen, there's just one other thing."

Peroff swung his feet up on the bed and lay down. "What is it?" he sighed.

"Well, Tom Glazer is back in Paris. So instead of coming directly back here to Rome, why don't you stop off there instead? It'll save Tom a trip, you know?"

"Look, I don't know. . . ."

"Just briefly, Frank. Make a quick stop to see Glazer, and also speak to the Customs people."

He was sitting up again. "What the hell for?"

"They just want to speak with you. Listen, I'll have Glazer call you himself. Stay there. Don't move."

The phone rang soon and Peroff picked it up again. He heard Tom Glazer's voice: "How're you doing, Frank? How's London?"

"Same as ever."

"Listen, it's *crucial* that you stop here in Paris before going back to Rome."

"How come?"

"A quick meeting, Frank."

"Is it really necessary? I mean, you were gonna visit *me*, you know, because I have the bills stashed at the villa, and—"

"It *is* necessary, Frank."

"How about the cover story?"

"Oh, we'll be getting right to work on it. That's important to you, right?"

He sent Stefano to Montreal, to pick up the Canadian driver's licenses and stolen credit cards from Bouchard, telephoning the underworld leader in advance to prepare him.

When the young man returned, they flew to Orly Airport in Paris, where Peroff expected to be greeted by someone from the Secret Service. Instead there was a message for them to continue into the heart of the city, to a small hotel just two blocks from the American Embassy. They checked in and, soon after, Glazer called the room.

"Hi, Frank. Welcome to Paris."

"Thanks. Are you coming over?"

"Listen, send your kid back to Rome."

"Why?"

"Because I won't be able to get over there until tomorrow."

"I wasn't expecting to spend the night here."

"It'll do you good. You'll be fresher in the morning."

Wary but still trusting, Peroff got off the phone and told Stefano to leave for Rome that same night. Then he picked up the phone and called Ruth, filling her in and telling her not to worry.

He awoke in the morning and dressed, and before nine o'clock there was a brief rap at the door of his tiny hotel room. When he opened it, an agent of the Secret Service stepped inside and asked if he was ready.

"I thought Glazer was coming here himself."

"My instructions are to take you to the Embassy annex."

Peroff hesitated, then took his attaché case and followed the agent downstairs to a car outside the hotel. They rode for about a mile and slowed down in front of a bank building. The agent swerved off the road and they went past the drive-in window to a courtyard. From there they continued into an alley, emerging in a tiny parking area. They left the car and walked to a five-story building, the Embassy annex, which was headquarters for the American investigative agencies in Europe. This one building in the heart of Paris housed the main offices for the Secret Service, the CIA, the Bureau of Customs, the FBI and the Bureau of Narcotics and Dangerous Drugs. As they walked inside, Peroff had the unmistakable sensation that he was heading into a labyrinth far from the outside world.

Marines were stationed inside the building at every turn, scrutinizing him as he kept pace with the agent. They came to an elevator, went up two floors, walked through another corridor and stopped in front of a large, unmarked door with a peephole. The agent pressed some buttons on a gadget on the wall, playing a coded tune that opened the door. They went through a long office area to still another door with a new gadget, this one requiring a different set of musical notes.

At last Peroff was brought into Tom Glazer's inner sanctum. The office walls were covered with photographs, mainly of Glazer himself posing with various Government officials who had inscribed warm "Dear Tom" notes on each one of them. Before being placed in charge of Europe and Africa, the Secret Service boss had been Lady Bird Johnson's bodyguard when her husband was President.

Glazer stood up from behind his desk, a tall man with a Mexican-Indian face, about forty years old, appearing friendly and in a pleasant mood. He said, "How are you? Have a seat."

Peroff sat in a chair several feet from Glazer's desk, the attaché case across his lap. He took out samples of Savotok's counterfeit American money and tossed the packet onto the desk.

"That's some of the stuff," Peroff said. "I got the rest of it in my house, back in Rome. Over four hundred grand."

"I'll have some tests made," Glazer said.

Peroff shifted in his chair, waiting to get down to the business of his cover story.

Glazer asked, "Have you talked to Bouchard?"

"I spoke with him from Rome, and my boy just went to see him in Montreal. He picked up some stuff for Nunzio."

"What about Savotok or Spellman?"

"Well, I talked to them by phone when they were here in Paris. But they went back to Canada."

"You sure they're still there?"

"To be honest, I haven't the slightest idea where they are."

"If you don't mind," Glazer said, "I'd like to have a couple of people sit in on this meeting."

Always the investigators, Peroff thought. Now they want to pump me for all I'm worth. "Sure," he muttered.

Glazer buzzed his secretary in the outer office, and within seconds a tall, easygoing man with a mustache entered. He was introduced to Peroff as Artie Jenkins of the Bureau of Narcotics and Dangerous Drugs (BNDD), in charge of the Paris office. Jenkins sat down in another chair and began to question Peroff about Conrad Bouchard, the late Louis Greco, on and on, until it seemed as if he were in a fairly new police station in, say, New York City, being interrogated. He answered to the best of his ability, his mind racing to anticipate where the conversation might be leading.

"You should know," Jenkins offered, "that Connie Bouchard is one helluva hot man in Montreal."

"I figured that."

"We're out to get his ass."

"Uh-hunh."

"Listen, Frank, did you ever know Savotok before this?"

"Nope. Never."

"Do you know any other friends of his?"

"No, except for one thing," he said, going on to explain that when Stefano had gone to Amsterdam with Savotok, to retrieve the suitcase, they had met with a man named Albert Abdul, from Canada, apparently an associate who ran an independent hashish ring. When Stefano had reported this information, Peroff had paid little attention.

"We'll have him checked out," Jenkins said.

I couldn't care less, Peroff thought. Let's just get to *my* business and we'll be done with it.

At this point another man entered the office. Well-built, also with a mustache, reminding Peroff of Elliott Gould in the movies but not as good looking, he introduced himself as Leonard Tobin of U. S. Customs, in charge of narcotics. Watching him sit down, Peroff took an immediate dislike to Tobin, sizing him up as a nasty cop without any sense of how to deal with someone like himself. He glared at Tobin, then looked at Jenkins briefly and, at last, appealed to Glazer as if to ask what was going on.

After a silence Jenkins began, "Frank, I want to tell you something. This counterfeit thing you came with—it's a very, very important thing. It's certainly important to the Secret Service."

"So why am I sitting here with BNDD and Customs?"

"Because," Jenkins replied grimly, "those guys are dealing with junk. There's a deal going. We know, from other sources, that there's a heroin deal moving. Now, we also know that Bouchard is behind it. From everybody we know in Paris, it's got to be Connie's boys."

Again Peroff looked over at Glazer for help, but the Secret Service boss maintained an impassive expression on his face.

"Well," Peroff said, "what do *I* have to do with it? Listen, let's put all our cards on the table, right?" He looked at Jenkins and Tobin, accusing them with his stare. "You're the G-men, okay? So you guys wear the white hats. Now, wait a minute, let me finish! You wear the white hats and me, I'm the bad guy. I'll wear the black hat. And you guys, you can get my background in five seconds, right? You pick up a phone and you know everything about Frank Peroff. And you know," Peroff said, standing up as his voice grew louder, "that Frank Peroff has never, *never* touched junk in his life! Of any kind!"

"We know that," Tobin said.

"So what in hell are you asking me questions about junk for?"

"We're not asking you questions," Tobin returned. "We're telling you facts, that's all."

"Frank," said Jenkins, "did Savotok make any long-distance phone calls from Italy?"

"That's a question," Peroff muttered.

"Please answer it."

"Well, yes, I think he did."

"Where from?"

"From the Excelsior, from my own house. Also from the hotel in Naples. I believe they were calls to somewhere else in Europe."

Tobin became excited and dispatched other agents to make checks on Savotok's calls. Peroff waited, smoking a cigar and trying to relax, and soon Tobin returned in triumph. "Listen, Frank, that's it! There's a deal! A heavy, heavy deal here in Paris, man, and you're gonna get in their pants for us!"

Peroff laughed. "What are you talking about? You gotta be crazy!" He turned away from Tobin. Appealing to Tom Glazer, he said, "You're asking me to play with Conrad Bouchard and those guys? Do some undercover shit with them? You *know* I'm going to refuse. What are you even *asking* me for?"

Jenkins and Tobin were talking at once, shouting over each other, while Glazer kept interjecting, and Peroff thought he was facing three madmen who had set him up to be trapped and confined, so they could pressure him without interference. He wanted to take his briefcase and run from the room, escape this building, flee from Paris, but there was no choice except to sit down and shake his head and laugh while they continued shouting and cajoling.

"You've *got* to do it!" Tobin screamed.

"Go to hell!"

"This is different!"

"You're damn right it's different!"

Tobin took him from Glazer's office over to the Customs section in the same building. There, Peroff was introduced to the chief of U. S. Customs for Central Europe, a big Irishman named Pete Murphy. He and Tobin started in again with Tobin appealing, of all things, to Peroff's "patriotic duty" to become an undercover agent for the United States Government.

"This is your chance," Tobin argued, "to really do something for your country! You can be a *good* guy, for a change!"

"Bullshit!"

"We could have busted you a long time ago, Peroff!"

"Yeah? Why didn't you do it?"

"Because we know you're a decent guy, and—"

"Oh, shut the fuck up, will ya? What do you think, that you can con *me?* You got nothing on me and you know it!"

Several other agents, from Customs and BNDD, walked in and out of the office over the afternoon. Tom Glazer and Artie Jenkins made a few appearances as well, but the only man whom Peroff respected was a short, cocky Italian agent from the U. S. Bureau of Narcotics, a quiet fellow named Tony Mercado. At one point Mercado came into the room without any pretenses and sat down in a corner to listen. Peroff looked over at him and stared at the drug agent's dark, penetrating eyes, thinking that maybe this was at least one man whom he could trust. For every fifty words out of Tobin's mouth, Mercado spoke only one or two, treating Peroff with courtesy and respect.

The worst moment of the afternoon was when Tobin and Glazer telephoned Ruth in Rome, without even asking for his consent. They picked up the phone in Pete Murphy's office and, before Peroff knew it, Tobin was saying to her, "Listen, Ruth, we really need your husband's help on this very important matter. *Please* make him understand, and convince him to do this for us . . . No, Ruth, he won't be in any danger. He can call you whenever he wants, and it'll only take a couple of days or else it won't happen at all . . . Right, Mrs. Peroff, this is a narcotics deal. You have kids, right? Think what these drugs can do to little children, Ruth! Now, you talk to him, ma'am, and tell him to cooperate, for his best interests. . . ."

His neck burning, Peroff went to the phone and said, "Hi, honey," now suddenly laughing at the thought that they would expect him to play games with her. "I'll talk to you later," he said, abruptly hanging up.

They called her back several times over the afternoon, with no results. It was a strong tactic, to use a man's wife as a wedge, but he knew they had no understanding of how tough a woman Ruth was.

It was a standoff. Told at last that he could leave, Peroff tried to find Glazer, who had disappeared following his last visit to Murphy's office. It was Glazer, after all, who had gotten him here on false pretenses. But, Peroff thought, he still owes me that cover story.

"Glazer left a message for you," Murphy said. "He says he'll see you in the morning."

Very convenient, Peroff thought. Well, I'll see the bastard first thing tomorrow, and we'll have it out. It's always nice to see Paris, gentlemen, but I'm flying home by noon, and you can make your narcotics bust by yourselves, not with me, no way, no way at all. . . .

He lay on his back in the small hotel room in Paris, unable to sleep through most of the night. He cursed Tom Glazer for having set him up for the trap. What they were asking him to do was far too dangerous, in the first place. A narcotics deal at this level, here in Paris, was serious business. Go undercover and risk the chance of being discovered? It was unthinkable.

In the morning he took a cab and got to the annex building before nine o'clock. Inside, he was told by a guard that Tom Glazer was not in the Secret Service section, but that perhaps he was in the U. S. Customs office. Peroff debated with himself, on the alert for another trap, but decided to try. A Marine came out and escorted him down the hall.

When he got there, he looked inside Leonard Tobin's office and saw, to his amazement, an array of heroin-related equipment and piles of samples and test kits set up on tables, as if Tobin were planning to hold a special-instruction class for him. The odor in the room was strong, so Peroff backed out and took a seat near the office of the Customs boss, Pete Murphy. A pretty French girl was typing at the desk and Peroff attempted, without success, to pass the time with some conversation. He felt ridiculous, totally alone, wondering why he didn't just get on a plane and leave Paris for good. The only thing keeping him was the cover story that Glazer had promised, but it was essential.

Murphy came out of his office and grinned, saying, "Hiya, Frank. Good morning." He pointed toward Tobin's office and said, "Why don't you go inside?"

"Stuff stinks in there," Peroff replied. "Where's Glazer?"

"Oh, he'll be here soon."

Now Leonard Tobin strode in with a serious, grim expression and manner. "Frank baby," he said in greeting, but Peroff looked at him coldly without speaking. "Come into my office, Frank. I got some things to show you."

Peroff shrugged and followed him. It was unbelievable, but he found himself listening as Tobin went through a long lecture, showing him books about narcotics and inviting him to sit down at the table, like a science student, to witness some demonstrations. Tobin showed him samples of opium, poppies, powder, explaining the intricate details of the process by which heroin is grown, manufactured and cut for eventual injection by addicts. Peroff was almost amused when he was led into another room where the lights went out and a film projector began running. The movie was about the evils of drugs, showing junkies suffering and dying from overdoses: "Teenagers and young children," the narrator warned, "whose lives are being destroyed by this insidious poison."

"You gotta be kidding," Peroff said when the film was over.

"Not at all," Tobin replied. "Frank, where's your compassion? I mean, if you don't care about your country, what about *feelings?* If you don't help us in this, do you realize how much damage will be done? To kids in the United States, from this one junk deal?"

Peroff said, "Why do you think I never went near that shit in my whole life?"

"Frank, we need your help."

"No way am I gonna put my life on the line, just so you guys can get some more trophies."

Back in Tobin's office, he again tried to learn the whereabouts of Tom Glazer, but was told that the Secret Service boss still had not yet reported for work. He sat down, rubbing his eyes, aware that the morning was dragging on. Artie Jenkins, the tall BNDD chief, came in with his colleague, Tony Mercado, who again impressed Peroff with his manner of quiet toughness. "Good to see ya," Mercado said, shaking his hand and looking him in the eye, treating him more like an equal than did any of the others. Several more agents sauntered in, stood around, stared at Peroff and otherwise contributed to the awkward, sullen mood in the room. He felt like a specimen under glass, a captive whose stubbornness was slowly feeding the frustrations of his captors.

Leonard Tobin loudly announced, "Frank, there's money in this for you."

Peroff wanted to laugh in his face. Instead he quietly replied, "Shove your money up your ass."

Tobin's expression turned ugly. "You know," he said, "you're a pretty active boy, Frank. The CIA has one helluva file on you."

"Yeah? Big fucking deal."

"Nobody's been *mad* at you," Tobin said, pacing the floor while the other agents watched. "Not until this point, anyway."

"Don't tell me who's mad! Look, you're keeping me here, right? What are you gonna do if I turn around and just get on a plane and get out of here?"

"You can do that."

"All right, great," Peroff shouted, standing up. "I'm gonna do that," he added, but a couple of agents blocked the way.

"What are you getting upset about?" Tobin asked.

"Look, there's ten of you guys in this room. Like I say, you got the white hats! I got the black hat! Far as you're concerned, I'm as bad as Connie Bouchard and Savotok and everyone else! So what the hell do I have to gain by sitting here talking to you? Why should I help you?"

"We're getting to the limit, Frank! We've been nice up till now! You want a bunch of charges all of a sudden?"

"What charges?"

"Back in the States, here in Europe—you could start having a *series* of problems, friend! The Italian authorities might just feel you've overstayed your welcome in Rome! And the FBI could take a sudden interest in you. We'll fix it so you can't live in *any* country, Mr. Peroff! Back home, the IRS will give you problems that you'd never believe could exist! You'll never be able to go back to the States!"

"Is that what this is? Blackmail? Well, go ahead! The answer is still no! No!"

In the midst of the shouting, Tom Glazer at last made his appearance, but before Peroff could confront him he heard Tobin scream, "What are you going to tell Savotok and Bouchard about the counterfeit money?"

"What?"

"You heard me!" Tobin retorted.

Peroff turned to Glazer, almost pleading, but Glazer said,

"That's right, Frank, there's no other way. This is too important. You walk out of here, fine, that's your privilege. But I have to warn you—we'll put out the word on that counterfeit money. We'll make sure Bouchard knows exactly how we got it. See, if you don't help us, how can we help you?"

As Glazer spoke, Peroff grew afraid for the first time. He cursed and swore at everyone in the room, but underneath he experienced the sinking feeling of having been totally beaten. It was an alien, nauseating sensation of helplessness, with the realization that he had walked into a situation unprepared, against all his previous self-training as a successful manipulator of other people. If they put out the word, he could face the wrath of the underworld, become a hunted man. He had an image of Louis Greco burning alive in the pizza parlor in Montreal.

There was still one card to be played. "Where *is* that counterfeit?" he asked. "It's in my house in Rome, right? You guys don't *have* it yet, so—"

"Frank," said Glazer, "*you* don't have the counterfeit any more. *We* do."

"No, I—"

"The money is no longer in your possession," Glazer went on, explaining that Nunzio Galli had gone to the villa and had taken the suitcase. Peroff could not speak. He glared with hatred at Tom Glazer, a man whom he had trusted, who had changed from a nice, easygoing guy into an uncompromising, hardened cop. In Peroff's view these men had no regard for him whatsoever. If the situation went on they would probably have the Italian authorities place Ruth under arrest. In Italy, the police did anything the Americans wanted. And right now he would put nothing past the Americans; they were capable of making any move against him that served their purpose. To them, he was not a human being but a criminal to be twisted, turned, used and then, no doubt, tossed away when he was no longer needed. No matter that he had reached out to them in the beginning; their grip was strong and they weren't letting go and he felt a part of his spirit go out of him. His ability to resist was slipping away, and he knew it would not be long before he was broken.

The threat against him was fourfold: no cover story in the papers; they would let Bouchard know that he, Peroff, had gone to the Government; he and his family would no longer be welcome in Italy; he could be extradited to the States for possession of the counterfeit money; once in the States, he could be harassed by the IRS.

After another hour of intense pressure he gave up and said, almost in a whisper, "Okay, what do you want me to do?"

III

Peroff agreed to perform one task only. He would try to find out if, in fact, a heroin deal was in progress. If there was, then Connie Bouchard had set up the contacts here in France. Savotok would be the architect of the deal, using Spellman as his courier for the narcotics between Paris and Montreal. In all probability, a third party had provided the financial backing or commitment.

He made his position clear to the agents: "You guys want to know *if* they're doing a junk deal, right? Well, that's as far as I'm going—period!"

Tobin said, "Now you've got to call Bouchard and Savotok."

"What'll I say?"

"Start with the truth, that you're in Paris. See if you can get them talking about junk."

Peroff nearly went after him with his fists. "For Chrissake, man! Are you breaking our deal already? I can't do that! What's the matter with you? The first thing, if I call Connie or Savotok, they're gonna ask me about the counterfeit! They want their money! And what am I supposed to tell them?"

"Well, Frank, that's your department."

"All right. But listen, I can't suddenly break my own character with them. I mean, I've got to just continue being myself, you know? If I *happen* to learn about their junk deal, fine, but don't ask me to go beyond that. It wouldn't work."

He was ushered into Murphy's office. They shut off all radios in the room and even the secretaries outside were told to stop typing, to give him complete quiet. The agents also gave him a special phone which could not be traced back to any Government agency or source.

"Take it from here," Murphy said.

He sat behind the desk of the Customs boss, surrounded by photographs, trophies, plaques—the kind he had seen on Glazer's walls. They play their game with these awards, he thought. Maybe that's what they're really in this for; maybe just for all the cheap, petty glory. It's a game, and right now I'm one of their pawns.

His insides had become wrapped up so tightly that he felt on the brink of bursting. They were all in the room—Murphy, Tobin, Mercado and a fourth agent named Walsh—and they were watching him, waiting for him to call Bouchard. He closed his eyes. He would have to make the call under entirely new circumstances and just hope that his new role as a spy would never be revealed or discovered. The first task was to give Bouchard a believable story about the counterfeit money. Then, to find the whereabouts of Savotok. Is he back here in Paris? Has he already done the heroin deal? Or what?

He gave himself time, concocting a tale—at the agents' suggestion —about how he had converted some of the counterfeit bills into Chilean money. He would say that he had left it hidden somewhere in Chile, and the balance of the counterfeit bills were locked in a hotel safe in Santiago. . . .

He dialed the number in Montreal and immediately recognized Bouchard's French accent and halting English. "I just got into Paris," Peroff told him. Then, fishing, he added, "Listen, Connie, I've been trying to find Savotok. He told me he was going to be here, but I don't think he is."

"No," Bouchard said, "He's back here."

So maybe, Peroff thought, the heroin deal is already completed.

"What's new?" Bouchard asked.

Obviously he was referring to the counterfeit money. Peroff hoped his story would hold up. "I wound up taking it to Puerto Rico," he began. "My kid, Stefano, went with me."

"So what happened?"

"We went to a friend of mine in San Juan. He went with us to Costa Rica. We all flew down there, you know? And in Costa Rica, we made a deal for Colombian emeralds."

"Yeah? You got 'em?"

"No, that deal went bad. We got caught."

"What?"

"Things got very tense. I had to make Stefano the fall guy. We went to see this old man in Costa Rica. Stefano gives him your stuff, and the guy starts counting it, and then he spots it! He can see that the bills are bad! So he reaches over and grabs the kid by the throat, and I had to pull him off. I calmed the old guy down, told him it was all a mistake, and we gave him back the emeralds."

"Shit!"

"But he returned our money, the bad stuff, and we left. It ruined the kid, though. I can't use him any more. He's a wipeout. I put him into a pad in San Juan, and he's still sitting there. The kid just didn't have the background for it, and he couldn't hold up. So he's still in Puerto Rico, waiting for me."

"You got *nothing*, Frank?"

"Hold on, Connie. I didn't have any courier at that point, so I flew down to Chile with my Puerto Rican friend, on a commercial flight. We worked some deals down there."

"Yeah? How much?"

"Well, I got between nine and ten million in real Chilean money. That comes to a little over a hundred grand, when it's converted."

"You got it with you? The Chilean money?"

"No, no. I had no way to get it out! I left it hidden in a good place, don't worry. But I'll have to wait until I can send a private plane down there to pick it up. That's restricted currency, you know."

He could hear Bouchard breathing heavily at the other end of the line. "Listen, Frank, come right over here tonight! Take a flight to Montreal. I'll get the cash, and you rent a plane. You can fly right down to Chile and get the stuff!"

"I'll call you back," Peroff said. When he hung up, he became overwhelmingly tired and dizzy. How can I follow through on this? Go all the way to Canada and fly down to Chile with one of Bouchard's hit men? And then what?

He stared at the agents and dialed the number in Montreal for Herman Savotok.

"I thought you were going to Africa," Savotok growled when he heard the Chile story.

Peroff's forehead had begun to perspire. He wiped it, then got set to talk back with authority and toughness. "Look," he yelled into the phone, "in the beginning, when I knew you guys were coming to Rome, I had no idea what you were bringing. I figured it would be traveler's checks! So that's what I was prepared for. And when you showed up with the counterfeit, I had to switch all the signals. See, there were two people involved—one guy in Africa, the other in the Far East. I called the African contact and told him it was counterfeit, not traveler's checks. He tells me to go to hell, but I get him to agree. Then I tell him I've got a guy that we're gonna use as a front man. But I can't find Spellman! Your man chickens out! So the contact finally tells me to go fuck myself, and I had to take Stefano with me to Puerto Rico. And I've just told you the rest of the story."

"All right," Savotok said. "The money is safe in Chile, though?"

"Yeah, it's safe."

"Did you tell this to Bouchard?"

"Yeah, I did. He says I should go right to Montreal."

In the silence, Peroff held his breath. If Savotok agreed, what then?

"Listen," came Savotok's voice. "Don't come to Montreal. Stay right there in Paris." Thank God, Peroff thought. "I'm leaving here soon. I'm coming over there," Savotok said, and those, Peroff knew, were the magic words. "Where are you staying?"

"I just got here, Herman. I'm near the airport, on the outskirts of Paris."

"Remember the hotel you called me at?"

Peroff did remember. The hotel in Paris where Savotok had stayed was called, of all things, the Hotel Rome.

"You mean," Peroff said, "the one that's got the same name as my city?"

"That's it. Go check in there."

"No, no. We shouldn't stay at the same place. I'll find another hotel."

"Okay," Savotok said. "But once you check in, keep calling the other place. Starting tomorrow morning, try every couple of hours. I don't want to say when I'm leaving here, but I'll be in Paris within the next thirty-six hours."

57

With great relief, Peroff hung up and placed another call to Bouchard, reporting Savotok's instructions for him to remain in Paris. Bouchard sounded disappointed, but made no objection.

His task—to create an appropriate reason for remaining in Paris —had been accomplished with the fabricated story of the Chilean money. It would require much discussion with Savotok. Now there was full justification for him to be among the heroin smugglers without ever becoming part of the operation. Beyond that, his job was to stay close enough to them in order to discover, if he could, how and when the deal would be carried out, assuming there really was one.

He had arrived in Paris on the first of February, a Wednesday, but not until early afternoon on Friday had he capitulated, agreeing to assume the undercover role. After calling Bouchard and Savotok from the Embassy annex, he checked out of his small hotel and moved into the P.L.M. Saint-Jacques at the agents' request. The P.L.M. was a large steel-and-glass structure on the Left Bank, with streamlined modern rooms.

On Friday night, after he had checked in, he called Ruth in Rome to bring her up to date. She confirmed that Nunzio Galli had indeed come to the villa and had taken possession of the counterfeit money. So it was true; the agents had made it impossible for him to disobey their instructions.

The next morning, Saturday, he began calling the Hotel Rome there in Paris, asking if "Monsieur Savotok" had arrived from Canada. It was about noon on Sunday when Savotok finally answered, directing Peroff to meet him at a Chinese restaurant later that evening.

Peroff immediately telephoned the Embassy annex and was told that the operation would be carried out jointly by the Americans and the French National Police, the latter being the equivalent of the FBI in the United States. But Leonard Tobin of U. S. Customs made it clear that his agency was supervising and directing everything, and that he himself was in charge.

"I'm the boss," Tobin said. "It's a Customs case, with BNDD assisting. And I'm your contact."

"I get the message."

"Call me later tonight, after you meet Savotok. When you get free, find a phone and ring me."

At about seven o'clock that night, wearing his heavy camel's hair coat because of the cold weather, Peroff took a twenty-minute cab ride through Paris to the Chinese restaurant. When he got out and paid the driver in francs, he wondered just how closely he was being watched. Normally he would look around for cops, but now he decided to stare straight ahead and ignore them. Act natural, he told himself as he entered the restaurant. I'm no private eye. No dope smuggler, either. If Savotok wants to talk about junk, fine. If not, too bad for the agents. There won't be any leading questions from me.

He checked his coat and looked across the crowded restaurant and recognized, at a rear table, Savotok's short but massive figure. Closer, he saw the grotesque eye that pointed off sideways beneath Savotok's balding dome. Two others were at the table, a man and a young woman. The man's back was facing Peroff, while the woman seemed to be with Savotok.

He noticed that Savotok was extremely well dressed this evening, wearing an expensive light blue suit. Savotok was gesturing to him with one of his ham-sized arms. The other man at the table turned around, and in an instant Peroff realized that this fellow *also* had a disfigured eye. He glanced from one to the other, making his way to the table and sitting down between them, almost mumbling to himself in amazement.

"Hey, Frank, great to see ya," Savotok was saying, with the familiar tough-guy voice from the side of his mouth, and Peroff settled into his chair, elbows on the table, wondering if these two men were perhaps members of an Ugly Club of some kind. Maybe, to join, you need a bad eye. A real whammy marble in your head, or else you don't qualify. Unbelievable, he thought, realizing that Savotok was still talking to him.

"This is Albert Abdul," Savotok said, introducing his companion. Peroff nodded at the man. In addition to the glass eye, Abdul had a huge scar slanting over his face as if he'd been cut open in a duel. He was perhaps in his midthirties, with curly, bushy dark hair. Peroff suddenly recalled that this must be the same Albert Abdul who ran the hashish ring in Amsterdam,

59

where Savotok had left the bulk of the counterfeit money before bringing it into Rome. Another junk man, Peroff thought.

"And this," Savotok went on, beaming, with a fat hand reaching under the girl's chin, "is Tonia. The best little woman I ever seen."

"Hello," Peroff said. What in the world, he wondered, has attracted her to Herman Savotok? He judged her to be a gypsy of some sort, in her twenties—a prostitute? No, probably not. She was wearing an expensive silver-gray dress, with her hair done up in a fancy manner, and she'd put on heavy makeup. This was no streetwalker; but undoubtedly she was costing Savotok a bundle.

"Order anything you want," Savotok said. "It's all on me, Frank, 'cause I'm enjoying myself tonight. See this kid, here? I love her, Frank. We both speak Hungarian. I never met a broad like this in my life. She makes me a happy man."

I'll bet, Peroff thought, trying to imagine the two of them engaged in sexual gymnastics. Tonia was giggling, clutching Savotok's arm, apparently not understanding a word of English.

"I'm paying for this meal in real francs," Savotok announced. "I don't use bad credit cards. I let Spellman pull that shit, but not me."

"Is Irv in town?"

"Nah. He'll be coming along, though."

Albert Abdul stood up and walked off to the men's room. Peroff was glancing at the menu of Chinese food when Savotok leaned toward him and said, "I'm gonna get the money for you to get the stuff out of Chile. I'll get you enough for a plane."

"Good," Peroff said. "I was going to fly over to Montreal, at first. Because I didn't know you were coming back to Paris. Connie told me to go on up to Canada."

"Forget him," Savotok said, almost snarling with contempt for Bouchard. "He don't deserve nothing! You don't listen to him."

Peroff had a quick image of Savotok and Bouchard fighting over the profits from the counterfeit-money deal. I'd love to see them at payoff time, he thought. They'd probably kill each other off.

"Look," Peroff said, "I'll go down to Chile and get the stuff. I'm taking my share, plus expenses. Then I'll throw the rest between you and Connie. You guys can handle it by yourselves."

"Okay," Savotok said. "What's your expenses?"

"Twelve grand will cover everything."

"You'll get it before you leave Paris."

Albert Abdul returned and sat down again, looking worried. He said to Savotok, "I gotta get out of here soon. It's been a rough week, Herman. I'm hurting for bread, too."

"Shut up. Relax, will ya?"

"I've done my job," Abdul complained.

"So enjoy yourself."

"I am, I am. We're gonna do the town. But where the hell is the Kraut? He should've been here by now. Why don't you call the Doctor again? Find out what's going on, ya know?"

"Look," Savotok told him, "the Kraut is coming tonight, with the money, and you'll be able to leave in the morning. So eat up and have a little enjoyment."

There were at least ten separate dishes of Chinese food on the table, for the four of them. While they ate, Peroff waited for more clues. The Kraut? The Doctor? It seemed as if he had walked into the opening session of a crazy game in which, on the one hand, he had to keep bluffing about the Chilean money hidden in Santiago and, on the other, he would have to piece together fragments of information about the heroin deal, if in fact one existed.

It took him several hours to get to a phone that night. By the time he made contact with Leonard Tobin of U.S. Customs, it was nearly three o'clock in the morning.

From the Chinese restaurant, he had gone with Savotok and the Russian girl and Albert Abdul to the Raspoutine supper club, a fancy Paris night spot with a continuous stage show of Russian dancers and singers. Savotok's girl friend left their table at the Raspoutine only to appear on stage a few moments later, performing a solo number in a high soprano voice. Savotok literally swooned, explaining to Peroff that he had met the Russian girl during his previous stay in Paris with Irving Spellman.

The night went on and on, with at least fifty Cossacks and gypsies stomping and parading while Herman Savotok, in ecstasy, tossed hundreds of dollars' worth of francs on stage after each act was finished. He kept buying fifty-dollar bottles of Dom Perignon champagne, toasting the orchestra and even singing along, until their table became the center of attention. Near one thirty in the morning, Savotok had spent more than two thousand dollars in French currency and had run out of cash, so he borrowed several hundred dollars from Peroff, who had been trying without success to sneak off to a phone.

The singing, clapping and stomping were still ringing in Peroff's ears when he got back to the P.L.M. Saint-Jacques. He had called Leonard Tobin at home from a pay phone, fearing that at any moment he might be seen; and now, at the door of his hotel room, the Customs agent appeared with Tony Mercado of the Narcotics Bureau. They came inside and sat down to debrief him, but there was very little specific information so far. Peroff had learned that Albert Abdul was a Turkish Jew whose wife and family lived in Israel while he himself had apartments in both Amsterdam and Montreal.

"He's the same guy with the hash ring," Peroff said, adding that apparently Abdul had been in Paris for at least a week, performing some task for Savotok. "As the night went on, he got real nervous, itching like crazy to skip town."

"Did you hear any straight talk?"

"No. A lot of *loose* talk. They're expecting someone they call the Kraut. And there's another guy, the Doctor, who's involved. And Spellman is still in Montreal, but he's coming here, too. That's all I can tell you."

"What's your opinion, Frank?"

"Well, look, they're not all meeting in Paris on *my* account, that's for damn sure. I don't know Albert Abdul, I never heard of the Kraut, and I got no idea who the Doctor is. I mean, let's put it this way," Peroff added, laughing, "if all these characters are here to see *me*, I'm in a helluva lot of trouble!"

Tobin was pacing around the hotel room while Mercado, the BNDD agent, quietly took notes.

"You'll have to keep at this," Tobin said. "By the way," he went on, "I have to go somewhere on a trip. Now, remember— this is a Customs operation, here, so your new contact will be one of my men. A guy named George Walsh. You met him before, in my office."

The following morning, Monday, he took a cab to the Hotel

Rome where Savotok was staying. The place was a dump. It was small, with glass front doors and a tiny lobby immediately within, and a winding staircase led up to the various floors with their cramped rooms. No more than three people—only two when one of them was Savotok—could fit inside the hotel's elevator. Half the residents were students of a nearby foreign-language school, mostly youngsters from Sweden.

He walked up to Savotok's room and knocked on the door. "Who's there?" came Albert Abdul's voice.

"Frank."

Abdul opened the door carefully, then let him in. Savotok was still in his robe, in the process of laying out his clothing so he could get dressed. Peroff took a seat while the two men resumed a heated conversation which apparently had been interrupted by his entrance.

"The Kraut should *be* here," Abdul exclaimed. "Where is he? You said he was coming in last night!"

"I know," Savotok said, pulling on his pants.

"Well, *do* something! I gotta leave! I've *done* my job."

"All right," Savotok said. He sat down next to the telephone and placed a call to Spellman in Canada. "Hello, Irv? Have you heard anything from either one of them? The Kraut? The Doctor? Okay, okay. Talk to you later."

When Savotok hung up, Abdul said, "So what's going on? What'd he say?"

"Relax," Savotok told him. "He said that all he heard was what I already told you. The Kraut has left. He's not in Montreal, so he's on his way. No sweat."

Peroff went with the pair for lunch and later that afternoon he broke free to call Tony Mercado, who instructed him to be at a coffee bar not far from the American Embassy. Peroff took a cab, nervous the whole way. Mercado was waiting for him in a booth at the far corner.

"I called you," Peroff told him, "because I don't want to deal with that Customs guy. I don't trust him. Besides, it's Tobin's own fault for leaving town."

"Okay," the BNDD agent said, pleased. "You and me. What's new?"

"Not much yet," Peroff said. "They're still waiting for this guy they call the Kraut. And they discussed the Doctor, who might be the Kraut's boss, but I don't know what the hell's going on at this point."

"If there *is* a deal," Mercado said, "I have confidence that you'll lead us to it. In the right way. You go ahead and do your thing."

Sometime during that night, the Kraut arrived in Paris and also checked into the Hotel Rome. Peroff first saw him at about ten the next morning, seated at a card table in the lobby with Albert Abdul. When Peroff walked in, the two were sipping espresso coffee, talking, and the Kraut was nervously fiddling with some checkers on the table.

He was a young man in his mid-twenties, with the face of a baby, wearing a black leather sports jacket and a white scarf with maroon paisley print and elegant fringes.

"Good morning," Peroff said.

The young man looked up. "You're Peroff?"

"Yeah."

"You're the big man with the airplanes, right?"

"Who are you?"

Abdul broke in. "I want you to meet my good friend Jules," he said, draping an arm around the Kraut. "This is a good man," Abdul went on in his thick Israeli accent. "Jules Handel, meet Frank Peroff."

"Where do you live?" the Kraut asked when Peroff had sat down at the card table.

"Rome."

"Ah, yeah, I'd like to go to Rome. Never been there."

"You should, then."

Peroff order some coffee and started more banter with the Kraut, intrigued by the contradictions between the young man's background and character. His parents, Handel explained, had been regimented, full-fledged Nazis. He himself was a Canadian, a member of the new and more open-minded generation.

While the three of them were talking, Herman Savotok appeared at the stair landing. He leaned over and yelled, "Come on up here!" Jules Handel immediately jumped from his chair and ran upstairs. Peroff followed, with Abdul behind him, although Savotok had meant his command only for the Kraut. By the time Peroff got up to the floor, Handel and Savotok were already inside the room, but the door was open. Handel was reaching into his jacket and pulling out large stacks of cash. There were four packets altogether, consisting of Canadian hundred-dollar bills, and Peroff estimated the total at somewhere near $150,000. Savotok grabbed the cash, flipping through it quickly as if to make sure the amount was correct.

If there was a heroin deal, then obviously the Doctor had sent Handel, the Kraut, from Montreal to Paris with the payment. If Savotok was the architect of the deal, using Conrad Bouchard's contacts here in France, then the Doctor was the financier. And Handel was merely the money courier who had just completed his mission.

"Wait for me in the lobby," Savotok said as he pushed Handel out of the room.

At the same time, Peroff and Abdul turned around in the hall and headed back down the stairs, with the Kraut behind them. In the lobby again, they resumed their conversation at the card table.

While Handel chatted about politics, Peroff tried to calculate the size of the deal. At $3,500 per kilo from the wholesalers here in France, Savotok could buy at least forty kilos of pure, uncut heroin. In Canada or the United States, the Doctor could get $27,000 per kilo from syndicates of organized crime, which would come to more than a million dollars for their efforts. The street pushers, of course, would eventually cut up the dope and realize up to $1.8 million per kilo, or as much as seventy million dollars spent in total by drug addicts.

Savotok came downstairs, dressed and in a hurry. He walked over to the table and said to Peroff, "How are ya this morning? Feel all right?"

"Sure."

Savotok turned to Jules Handel. "Let's talk," he said, motioning to the corner of the cramped lobby. The two immediately got into a heated discussion. Handel's face was twitching as he whispered, and Savotok said aloud, "Watch that talk!"

"Look," Handel replied, "if you got any complaints, you know where to make 'em. You call Montreal, and—"

"Shut up!"

"I don't work for you!"

With that, Savotok grabbed the Kraut by the front of his jacket, lifting him up on his toes. "Idiot," he said, proceeding to slap Handel on the face with his free hand, back and forth, the noise echoing around the lobby.

"Look," Savotok shouted, "I'm not gonna warn you any more! Next time you're gonna get it all!"

Handel had made no move to defend himself. He was bent over, holding his face, terrified and about to weep. Peroff pretended that he had barely noticed the scene, while he wondered what the argument had been.

Savotok shouted to Abdul: "If a call comes in, I'll be back in an hour."

Abdul nodded. In another second, Savotok was out the door, perhaps going to meet the French suppliers to give them the money.

That afternoon, Peroff called Tony Mercado from an obscure phone booth. The agent wanted another secret meeting. Hoping he wasn't being watched, Peroff met with him up in his room at the P.L.M. Saint-Jacques.

"What's going on?" Mercado asked, rubbing his mustache.

"It's a zoo," Peroff said, quickly going over all the facts, the key one being that Handel had delivered about $150,000 in Canadian cash to Savotok.

"We've been getting information through another door," Mercado said. "The word is that the deal is for fifty kees."

"Fifty!"

"That's just what we hear."

"Listen," Peroff said, "what happens if all of a sudden these guys get busted? What protection do I have?"

"Don't worry, Frank. You just do what we tell you."

"Okay, but a guy like Savotok would try to *shoot* his way out, you know? I'd be caught in the crossfire!"

"If you do what I tell you, Frank, nothing like that will happen. Just stay in touch—if you can."

When Peroff returned to the Hotel Rome in the early evening, Jules Handel was waiting for him in the lobby. The Kraut gestured to him, so Peroff wandered over to the card table and sat down.

"I have to ask you something," Handel said.

"Go ahead."

"What's involved in getting this money, uh, down there in Chile?"

"Wait a minute, friend. What do *you* know about it? What business is it of yours?"

"Well, we paid for it."

"Hunh?"

"That's our stuff. That money belongs to us. Savotok came to us and told us there was a deal for half a million in counterfeit, so we gave him the money to buy it."

"Who's we?"

"Me and my partner," said Handel, who was almost certainly inflating his true stature. But there was no reason to disbelieve what he was basically saying: Savotok had gotten his money from the Doctor in order to pay for the original $500,000 worth of counterfeit American bills. Bouchard had provided the printer in Montreal and, no doubt, he had also supplied the heroin contacts here in Paris; but it was the Doctor who had put up the cash for both deals.

"Look," Peroff said, "you should know what the situation is down there. I mean, in South America—"

"We *do* know," Handel said. "I had a long discussion with Herman today. We have an awful lot of business down in Bogotá, Colombia. We know some heavy people in some of those countries. So maybe we'll send *our* man down to get it. One of our guys."

"No way," Peroff told him. "When that money comes out of there, it's *me* that's taking it out. I don't trust nobody. This is my game."

Handel fell silent. He started to argue further when Albert Abdul came downstairs with Irving Spellman who, Peroff realized, must have arrived in Paris within the past few hours.

"Hey, Frank," Spellman giggled. "Come on, we're going for coffee."

The four of them walked out of the hotel and down the block to a coffee bar, where they took a table together. When they had ordered their coffee, Handel leaned toward Spellman and said, "Look, Irv, I want you to know something. Savotok is a slob! I mean, he started getting rough with me! And he's got no *right* to do that. Who does he think he is?"

67

"Take it easy," Spellman replied. "Calm down."

Abdul spoke up. "I was scared last week," he confided to Spellman. "The whole week, you know? I was watching that car, and leaving my hotel room all the time, going down there to make sure it was okay. I was getting crazy."

Peroff listened to the conversation and noted a growing urgency among them. Without Savotok around to play the bully, both Abdul and Handel were letting off steam, unloading their frustrations upon Spellman instead.

"Don't worry," Spellman told them. "I'm getting the paintings soon. Everything'll be fine."

At dinner that night, they were all seated around a large table in Le Western, a ranch-style restaurant in the Paris Hilton. Spellman was talking to Albert Abdul and the Kraut, but suddenly he turned to Peroff, frowning, and yelled, "You *owe* us, ya know! You *owe* us!"

"What are you talking about?"

"Chile! You ever heard of Chile?"

"What are you, a maniac?"

"Come on, Frank! Why did you leave that money there, eh? Where are your brains?"

"Look," Peroff said, "you were supposed to be the courier in that thing! But you chickened out! Where were *you?*"

"It's not my fault! I never agreed!"

"So just mind your business."

"You're an idiot!"

Peroff glared at him, then said quietly, "Watch your mouth."

"Well you owe us! If you weren't so stupid, you—"

"No more mouth!"

"Idiot! You—"

Peroff stood up, knocking over water glasses and drinks as he lifted Spellman out of his chair. He picked him up, holding onto his tie and shirt, ripping off buttons, and threw him toward the wall of the restaurant. He lunged, ready to smash Spellman with his fists, when he felt Savotok's huge hands grip his shoulders from behind.

"Relax," Savotok roared. "Sit down, Frank. And you! Hey, Irv, keep your mouth shut!"

Shaken, Peroff waited until everyone else sat down before he resumed his own place at the table. The dinner proceeded for a while on a quieter note and, at one point, Savotok said, "Hey, Frank, Handel wants to discuss something with you."

Peroff turned to the Kraut, who was seated at his left. Handel said, "How hard is it, going into South America? And coming back into the States?"

"In a private plane?"

"Yeah."

"It's a helluva lot easier than going from Europe."

"How much would it cost to charter a jet and do it?"

"What for?"

"Look," Handel said, his voice lowering, "we got forty kees of coke in Bogotá. Me and my partner. It belongs to us."

"That's not my business," Peroff said. "You're looking the wrong direction for that kind of shit. If you talk about paper and stuff like that, sure. But what you're talking about is another story."

"What would it take for you to do it?"

Peroff hesitated, then decided to play along. "Well, I would want at least a third split. But you can't charter a jet with no money. The expenses would be up around forty grand."

"That much?"

"It depends. I'd have to go out and look for a plane. And make a deal. I can't tell you exactly."

"To make your start, to *begin* going out to do this, what would you need? I mean, if I get an agreement on the third split, what would it cost to tie up a deal with you?"

"You'd have to get me at least between ten and twenty grand. I don't even think ten would do it, to go under contract for a plane."

"All right," Handel said. "I have to talk to Montreal."

Peroff poured himself some more coffee. Soon his attention was drawn to Spellman, who was describing something in great detail for the benefit of Albert Abdul. From what Peroff could gather, Spellman had used the twelve suitcases full of merchandise, which he had purchased in Rome on stolen credit cards, to transport fifteen kilos of heroin from Paris to Montreal! Was that a separate deal or part of the current one?

"Anyhow," Spellman was saying, "my paintings are almost ready to be picked up. Also I'm getting some special shipping containers, you know? For rolled canvases. Beautiful stuff, and—"

There was an awkward silence. If Peroff wasn't mistaken, Savotok had just kicked Spellman under the table.

Peroff sat in the lobby of the Hotel Rome the following morning, at the card table. With him was Jules Handel, complaining that Albert Abdul had left Paris unexpectedly during the night. The Kraut added, "I'd like to get the hell out of here, myself."

By this time, Peroff himself was ready to quit and leave. As far as he was concerned, there had been little or no progress in getting hard information. The entire experience could go on for weeks, and, besides, he had growing apprehension over being caught as a spy.

An hour ago, he had called Bouchard in Montreal, from the P.L.M. Hotel, just to keep up appearances with the French Canadian.

"I'm sitting here like a dummy," he had told Bouchard. "All I'm doing is waiting. But they're coming up with the bread for Chile."

"Good, good," Bouchard had replied. "The minute you get it, Frank, come here. Don't do nothing. Come here first."

Bouchard had sounded eager and desperate. There was no question that he and Savotok would have to kill each other before they would be able to split up the Chile money in a fair manner. So far, Peroff had told them that there was $120,000 worth of Chilean money, hidden somewhere in that country. After his costs were taken out, Peroff supposedly would get 60 percent. The estimated expense was $12,000, leaving about $108,000. Peroff's share would come. to $65,000 while Bouchard and Savotok would be fighting over the remaining $43,000, which really belonged to the Doctor. Bouchard was hurting for cash so badly that he was ready to steal it all, if he could, even though this was his way of making up for the previous heroin fiasco, when the Frenchman had fled.

All this nonsense, Peroff thought, when there isn't any money in Chile in the first place.

"When did the others say they'd be back?" he asked the Kraut.

"Soon," Handel said.

It was clear that Savotok and Spellman did most of their important business in the early morning. Savotok was probably meeting with the French heroin suppliers, while Spellman could be off seeing about his paintings with their special shipping containers.

"I had a conversation with Montreal," Handel said.

Peroff sipped his espresso. "Yeah?"

"We got a deal, Frank. Money is coming. There'll be bread for you to do the thing in Chile. But you might want to hold off on that a bit."

"Why?"

"Well, I'll be leaving in a couple of days. Maybe you should come back with me, up there, and maybe we can get the whole forty grand for the other deal."

The young man was referring, Peroff knew, to the job of flying cocaine out of Bogotá, Colombia.

"At any rate," Handel went on, "we can make an agreement now, because there's gonna be enough to wrap this up between the two of us. For you to begin, anyway. But you need to come with me to Montreal for a meeting."

Peroff tried to stifle his panic. "I'm not going to Montreal right from here. I want to go home for a few days."

"Maybe in a week?"

The conversation abruptly ended when Irving Spellman came through the glass doors into the lobby. "Come here," he told the Kraut.

Handel got up and followed him through the glass doors to the sidewalk just outside the hotel. Both men had loud voices, so that Peroff could hear them, but not distinctly. He stood up, slowly moving near the doors.

Spellman: "It'll be a couple of days."

Handel: "It should've been over by now."

Spellman: "Fifty kees, you know? It takes time. I'm picking up the paintings tomorrow morning."

Handel: "Okay, but—"

Peroff quickly moved away, resuming his seat at the card table as they came back through the door. The pair sat down again, ordering more espresso. Fifty, Peroff thought. And he's picking up the paintings tomorrow. But what the hell is supposed to happen?

71

Spellman was pulling a contract of some kind from his jacket. He spread it on the table in front of the Kraut, saying, "Go down and take care of this. Pay another week on the car."

"I ain't got nothing to do with that."

"Look, you have to do it. Don't start another fight. Calm down."

"All right, all right," said Handel, his baby face looking haggard and frightened.

Spellman stood up and immediately walked back out of the hotel. Peroff watched the Kraut fold up the car-rental contract.

"Come on," Handel said. "Let's take a ride."

They hailed a taxicab and Peroff climbed into the back seat with the Kraut, who was muttering about Savotok again.

"You're upset?"

"I'll fix his ass."

When the cab stopped after several minutes, Peroff saw by his watch that it was almost noon. They were at a Hertz car-rental garage. He followed Handel into a tiny office building on the corner. At the counter, Handel took the lease from his jacket and spread it out. The contract, Peroff saw, was for a white Peugeot. It had been leased under the name of Albert Abdul, who had signed at the bottom.

"One more week," Handel told the Hertz woman. "I'll take care of it right now."

They went back to the Hotel Rome, the Kraut rushing into the lobby and upstairs. Peroff joined him as he was knocking on Savotok's door. When it opened, Peroff saw that Savotok was sitting in bed naked, groaning from a severe case of influenza. Stepping into the room, he now realized that Tonia, the Russian girl, was on the bed with him and that she, too, was naked. She was kneeling over the stricken Savotok, holding a bowl in one hand and feeding him spoonfuls of steaming chicken soup.

"Hi, Frank," Savotok moaned. "I'm sick as a dog. Look at this broad, will ya? Nobody ever did this for me."

"You okay?"

"I got the flu. The fucking flu."

The Kraut was pacing around the room. "I did what you wanted," he said. "It's taken care of."

"One more job," Savotok said.

72

Handel slammed his fist down on the desk. *"What* more?" he asked. *"What? What?"*

"Take the keys," Savotok ordered, "and go down there and move the car. Put it on the other side of the street."

Handel protested, but when Savotok jerked his head up as if he might suddenly attack him, the Kraut flinched and said, "I'll do it! I will!"

Peroff followed him out of the room and down to the lobby again. Spellman came in the front door and immediately he and Handel held a private conference in the corner. At one point Peroff heard Spellman say, "The car's been okay all this time, so don't worry."

Whimpering and complaining, the Kraut left the hotel. Spellman and Peroff exchanged brief grumbles, avoiding the touchy subject of the money in Chile. After a few more minutes, Handel returned and said, "I moved it to the other side of the street. Up the block."

They were seated around a table at a fancy Paris restaurant: Herman Savotok, the Russian girl, Irving Spellman, Jules Handel and Frank Peroff. Missing was Albert Abdul, but a new addition to their party was a lovely but naïve Swedish girl whom the Kraut had picked up at the Hotel Rome. Apparently she was one of the students staying there while studying French at the nearby language school.

Peroff tried to enjoy the food despite the fact that he had been unable to reach Tony Mercado. He had called from the P.L.M. Hotel and left a message that he would try again later in the night.

"I've had a couple of conversations with Montreal," the Kraut told him.

"Good."

"I think you're going to make it possible for us to stop playing piecemeal. We're involved with too many people," Handel went on, referring to the Doctor's cocaine-smuggling operation between Canada and South America. "We're going to do some heavy things when you get up there."

When the huge meal was over, Savotok, who had recovered somewhat from the flu, announced that they were all going over

73

to the Lido on the Champs-Élysées to watch another spectacular floor show.

"I'm tired as hell," Peroff said. "I'm going back to my hotel and get some sleep."

"We'll go with you," Handel said, taking the Swedish girl by the arm. While the others went on to the Lido, the three of them took a cab, first stopping at the Hotel Rome, where Handel said, "Let me just drop her off here, and I'll come with you, Frank."

"Why?"

"I'd like to see where you're staying. Maybe I'll move in there myself."

Peroff shrugged. It was a chance to get more information. He waited until Handel had dropped off the Swedish girl, then told the driver to continue on to the P.L.M. Saint-Jacques.

"Thank God I met you," Handel said.

"Hunh?"

"You're one of the smartest guys I've ever met. You're gonna mean the biggest difference in my life."

He doesn't know how right he may be, Peroff thought, as the cab pulled up in front of the large modern hotel. As they walked in the darkness toward the front door, Peroff glanced around to see if they were under surveillance. It had been his normal habit, but so far in Paris he had reversed himself, actually trying hard to *avoid* spotting any French National cops who might be watching, especially when Savotok was around. Whenever he had walked out of a restaurant, for example, he had kept his eyes straight ahead. But now, with Handel, he forgot himself and looked up and down the block. Nothing except a tiny gray truck, probably delivering something.

Up in his spacious room, he and Handel settled down on separate beds, pouring drinks and chatting. The Kraut seemed tense from the day's events, needing to talk and unwind, so Peroff just listened. The young man spoke about his life and how he had been raised by Nazi parents. At one point he said, "You know, I got a lot of kids working for me."

"In Canada?"

"Yeah. We got a pretty good-sized group up there."

"What do you mean? What kind of business?"

"You know. We fool with coke, hash, grass, whatever."

"You actually got the pushers?"

"Yeah. The problem is, most of 'em are hooked. I hate junkies—worst animals in the world. You can't trust 'em. I use 'em because I have to."

"If I were you," Peroff said, "I'd quit that whole business."

"You never did junk?"

"Never. I'm a paper man, and I've done a helluva lot of things, baby, but I never fooled with junk. You do that, you're killing people."

"Well," Handel said, "it's an economic thing. Look how much money goes into circulation. Look how many people would be out of jobs."

"Who, pushers?"

"Listen, by dealing in junk, we're helping to satisfy a basic need that people have."

The kid is crazy, Peroff thought. The Doctor must have brain-washed him.

"We're performing a service," Handel went on.

Peroff poured some more liquor into the young man's glass. The conversation went on for another hour. He probed the Kraut's mind in the manner of a psychiatrist, learning that Handel still believed that Hitler's views had been correct.

"You know," Peroff said, "that I'm Jewish?"

"Yeah, but you're not a weak man. I'm not talking about race! I'm saying strong versus weak!"

At last he walked Handel to the elevator, convinced that the young man was mentally unstable. To be safe, he waited a few minutes before picking up the phone in his room and calling Tony Mercado at home, telling him he was alone and it was all right to come over.

"Come on," Mercado said. "What else?"

The agent was hunched over the desk in the hotel room, taking notes, while Peroff sat on a bed and tried to remember all the details from the past thirty hours. There was the $150,000 from the Doctor to Savotok, delivered by Handel. That information had been relayed to Mercado already. Then there was the specific mention by Spellman that the deal involved fifty kilos, and also his references to paintings with special containers.

"They gotta be doing it in stages," Mercado said. "Maybe ten, fifteen kees at a time. You think in the paintings?"

"Probably."

"But where's the shit?"

Peroff went over and over the events in his mind. "We went to Hertz this afternoon," he said.

"Who did?"

"Me and Handel. He paid another week on Albert Abdul's car. He was real upset, and—"

Mercado looked up from his notes. Peroff had cut himself off, because the answer had struck him all of a sudden—the car!—and now everything began to have meaning.

"That's it," Peroff said. "The stuff's in the car! He was *nervous* when we went to Hertz! Then he was *really* pissed off when Savotok told him to move it!"

"Wait," Mercado said, furiously taking notes. "Slow down, start again!"

"Son of a bitch," Peroff was saying. "That's gotta be it, Tony! That's why he was nervous! He didn't want to move that car!"

"What kind?"

"A white Peugeot."

"Why didn't you tell me before?"

"Because," Peroff exclaimed, "it didn't piece together in my mind until now! But it fits! Abdul said he'd been watching a car for a week—but I didn't know what the hell he was talking about!"

For the first time, it was clear that the French heroin suppliers were using the white Peugeot as a dropping point, and that they already had placed some of the load inside it. Why else would Abdul and Handel have been so nervous and upset? Somehow, the drugs would have to be transferred from the car to the paintings, which then would be shipped to North America.

"You're right," said Mercado, unable to conceal his excitement. "That's gotta be it. That's our only shot in this whole case. It's either in the car or we're in trouble. Which Hertz place did you go to?"

"How do I know? We got into a cab. He'd already given the driver an address. I'll tell you this—it was between five and eight minutes from the hotel. It was a corner building, right at an intersection. . . ."

Mercado took more notes and picked up the phone, but he stopped himself and said, "I gotta get moving. Call me tomorrow, as early as you can."

Before leaving the P.L.M. Hotel in the morning, Peroff tried to reach Mercado again, but without success. Apparently the agent had not even gone home after their conversation the night before, nor had he showed up at the office. He was "out in the field" somewhere, probably trying to locate the white Peugeot.

Peroff arrived at the Hotel Rome by eleven. Jules Handel was in the lobby, and Irv Spellman came down the staircase and said, "Come on. Let's take a walk."

Without speaking they followed him outside, and Peroff wondered when Spellman would go pick up his paintings. At this point it was only a matter of timing. How soon? If a segment of the fifty kilos was already inside the car, and if Savotok had already paid the Frenchmen, what was to stop the entire deal from reaching its climax? Only the paintings, Peroff thought.

He and the Kraut hurried alongside Spellman as they walked at a brisk pace. After a few blocks, Peroff began to enjoy himself, forgetting momentarily his dangerous role as a spy. It was pleasant, strolling now into an open market with fruit and vegetables and all sorts of items for sale. Spellman abruptly stopped to buy a fried chicken leg. Then he waved it at them and said, "Let's go, come on. Mmmmm, this is good! You like a bite, Frank?"

"Nah."

They came to a small public square at which five streets intersected. Spellman halted in the middle, eating the remainder of his chicken and tossing away the bone.

"It's a beautiful day," he said. "A bit chilly," he added, when suddenly a black car roared from one of the streets into the square and screeched to a stop beside him. He was saying, "I really like Paris," but now the rear door of the car was opening and, still talking, Spellman backed in, slamming the door shut after him. The car raced off.

Peroff was standing in the empty square with Jules Handel. It had happened so fast that he had been unable to speak. Spellman was gone. "What was that?" he asked.

The Kraut shrugged. "Let's go," he said.

On their way back to the Hotel Rome they stopped for lunch and Peroff excused himself and went to call Mercado again. The paintings were probably being picked up by Spellman at that very moment, which meant that anything could happen right away. Again, however, Mercado was unreachable, still out of his office and not at home either.

Over lunch, the Kraut said he had been in touch with Montreal again. "Are you sure," he asked, "that you don't want to let *our* people bring out the Chile money?"

"Look," Peroff said, "let me tell you something. I don't know you from Adam. I mean, you're a nice guy and all that crap, but I got only one deal. And that's with Connie. When the time comes, I'll get that money out *my* way. It's really got nothing to do with you, or your partner, or anybody else."

The Kraut held up his hands, indicating that he wouldn't press the point any longer. Apparently the Doctor had urged him on the phone to make one final overture to Peroff, but now the issue was settled.

The two split up after lunch and Peroff went back to his own hotel. Once more he tried to reach Mercado without success. It was just possible that the paintings had been picked up and that the heroin deal was being carried out. No doubt, he thought, that Mercado and the French police are keeping watch on that car—if they've found it.

He returned to the Hotel Rome and, as before, Handel was alone in the lobby, seated at the card table. Peroff approached him and asked, "Where are the others?"

"Savotok's out. But Spellman just came in, with a young girl."

"Yeah?"

"He said she's the daughter of a friend of his. In fact," Handel went on, "he said she works at the Lido! One of the dancing girls!"

"How old?"

"Sixteen!"

"What's he doing up there with her?"

"Who knows?"

Peroff sat down at the table and poured some espresso coffee, thinking that Spellman might have brought the paintings back here or somewhere else; but if he's up there with a girl, there must be time to kill.

"He's an old man!" Handel exclaimed. "What's he doing with a little kid like that?"

"He's a lecher."

"But how did he *do* it? I mean, get her up to his room?"

"I dunno. Money. Just like Savotok, with his Russian broad."

They sat in silence, Peroff noticing that the Kraut had become disturbed over the thought of Spellman with such a young girl. Then, without warning, they heard a loud noise, not quite a scream but a cry of pain, from upstairs.

"What's going on up there?" Handel whispered.

Another muffled cry echoed down and Handel jumped to his feet. Peroff watched him bound up the stairs. Moments passed and the Kraut came racing down again, out of breath, his face quivering.

"She's crying!" he exclaimed in a whisper. "I listened at the door, man, and she's going through a whole thing in there! He's *raping* that broad! She's struggling and crying, and Frank, we gotta do something!"

"Sit down. Just mind your business," Peroff said. "The girl went up there with him, right?"

"Frank, he's raping her! I swear!"

"You're crazy," Peroff replied. "What's the matter with you? That's his friend's daughter! I mean, even *that* old bastard isn't gonna rape her. Something must be wrong with the girl."

Handel sat down, but then came another cry, this one more of a scream. The Kraut sprang to his feet, unable to bear it any longer, and he bolted up the stairs. This time, Peroff could hear him banging on Spellman's door and shouting, "What are you *doing* in there? Open up! Stop!" In another moment the Kraut was leaping back downstairs, panic-stricken, pacing back and forth.

"What'd he say?" Peroff asked.

"He told me to get away and mind my own business! I'm telling you, I heard it! He's raping her, and she's *crying!* You don't even have to go near the door! You just walk up to the landing and you can hear everything! Go on, Frank! Go up and listen for yourself!"

"Forget it," Peroff said, thinking that Handel was inflating the entire incident.

"I'm calling him," Handel said, going to a house phone in the lobby. "Give me Mr. Spellman's room! Quick! Hurry!"

But Herman Savotok entered the hotel with his Russian girl

friend. Handel slammed down the phone and shouted, "Herman, listen, Spellman is up there with a broad and—"

"Shut up!" Savotok yelled. "I'm going up to get dressed, and then we're going to dinner."

"But—"

"Hey," Savotok shouted, holding up a menacing hand. With that, he led the Russian girl into the tiny elevator and disappeared.

Handel lifted the house phone again and got Spellman on the line. "Hey, Irv, listen, we're going to dinner! Come on down here!"

For the next ten minutes, the Kraut could hardly sit still. Peroff was fascinated and somewhat amused by the young man's reaction. Underneath, he thought, the kid has some real feeling of right and wrong. Or else he's got a helluva hangup.

"Son of a bitch," Handel muttered. "He's a low, low life. I'm gonna kill him. He's raping that young kid. . . ."

Peroff looked up and saw Spellman on the landing, with an embarrassed expression on his face, and with him was the girl, who had golden hair and such a lovely face that it was almost unreal. Like a goddess, Peroff thought. She was crying and shivering, unable to control herself. She obviously had tried to clean her face, but the mascara had run all over.

"Hey, Frank," Spellman whispered. "Come over here."

Peroff got up while the Kraut shouted, "You raped this kid!"

"Sssssh! Come on, Frank! You understand!"

"But you told him that she's your friend's daughter!"

"Yeah, that's right! I know the guy for years!"

"You son of a bitch!"

Spellman's frown dropped deeper than ever. At this moment, Handel's Swedish girl friend walked into the hotel and Savotok came out of the elevator with Tonia, the Russian girl.

By now Peroff felt that he was part of some wild vaudeville act. He watched the Kraut rush over to Savotok and exclaim, "Spellman just raped this French girl, here! He *raped* the broad! Look, Herman, she's still crying!"

Savotok's face turned uglier than usual and he turned on Spellman, shoving him quickly across the floor. "What are you trying to do, eh? Get us all locked up? What's the matter with you? Are you stupid? Dummy!"

Spellman protected his face with his hands while Peroff and

Handel tried to conceal their laughter. Then the whole crowd—Savotok, Spellman, the Kraut, the Russian girl, the French girl, the Swedish girl, and Frank Peroff—adjourned for dinner.

It had been at least twenty hours since he had met with Tony Mercado the previous night in his hotel room. Peroff remained calm during dinner until he heard Spellman remark to the Kraut, "You can return the car by noon tomorrow."

That was all he needed to hear. Now it was certain that the first stage of the heroin deal was about to be completed. By tomorrow morning, the load of narcotics would be taken from the white Peugeot and placed inside the paintings for shipment out of France. For a while Peroff sat there with the whole cast of characters, then excused himself to call Mercado. It was a dangerous call to make from the same restaurant, but necessary. Neither Mercado's wife nor his office, however, could reach him.

When Peroff returned to the table, he glanced over at the French girl whom Spellman apparently had raped. Her eyes were still red from crying.

"Hey, Frank," Savotok was saying.

"Yeah?"

"Irv and I are going on a little trip."

"Where to?"

"Austria. We're taking off tomorrow. Listen, you'll have your money for the Chile thing before we go. But I wanted to mention something else."

"What's that?"

"We're stopping off in Rome, first, to get your Cadillac."

"What?"

"We want to *buy* it, Frank. When the Chile money gets here, we'll throw in enough for the Caddy, too. We'll fly to Rome tomorrow night. I'll go to your house and pick up the car."

Peroff imagined Savotok and Spellman going to his house without him there. Ruth would be at their mercy when they showed up, and the mere thought of it made Peroff almost delirious. For the first time he was gripped by fear, not so much for himself but for his family. Got to find Mercado, he thought. Got to get back to Rome, to Ruth and the kids! Got to get away from these people!

He was almost numb when the group left the Chinese restaurant and proceeded in two taxicabs to the Folies Bergère. He sat in the music hall, hardly noticing the dancing girls with their skimpy clothing up on stage, thinking that everything would be over by tomorrow. But how? Exactly *what* would happen?

Outside the Folies the group split up. Peroff hailed a cab with Handel and his Swedish girl friend. They rode through Paris while the Kraut begged Peroff to join them for a couple of drinks. Peroff tried to refuse, arguing that he felt nauseous, but they stopped off at a tavern called the English Pub and he went with them.

"Tell me more about the jets," Handel said when they were at a booth in the pub. "And the gold smuggling, too."

Peroff started to reminisce, but the faces of the Kraut and the Swedish girl began to seem distorted. He could not control his nerves, becoming increasingly dizzy, unable to keep his mind focused on the conversation. He took a sip of beer, but could not swallow. At last he excused himself and rushed outside, wandering off in the darkness.

He found himself walking quickly through an ugly section of Paris, his heart pounding as he searched for a public phone booth. By now it had to be nearly one in the morning. The narrow street through which he was hurrying was lined with drunks leaning against a brick wall. Then he passed a group of men dressed in weird clothing, flamboyant homosexuals, and one of them yelled at him in French. Peroff kept walking, holding his hand inside his jacket pocket as if he had a gun.

It was a long block, seeming endless. At the corner he saw a drugstore that was open. He went inside, looking around for a phone. The place was large and crowded, mainly with young men and women, and Peroff took a stairway leading up to a small coffee shop where people were waiting in line for three telephones on the wall. He fumbled for change, and at last a phone was free. He had written Mercado's home number on the inside of the waistband of his underwear, just in case he was ever searched for stray slips of paper. He glanced at the number to be sure of his memory, dialed, and Mercado's wife answered.

"Tony there?"

"No. Is this Frank?"

"If he calls in, tell him I'm trying to find him."

"I haven't seen him myself for almost two days."

Peroff hung up and dialed the Embassy number. He was put on the line with Artie Jenkins, chief of the Narcotics Bureau, at his home. "Where the hell is Tony?" he asked.

"Out in the street somewhere. I haven't seen him for over a day."

"If you reach him, have him call me at the P.L.M."

When he hung up he walked slowly downstairs to the lower part of the drugstore and outside, thinking of what he should do. He walked back the way he had come, passing through the same dark street, and returned to the English pub. Jules Handel was still there, but the Swedish girl apparently had met up with a previous boyfriend. The Kraut was drinking heavily, depressed.

"I got the flu," Peroff told him. "I don't know what the hell it is, but I'm going back to my room."

Handel was almost completely drunk, nodding and paying little attention to him. Peroff walked outside, hailed a cab and started to give directions for the PLM. Instead, however, he found himself saying, "Hotel Rome, s'il vous plaît."

"Qu'est que c'est l'addresse?"

Peroff leaned forward from the back seat to give the address and somehow explain how to get there. Instinct told him that Tony Mercado was nearby, keeping watch on the white Peugeot which was parked in the same block as the hotel. He told the driver—half in English, half in poor French—to slow down when they came near the Hotel Rome.

"But when we get there," Peroff said, "don't stop. Keep going past it."

The cab driver shook his head. "Ne parle Anglais," he muttered, now taking a wrong turn and approaching the hotel from the opposite side. Peroff repeated his message, still leaning forward and gesturing to him, speaking in Italian and Spanish to break the language barrier. When they came toward the hotel he motioned to the driver to keep moving slowly in the darkness. No sign of anybody. A lot of parked cars, one of them the Peugeot, but which one?

"Keep going," he said, giving hand signals over the driver's shoulder. "Around the block."

As they turned the corner, he noticed a small gray truck, more like a tiny van, and in a fleeting second he remembered the same little truck parked outside the P.L.M. Hotel the other night. There was someone in the truck, but now the cab had gone by and Peroff hadn't been able to see who it was. He sat back while the cab continued to circle the block.

"Encore," he told the driver, and now the cab moved past the front of the hotel again. As they approached the corner, Peroff leaned forward and said, "Slow, easy. Okay—stop!"

The driver understood, slamming on his brakes. They were no more than twenty paces from the gray truck. Peroff waited, staring at the man inside it. The guy has to be an agent, he thought. What else would he be doing here at this hour?

"Uno momento," he told the driver. "Wait here. Don't move."

The cabbie nodded and picked up his newspaper, starting to read. Peroff opened his door, stepping out, thinking, Well, okay, here goes. He slowly walked toward the tiny gray van, wondering what he would do if Savotok suddenly appeared. He noticed that the truck driver was dressed in a suit and tie—absolutely the wrong costume for a delivery man, but typical of cops who do surveillance work.

The truck's window was closed, so Peroff bent down slightly and rapped on it with his fist. The man looked at him and gestured as if to say, What the hell do you want? Peroff motioned for him to roll down his window. The man hesitated, trying to act nonchalant. But then he complied.

"Mercado!" Peroff yelled. "Where's Tony?"

"Ne parle Anglais!"

Peroff pointed to himself. "Parlez Mercado!"

"Ne parle Anglais!"

"Aw, cut out the bullshit!"

"Ne parle—"

"Look, I want to speak to Mercado! He's an American! Me, too! Americaine! B-N-D-D! How's that? Embassy! Mercado! Americano! Narcotics!"

The driver was obviously upset at having his secret surveillance so rudely interrupted. Peroff realized that he had been speaking too loudly, so now be began to physically act out his message right there in the street. He pointed under his nose to demonstrate the fact that Mercado wore a mustache. He made as if he were injecting heroin into his arm, to show that Mercado was a narcotics agent.

He found himself actually doing an imitation, crouching a bit to approximate the agent's height and strutting around in Mercado's cocky manner. At last he even drew an imaginary gun.

"Heroeeeen," he whispered. "Narco!"

The man in the tiny truck suddenly nodded and gestured toward the cab driver. Peroff turned, thinking, I'll drag him over here—but for what purpose? How can the cabbie act as a translator if he can't understand English either? Peroff ran back to the taxicab. He opened the door and grabbed the driver by his shoulder and pulled him out, then dragged the bewildered man to the truck.

"Policia," he told the cabbie. "Talk to him! Parlez!"

Now Peroff stood to one side while the two Frenchmen conversed. The man in the truck—obviously a French agent, started giving the cabbie some detailed instructions. The cab driver was nodding, growing more excited. He motioned for Peroff to follow him back to the cab, actually pulling *him* by the arm, thoroughly in command of his unexpected assignment for the French National Police.

Peroff climbed into the back seat of the cab again. He sat frozen while the cabbie drove down the block and abruptly swerved to the side, cutting his motor and headlights. Although it was too dark to read, the cabbie lifted a newspaper in front of his face as if he, too, were a secret agent.

The minutes went by slowly. In the silence, Peroff waited and wondered what was supposed to happen now. Headlights began to appear from behind them and then the gray truck pulled alongside the cab. The agent and the taxi driver discussed something in French, and within seconds the cabbie was following the truck around the block. Peroff had lost track of time and place, but he noticed that they were slowing down at a section of grass and trees between two streets.

There was a paved area as well. In the darkness, Peroff saw a parked car. Then another one, alongside it. He squinted and saw, to his amazement, two more cars, then a fifth and sixth. Looking harder, Peroff realized that there were several men in each car. He rolled down his window and heard the crackling of police radios and walkie-talkies, and it struck him with full force that he had come upon a huge task force of French federal agents. They were lined up in rows, almost as if they were in a parade, obviously waiting to move in on the white Peugeot and the Hotel Rome around the block. Then Peroff made out the familiar figure of Tony Mercado, weaving his way through the cars and coming toward him.

Mercado joined him in the back seat of the cab, telling the driver in French to ride around while they talked. He said to Peroff, "Thank God you had the brains to come find me! I've been trying to get you all day!"

"Same here. I called you several times."

"We've been waiting for a signal to move in. That guy in the gray truck is a lookout," Mercado said, now bursting with laughter.

"What's so goddamn funny?"

"Jeez," Mercado said, unable to hold back. "What the hell did you do to him? He's a French National—one of their top men! And you just *ruined* that guy!"

"Hunh?"

"You ruined his whole year! He thought he was so *cool*," Mercado said, now crying with laughter. "Holy shit, this has never happened to them before. That guy'll never recover! He'll *never* be the same again. I mean, here comes one of the *bad* guys—walking right up to his window!"

"I ain't one of the bad guys," Peroff reminded him.

He started to outline the day's events. He described how Spellman had taken a walk, probably to go pick up his paintings, and how he had disappeared in a mysterious black car. Then Peroff mentioned how Spellman had returned to the hotel with a French girl, a dancer at the Lido, who was only sixteen, whom he apparently raped.

"You're kidding," Mercado said. "Well, we'll take care of him at the right time."

"Tony, I'm worried. At dinner tonight, Savotok says he and Spellman are gonna take a goddamn trip tomorrow. I guess they plan to mail the stuff in the paintings, while they go to Austria or somewhere. But first, they're flying down to Rome to get my Cadillac! Listen, I don't want them going near my wife!"

Mercado looked at him with a curious expression. "Frank," he

86

said, "don't worry. Spellman ain't going nowhere. Believe me. He's not leaving France. And Savotok ain't leaving, either. Neither is Handel. *Nobody's* leaving here. Not for a long, long time. Maybe never."

"You found the junk?"

Mercado nodded. "After I left you last night, we found the Peugeot and opened it up. Ten kilos! Made some tests, took photos and left it there. Now all we do is wait. We got agents all over this place. It's coming, man. I've been out here ever since I left your hotel room thirty hours ago."

"Spellman told the Kraut he could return the car by noon tomorrow."

"Are you sure?"

"That's what I heard."

"Ah, man, that means we might be waiting all night again!"

"What should *I* do?"

"Just go back to your hotel. Understand? We have to do this a certain way. Otherwise we'll have some problems."

"What do you mean?"

"Look, Frank, just get inside your hotel room and lock the door. In the morning, don't order breakfast—nothing! Just stay there!"

"Why?"

"Because if you're *with* these guys when they get busted, it's no good!"

"Now you tell me!"

"Look, Frank, the French cops aren't gonna come *looking* for you. They don't *want* to arrest you. I mean, they got no intent to do that. They know who you are! But they'd be *forced* to bust you, if you were with Savotok and the others."

"Ah, Jesus—"

"But as long as you follow *my* directions, nothing is gonna happen to you! I want that clear, man—just don't go looking for anybody."

"So what now?"

"Go back to your hotel. At ten in the morning, make a call to Savotok. Tell him you're fed up waiting for the money for Chile. Say you're leaving Paris right away. You're going home and calling it quits. But don't move!"

Peroff fell silent in the back seat of the car. He dropped Mercado off at the scene of the police stakeout and instructed the driver to take him to the P.L.M. Hotel. It was past three in the morning.

He gave the driver a generous tip, then went directly up to his room and bolted the door. Unable to sleep, he placed a call to Ruth in Rome.

"Hi," he said.

"I was lying awake in bed," she replied. "Thinking of you. Don't tell me, Frank—I know something's about to happen. Or else it's already taken place. Am I right? Frank? You're okay?"

"I'm fine, babe. You're right, though. Listen, I don't want to say anything over the phone. Just hold on, because that's what *I'm* doing."

"Be careful."

"You know I will. How are the kids?"

"They miss you, but they're fine."

When he got off the phone he lay down, still dressed, waiting for sunrise. It was Friday, the tenth of February, which meant that altogether he had been in Paris for nine nights. Before that, he'd been in London. The whole experience had turned into a bad dream.

The time passed slowly, especially after seven o'clock. But he waited and, as instructed, called the Hotel Rome at exactly ten. He asked for Savotok's room, but Spellman answered.

"Let me speak to Herman."

"He's not here," Spellman said. "He'll be back in half an hour."

"All right. I'll call again," Peroff said, setting down the phone. He hated the situation of being so isolated. What would happen if, say, the Kraut showed up here at the P.L.M.? Would the French police be right behind? In that case, what happens to me?

At ten-thirty he placed his second call, but again Spellman answered. "Try in fifteen minutes," he said.

"I'm coming over there right now."

"No! Stay away from here!"

"Listen, Irv, when do I get my bread for Chile? How long am I supposed to sit here?"

"Not much longer."

"Well, I've had it. The whole thing stinks! You guys are playing games with me! I don't know what the hell you're doing, Irv, but it don't matter any more. I'm catching a plane. You tell Savotok that I'm leaving."

"No, wait! Frank, call again in twenty minutes, okay? Herman will be back here by then."

"All right, but that's as long as I'm waiting. After that, I'm taking off."

Past eleven he made his third call, but this time the operator at the Hotel Rome refused to put him through to Savotok's room. There was a pause, and then another male voice said, "Qui parle? Qui parle?"

"Monsieur Savotok, s'il vous plaît."

"Qui parle?"

Peroff hung up. He called again ten minutes later, with the same result. Trying to envision what was taking place over there, he picked up the phone once more and dialed.

"Oui?"

"Monsieur Savotok?"

"Qui parle?"

"Mickey Mouse," said Peroff, slamming down the phone and starting to pace around the floor of his hotel room. He wanted to do something more, to reach out to the Embassy or to someone, feeling cut off, trapped—and at exactly eleven-thirty the phone rang.

"Yeah?"

"Frank?"

"Who's this?"

"George Walsh, Customs."

"What's up?"

"You sit tight. Don't open that door. And wait for another phone call."

That was the extent of it. Peroff waited, totally frustrated by his lack of knowledge. Forty-five minutes later, Tony Mercado called and said, simply, "It's all done, Frank. Nobody got away. It went beautiful. It's over."

"What now?"

"Stay put a while longer. I'll call back with instructions. I don't care who else calls you—if it isn't me, I don't want you out of that room."

Peroff had the terrible feeling that he was the most uninformed man in the world. If the arrest already had taken place, what then? Will my name appear in the papers? As a conspirator? He imagined that it would be broadcast all over Europe that Frank Peroff had been involved in a heroin deal, barely escaping France or whatever. Such publicity was just what he didn't need, even if he *did* avoid going to jail and being exposed as an undercover agent.

It was past one o'clock in the afternoon when he received final instructions from Tony Mercado to leave the hotel and go by cab to the Embassy annex. The orders were clear and specific: pack your bags, go downstairs, pay your bill, walk outside to the corner, hail a taxi and go *straight* to the annex building without, if possible, attracting any attention.

Once he was in the cab, however, Peroff could not resist returning to the "scene of the crime"—an impulsive urge to regain control over events which had taken place beyond his awareness. He told the driver to take a long detour past the Hotel Rome. When the cab drove slowly by, he looked out the window and saw that the lobby was crammed with men in plain clothes, undoubtedly French cops.

Satisfied that he had seen it with his own eyes, feeling somewhat like a schoolboy who had disobeyed the rules, Peroff instructed the driver to proceed directly to the Embassy annex.

He was taken by a guard up to the U. S. Customs section. When he got there, George Walsh greeted him and brought him into Leonard Tobin's office. Several other Customs agents entered the room, including Tobin, who apparently had just returned from his trip out of town. There were no smiles, no words of congratulation in the room; the scene reminded Peroff more of a wake than a celebration.

Tobin was approaching him; Peroff waited, wondering what to expect, when Tobin yelled, "I told you! I *ordered* you!"

"Ordered me what?"

"I told you that *Customs* was handling this case! Not the BNDD! It was *our* case!"

Tobin was lunging at him with his fists clenched. Peroff stood his ground, shouting, "You should have *stayed* here!"

"You son of a bitch!" Tobin shouted.

"You weren't even here!" Peroff said. "It's not *my* fault!"

Tobin's boss, Pete Murphy, came over to break up the shouting match. He called Tobin into his office for a private conference. At the same time Peroff turned and noticed that Tony Mercado was also in the room, the only BNDD agent on hand, and it was clear why the Customs men were so sullen. Mercado and the Narcotics Bureau were claiming the entire credit, on the American side, for whatever had taken place that morning.

"Come on," Mercado told him. "Let's go up to *my* office."

He followed the dark-eyed agent up to another floor, and here, in the BNDD office, the celebration was in full swing. It was as if World War Two had just ended, the agents all smiling and slapping Peroff on the back, even though he was unsure of what had happened and was still burning from his confrontation with Tobin.

"Have a cigar," someone said.

"Hey, Frank, have a drink."

"Will somebody tell me what happened!"

Tony Mercado sat down with him and described the scene at the Hotel Rome that morning. Somehow, Herman Savotok persuaded Jules Handel, the Kraut, to leave the hotel and go outside to the white Peugeot, in order to pick up the heroin by himself. Handel did so, apparently more terrified of Savotok than by the prospect of being caught with narcotics. Under surveillance every step of the way, with French agents inside the hotel and on the street, Handel walked to the car. He opened up the front door and went under the seat for something—no one could figure out what. He closed the car door and then, nonchalantly, walked to the rear. He lifted up the trunk, reached in, and grabbed a suitcase.

"He was nervous as hell," Mercado said. "He was glancing around scared shitless, but he couldn't see a single cop. They were all over! Well, the kid's not a real pro. Anyway, he takes the suitcase and walks back into the hotel. At that point all the cars started moving around the corner."

Handel went up to Savotok's room with the suitcase. He stepped inside and within half a minute there were at least a dozen French cops in the hall, outside the door. Mercado was the only American officer on hand when the passkey was turned in the lock and they burst into the room.

As Mercado described it, the scene had been a kind of living tableau, all the participants paralyzed in position for several long seconds of silence. Herman Savotok was naked, sitting on the edge of the bed with one foot in his underpants, apparently just beginning to get dressed in a hurry because the heroin had arrived. The Russian girl was there, too, and she was naked also, lying in the bed beneath the covers. The paintings were all over the room, dozens of canvas rolls on the desk and floor, along with the special shipping containers. The suitcase was on the far end of the bed, open, and Irving Spellman was bent over it with his hand reaching inside to grab the heroin. Jules Handel stood next to him.

"Spellman's frown fell right down to the floor," Mercado said, laughing. "Oh, man, did he look miserable! Handel was just in shock, you know? He started whimpering about wanting to call his lawyer. The Russian broad got hysterical. The big mouth, though, was Savotok. He says, 'Get your fucking hands off me,' you know? He says, 'I don't know what the hell's going on here,' and so forth, and he actually wanted to fight his way out! Then he saw how many cops were there, so he gave up. But he really acted the big shot. The French guys were ready to blow his head off. There he is, no clothes on, and he's gonna fight 'em all! One guy stuck the point of his gun up Savotok's nose. Right up the nostril!"

At this point, Mercado reported, Irv Spellman made a move to run. He closed the suitcase, picked it up, and then found himself in a brawl.

"They fixed him for that rape," Mercado said. "Three French cops really worked him over, right on the spot. They gave him a couple of good shots in the gut. He collapsed like a baby."

Spellman, Savotok, Handel and the Russian girl, who would be held for questioning, were taken immediately out of the hotel and whisked away in separate cars. They were brought to police headquarters in Paris and taken into separate emtpy rooms, each one with just a chair, and interrogated right away. In France, the police had four days in which they could do almost anything to prisoners arrested on any kind of felony charges, before having to bring them before a judge.

"They don't even have to tell anybody that they *got* 'em," Mercado explained. "No lawyers, no phone calls, nothing. They can starve 'em, torture 'em, anything. On Tuesday, they'll bring 'em before a jail magistrate and turn 'em over to the French Government. Then, your friends go to prison."

The load of heroin in the suitcase amounted to ten kilos or twenty-two pounds. It represented only one part of the fifty-kilo package, but it was enough to put Savotok and Spellman and Handel away for twenty years.

"How about some lunch?" Mercado asked.

"I just want to get out of here and go home."

"Sure, but first we'll eat."

They went back down to the Customs office, where Leonard Tobin officially apologized for his outburst. With Tobin and Mercado, Peroff rode to the main Embassy, where they entered a lavish dining room. They ordered roast beef sandwiches and French beer and ate on a coffee table, seated in huge, comfortable chairs.

Later, at the annex building, agents of Customs, BNDD and even the Secret Service got into a huge squabble over which bureau deserved most or all of the credit for the arrest. Peroff sat there and waited, disgusted at the rivalry, until it was agreed that Customs and BNDD would split the glory evenly.

Before leaving, Peroff confronted Tom Glazer of the Secret Service. Glazer agreed, at last, to issue the cover story about the counterfeit bills. Now, the fake press release would also have to say that someone had been caught with Chilean money in Santiago.

IV

On that Friday night, the tenth of February, 1973, Peroff landed at the Rome airport and took a taxicab to his villa outside the city. It was as if he had just returned from the wars, with Ruth running over to greet him at the door, with the two daughters and the little son surrounding him and asking for details of his trip. Peroff slumped into a chair and began answering questions, but soon the exhaustion crept up and he felt as if all the pressure of the previous ten days was seeping out of him. He barely made it to bed, falling asleep with his clothes on.

He remained in bed for the next two days, the entire weekend, talking on the phone to Nunzio Galli at the American Embassy in Rome a few times. Tony Mercado called from Paris to say that the French National Police had gone out on Saturday and, based on prior surveillance of Herman Savotok, they had rounded up five of the heroin suppliers in various parts of the city.

"One of 'em was from a lab in Marseilles," Mercado went on. "And are you ready for this?"

"What?"

"Fifteen more kees!"

"Yeah?"

"That makes twenty-five, Frank! So we got half the load!"

Peroff lay in bed with the phone held to his ear, his mind spinning with the figures. Three Canadians and five Frenchmen arrested, plus twenty-five kilos of pure heroin confiscated. It had to be one of the biggest busts in a long time.

Press coverage of the arrests was held up deliberately by the authorities for at least three days, enabling Peroff to call Bouchard with a line. He would have to come up with a careful, convincing explanation of why he alone, aside from Albert Abdul, had escaped the French Nationals. All during Monday he was on the phone with Mercado in Paris and Galli in Rome, working out the details of a plan. On Tuesday morning, knowing that the news had just broken in Montreal, and dreading the thought that Bouchard suspected him, Peroff placed the call.

Alone in his office at the villa, he worked himself into the role that would have to be played without the slightest discrepancy or false note. "Hallo," came Bouchard's voice with its Continental lilt, from four thousand miles away.

"It's me. Something's wrong."

"Yah?"

"I almost got it."

"Got what?"

"I don't know, Connie. There was trouble! Something's definitely wrong. I'm on the run."

"Where are you calling from?"

"Rome. Just got back today. Took me four days to get here."

"Why?"

"Well, Connie, it started on Friday, in Paris. I tried to call Savotok's—"

"Don't mention names on this phone! No names!"

"Look, those bastards almost got me! I *know* something's bad. I tried to call their hotel—all of a sudden, somebody gets on the line and wants to know who's calling. That happened two or three times."

"Yah?"

"I got panicky. I just packed up and ran. I rented a car and started driving to Switzerland. Drove two days and abandoned the car, and then I tried calling those bastards again, but the guy got on—he's speaking to me in French—and he still wants to know who's on the line. So I hitchhiked for two more days. Went through the Alps until I could get a train."

Bouchard questioned him closely about what he had just said, forcing Peroff to make up dozens of details. At last, apparently satisfied, the French Canadian said, "It's in the papers here."

"What's in the papers?"

"They're busted. They're all in the can."

Now Bouchard proceeded to read the stories to Peroff over the phone, translating from a Montreal paper written in French. After each sentence, Peroff let out short exclamations of surprise, as if he were hearing it all for the first time.

"Frank, did they ever discuss the deal? In front of you?"

"Never, Connie! Look, I knew these guys—I mean, I'd gone out to dinner with 'em and everything else—and I knew they were talking about dope. But I had no *idea* they were doing a deal. Not right then! You know what I mean? The impression I got was that Savotok was looking for a contact. But there was never—I mean, no way that I knew there was a dope deal going on there. If I'd known, I would've been out of there so fast—I mean, no way, Connie. That's the truth."

"It's on the front pages here."

"Connie, is my name in the paper?"

"No. Abdul's name got in, though. It says he escaped. And it says something about a fifth man, ya know? But it doesn't mention you by name."

"Well, thank God. Listen, Connie, did *you* know there was a deal?"

"Me?"

Peroff nearly laughed at Bouchard's innocent tone of voice, replying, "Yeah, Connie, you!"

"Hell, no, Frank! If those bastards did what I *told* 'em to do, they wouldn't be in trouble! But they went and did it their *own* way."

"You mean—"

"Look, Frank, I told 'em *who* to deal with and *how* to deal. And they wouldn't be in trouble if they did it my way. I'm waiting on a call from my man in France. I'm going to find out what happened."

There was a pause. Did Bouchard suspect?

"I want you to come here right away," Bouchard said at last. "It's very important. Let's worry about the bread we got, ya know?"

Peroff felt somewhat relieved. Bouchard was referring to the money in Chile, apparently more concerned about that than anything else. Either that, Peroff thought, or he wants me up in Montreal so he can put a bullet in my head.

"Nah," he said. "Listen, Connie, I just spent four of the worst days in my life. I'm going to sleep for twenty-four hours, and then I'm packing a bag."

"Come here."

"No, I'll be in touch. I don't even know if the cops are outside my door right now! I can't discuss a thing."

"You don't have to run, Frank. Get on a plane and come here. I'll meet you at the airport myself."

"No, look, I'm going someplace where I'm cool. You'll be seeing me soon," Peroff lied, "but I need a couple of days to find out if I'm hot."

Bouchard understood. "Yah," he said. "But when you do come here, go through the States first. I'll be waiting for you, Frank."

While Peroff was phasing out his relationship with Bouchard, anticipating his cover story for the nonexistent Chilean money, the United States and Canadian agents were already making new plans for him. First, Nunzio Galli asked for a meeting so he could hear firsthand Peroff's account of the Paris experience. Galli told him to drive his maroon Audi and to park it on the Via Veneto in the heart of Rome, and then to call the Embassy from a public phone booth. Soon after, Galli and another U. S. official would walk up the street. Peroff was to keep an eye out for them until he was sure they could see him; then, he should walk directly back to his car and get behind the wheel. They would join him immediately afterward.

The appointment was set up for Wednesday morning, the following day. Meanwhile, Peroff made an effort to spend some time with his wife and family. The three children came back from the Overseas School and, on Tuesday afternoon, he took them on a drive into the countryside. They went to visit an old farm, buying fresh eggs and homemade wine. The kids loved the sight of several baby lambs on the farm, and later Peroff took them for a long walk on a dirt road, stopping to chat with farmers and feeling as if he'd been holding a deep breath that was just beginning to be let out. In the evening they drove up to the mountainous area southeast of Rome, near the so-called Summer Vatican, and they went to a little hotel with excellent food and a terrace with a magnificent view.

When Peroff met with Galli the next morning, the Customs attaché showed up with a colleague named Sam Covelli. The two agents climbed into the car with him and Galli said, "Start driving." Peroff drove up the Via Veneto and began cruising around so they could talk in private.

Covelli was a tall man with slick black hair and a thin mustache, looking more like an Italian mobster out of some movie than a cop. But his background was impressive. Apparently he was one of the outstanding U. S. narcotics agents in Europe, and in fact he was quick to take almost full credit for the arrests in Paris. "I'm the one," Covelli began as Peroff drove. "I couldn't be up there, Frank, but as soon as I heard about Savotok, I knew there was a junk deal. I'm the one who called Paris and told 'em."

After that introduction, Peroff answered all of Covelli's questions about the scene in Paris, unloading the details in expectation that this would be the end of it. It took him no more than half an hour. The two agents seemed satisfied and asked to be dropped off on the Via Veneto again. Before they left the car, Peroff reminded Galli that he had spent $8,000 for the passports and other documents, not to mention expenses for hotels and planes and so forth.

"You'll get it," Galli said. "But it'll take time."

Peroff hardly cared how long it would take. Driving back to his villa, he allowed himself to envision another long yachting trip on the Mediterranean with his family. He would negotiate with the Zambian officials and come away with good cash and probably some strong assets, and his other business deals could be made to thrive as well.

But his relief was shortlived. Leonard Tobin and Tony Mercado called him from Paris that same afternoon and announced that his patriotic duty had been extended to include another trip, this time to Montreal. It wouldn't be a "new" operation, just a continuation of the one in Paris, merely a "fishing expedition" to tie up all the loose ends. He would have to spend some time with Connie Bouchard to see if he could learn the French Canadian's plans.

"Look at it this way," Tobin explained. "This was supposed to be a fifty-kee deal, right? And you helped us to get twenty-five in Paris. Now, that's only half. Who's gonna come get the rest?"

Peroff tried to interject the fact that Irving Spellman had already smuggled fifteen kilos into Montreal inside his twelve pieces of luggage, but the agents dismissed that information as if they hadn't heard it. There was no way, Peroff realized, that their pride would allow them to admit that they might have let anything slip through their fingers.

The agents were certain that if the Doctor in Montreal wanted to recover his losses, he would have to make Bouchard a full partner.

"Because," Tobin explained, "there's no more Savotok, no more Spellman, no more Handel. The Doctor's setup is crippled. So Bouchard can muscle in on the other twenty-five kees. If he does, we want to know who he'll send here to get it, and how."

Beyond that, Bouchard would be eager to see Peroff and try to get the full share of the "Chilean money" for himself. That situation, on top of Peroff's closeness to the underworld leader, provided the perfect means to learn what, if any, moves Bouchard might make.

The next day, Peroff was picked up by Nunzio Galli and taken into the Embassy building in Rome through the back door. In Galli's office, with Covelli again, there was a brief discussion of the new plans. "One more time," Galli said with a smile. "A one-shot trip, just to see if we can get the information."

Peroff shook his head, cursing more out of weariness than anger, and he said, "Haven't I done enough already? Is this more of the same blackmail?"

"No, no," Covelli assured him. "You'll be in Montreal for three days at the most. Hang around with Bouchard, see what develops. See if he talks about a new junk deal."

"How do I know I'm not committing suicide? Maybe Connie suspects me! I could be walking into a setup!"

"You'll be protected," Galli promised. "The Mounties up there will cooperate. And that's another thing, Frank. They're very, very anxious. They want to get the Paris story from you, and they're dying for any more information on Bouchard. But honestly, Frank, that'll be the end of it. After this, it's over."

"What if I refuse?" Peroff asked, only to be greeted with silence. When he tried to get them to talk about his cover story, he was told to call Tom Glazer about that. He reached the Secret Service in Paris, but received word that Glazer was unavailable. Peroff could sense the implied threat. The consequences of refusing further cooperation were unspoken.

"Just this one trip and you're done," Galli told him.

"That's what worries me," Peroff said.

The agents suggested that he start growing a beard to make himself more identifiable. Surveillance teams of Mounted Police would be following him wherever he went in Montreal with Bouchard. If any shooting started, the Horsemen would have a better chance to avoid aiming at him if he was wearing some hair on his face. It was a small consolation.

The ticket given him by Customs was for a flight to Paris and then direct to Montreal. For Ruth, it would mean more waiting and worrying, and it took on a greater element of danger because this time her husband would be leaving the European continent. Galli promised to watch after the family, specifically to call Ruth each day to make sure she was all right.

Peroff left Rome the day after his meeting at the Embassy. It was midday on Friday, the seventeenth of February, when the plane concluded its brief flight at Orly Airport in Paris. When he walked into the terminal building, he saw the familiar figures of Leonard Tobin and Tony Mercado waiting for him. "Long time, no see," he quipped as they shook hands and strolled through the airport crowd. They went to a restaurant inside the building and took a table in the rear.

Tobin began, "So what are you gonna do for us in Canada?"

Peroff laughed. "Come on," he said. "Be serious. I'm ready to go back home, that's what. Stop the bullshit, okay? I mean, don't try to con *me*."

Embarrassed, Tobin explained that his contact in Montreal would be the U. S. Customs attaché, Hal Roberts, who specialized in narcotics.

"Wait a second," Peroff said. "When I spoke to Bouchard, he specifically told me not to fly there direct. He said to go through the States, as a precaution. So that's the first thing we'd better straighten out."

Tobin agreed to have the flight ticket altered to include a brief stay in the Boston airport before Peroff continued up to Canada.

Another U. S. Customs agent, Joe Walker, would be told to handle the stopover.

"Another thing," Peroff said. "Bouchard is waiting for me to show up. He's very anxious about the Chile thing. Now, he doesn't know what plane I'll be on, but I wouldn't put it past him to have guys looking for me at the airport. And I wouldn't want to be seen with any cops when I get there. I mean, if that happens I'll get a bullet so fast that—"

"Okay, okay," Tobin said. "We'll sneak you in there completely unnoticed. You get off the plane in Montreal, and Hal Roberts will take care of it. You'll be invisible."

They left the restaurant and went to get Peroff's ticket changed. The only plane leaving soon for Boston was completely filled, so Tony Mercado got hold of the airline manager and promptly arranged for a passenger to be taken off that flight. At the gate, Mercado pulled Peroff aside and said, "Listen, Frank, don't worry about a thing. We just want to know if there's any inkling at all of Connie's plans. If you can find out *who* is coming to Paris, that's enough. You don't have to get any more involved than that. Who's gonna come get the rest of the shipment—that's all we want to know."

Tobin reminded him of the two Customs agents' names: Joe Walker in Boston, Hal Roberts in Montreal. Then Peroff rushed to get aboard the plane.

Peroff landed at the Boston airport in the early afternoon. He spotted Joe Walker with no trouble. The Customs agent, waiting as promised, was an oldtimer like Galli, an affable man with a slight build and graying hair, wearing a tan raincoat and having a certain look about him that immediately fit Peroff's image of a cop. Walker explained that the airport was filled with chaos because of delays and cancellations of flights.

"But you have priority," he added. "You got a seat on the next plane, no matter what."

Walker took him to meet the senior Customs official at the airport and a seat was arranged.

"They'll make your entrance at Montreal very discreet," Walker said as they rushed to the gate. "You won't even be noticed. I'll notify the people in Canada exactly what time your plane should arrive. Hal Roberts will handle everything at that end. He'll have a complete description of you. And he'll meet you right away."

Peroff was dressed in a distinguished-looking suit and a tan overcoat. He was wearing, as usual, the dark glasses. By size alone, he would stand out in any crowd, and already his face had the stubble of a Vandyke beard.

The flight to Montreal was just over an hour. When the plane touched down and rolled toward an exit gate, Peroff took a deep breath and prayed that neither Bouchard nor his henchmen would be waiting for him. If so, he would have to go right past Roberts, who had better be smart enough not to approach him. It was nearly three thirty. He let most of the passengers leave ahead of him, then got up and followed them off the plane, his nerves jumping as he walked down a ramp into the terminal building. Suddenly he heard a commotion at the far end. Looking ahead, he saw a U. S. Customs officer in full uniform, a young man in his early twenties, who was asking various male passengers in a loud voice, *"Frank Peroff? Are you Frank Peroff? Sir? Frank Peroff?"*

Pero: steadied himself and waited until the rest of the crowd had passed him on the ramp. He walked slowly toward the young Customs agent, glaring at him, and quietly said, "I'm Peroff."

"Oh! I have a message for you."

"Uh-hunh," Peroff said.

"Mr. Roberts will be about half an hour late. You're to proceed to the Customs office. It's next door to the Eastern Airlines counter. Go there as soon as you get your bags."

Peroff continued to stare at him, wanting to grab him by the throat. Instead he softly replied, "Thank you" and walked right away from him, nervously heading toward the baggage-claim section. He stood among the crowd, muttering to himself and wondering if already he had been seen by Bouchard or his people. Not only does the guy shout my name out loud, he's wearing a full uniform! And Roberts is thirty minutes late? He waited for his bags, glancing around, back and forth, when his attention was drawn to the Canadian Customs desk. A man in an overcoat, with an attaché case, had just walked over there. Peroff watched him take off his overcoat, revealing a U. S. Customs uniform. Roberts? The man gave his briefcase and coat to the Canadian officers, turned, and stared over at Peroff. Then he started walking in the wrong direction through the Customs aisle, into the crowd, looking right at Peroff as he approached. Returning his stare, Peroff waited for the man to come to him. In a few moments they were facing each other just inches apart.

"Frank?"

"Yeah."

"I'm Paul Brady of U. S. Customs. I'm the senior inspector. I just came down, on my way home. I wanted to make sure you got the message that Roberts will be late."

"I couldn't *help* getting it," Peroff replied. "The guy was standing at the edge of the ramp, there, yelling my name."

"Well, I'm sorry about that. All I know is that Roberts said to make sure you got the message."

"Thank you," Peroff said, wondering what anybody could do to him if he simply got back on another plane and left. He picked up his two bags and made his way to the upper level of the building. He strolled alongside the Eastern Airlines counter, searching for the U. S. Customs Office, but it seemed to be nowhere. He wandered back and forth, mumbling to himself again, realizing that all sorts of people were staring at him. At last he saw, to the left of the Eastern counter, a small sign—"U. S. Customs"—on a far door.

For several minutes he stood wondering how to accomplish the feat of getting back there. The Customs office was at the rear of an area where officials pre-inspected luggage that was destined to go directly into the United States. To get there, one had to climb over a low counter, perhaps a few feet high. Peroff stalled, trying to make up his mind whether to do it. The task would be anything but inconspicuous, to say the least.

Glancing around, he made up his mind and threw his bags into the inspection area. He waited a few seconds, then jumped over the low counter and, aware of how ridiculous he probably looked, scooped up his luggage again and quickly walked into the Customs office.

Several inspectors came up to him and one said, "Hey, nobody's allowed back here," and another asked, "Can we help you?" They circled around him, curious, with no idea of who he was, a third man asking, "What are you doing here?"

"I'm waiting for Hal Roberts."

The inspectors soon left the office, only to be replaced by several others who were coming onto the new shift. Now the questioning began all over again. The inspector who was in charge persisted until Peroff repeated that he was waiting for Roberts.

"Oh. Does he know you're supposed to be here?"

"Yeah. He knows."

"All right, then. Make yourself at home."

Peroff sat down on an old leather couch near a row of lockers. The senior inspector's tiny office was right next to him. Peroff waited for half an hour, refusing to answer any more questions.

"What's your name?" the senior man asked.

"Frank."

"Well, Frank, I'm sorry there's no coffee. The pot's not working."

When a full hour had gone by, Peroff asked him if he would try to reach Roberts by phone. The inspector placed a call and spoke to Roberts' wife, who said he was on his way to the airport. A while later, Roberts himself called and left word that he would arrive shortly.

Peroff took the phone. "Look, this is crazy. I've gone from Rome to Paris to Boston to here, and I've been inside this airport for almost two hours."

"Sorry," Roberts said. "Twenty minutes more and I'll be there."

"Okay. Listen, I'm thirsty as hell. I'll be in the bar."

"I'll recognize you, Frank."

Peroff hung up and hurried to the airport lounge. He ordered a drink and gulped it down in anticipation of Roberts' speedy arrival. After twenty minutes, he rushed out of the bar but no one came over to greet him. Disgusted and somewhat bewildered, he wandered over to a bench and sat down to wait again. An hour passed, then thirty minutes more, until it was after eight o'clock at night. It had been more than four hours since Peroff had arrived in the Montreal airport and still there was no Roberts.

From his position on the bench he surveyed the crowd, noticing two men sneaking glances in his direction. The one wearing a tan raincoat was perhaps in his forties, and the younger man had long hair in the style of a hippie. Peroff had no idea whether they were Government agents or members of the underworld or neither. His arrival in Montreal had been reduced to a nervous wait on a bench while the two strange men watched him from a distance. By now he had sweated through all of his clothing.

At about eight-thirty, Hal Roberts made his appearance, walking over to Peroff and introducing himself, profusely apologizing for being so late. He was a slim man of average height, wearing a bushy mustache.

"Look," Peroff said, "I've been going cuckoo here. I don't know what the hell's going on. Guys are looking at me and everything else."

"Relax, there's no problem," Roberts said, explaining that he hadn't been notified about the arrival of the plane until it was actually landing. Even so, Peroff could not understand how it had taken him more than four hours to show up.

"Who's watching me?" he asked.

"They're both on our side."

"The guy in the raincoat?"

"He's a Horseman."

"And the hippie?"

"A BNDD agent."

As if on cue, the two men among the crowd began giving hand signals to Roberts, who turned to Peroff and said, "Follow me." They walked over to the airport lounge and took a table at the far corner. Peroff started to relax for the first time. A minute later, the long-haired agent from the Bureau of Narcotics appeared and quietly took a seat. Another period of silence went by and then the Mountie in the tan raincoat came in. He, too, sat down at the table, introducing himself as Jean Sourbier.

Peroff mentioned that he needed some water to quench his thirst, but the agents looked at him with worried expressions on their faces. When Peroff asked what the matter was, Sourbier spoke in a low tone, almost a whisper: "We aren't sure, but Connie might be here in the airport."

For a moment Peroff closed his eyes, a knot forming in his stomach as he listened to the three men discuss how to deal with the possibility that Bouchard was actually nearby. They decided to split up and meet again fifteen minutes later, in a more private cocktail lounge on the top floor. The Mountie and the BNDD agent left immediately while Roberts explained, "Bouchard doesn't know me, so it's safe if you and I go up there together." Peroff followed him through the airport to the upper-level lounge, thinking that so far this entire experience had been one long series of blunders, any one of which could have been fatal. Even when the two agents returned to say that Bouchard was not in the airport, Peroff was wishing he could get back on a plane and go home.

The meeting in the private airport lounge was brief. Peroff capsulized his Paris experience for Roberts and the other two agents, who mentioned that Albert Abdul had returned here to Montreal. His apartment was raided following the arrests in Paris, and he was taken into custody, but the Mounties were letting him go on bond.

When the discussion ended, Roberts drove Peroff into downtown Montreal, letting him off about half a mile from the Sheraton Mount Royal Hotel, where a room had been registered in his name. Peroff took a cab the rest of the way, signing in at the desk by himself. A bellboy brought him up in the elevator to his room, which turned out to be a huge, palatial suite with a king-size bed and a separate living room complete with couches and coffee tables. After the bellboy left, Peroff glanced at his receipt and noticed that the agents had gotten him a rate reduction of at least 60 percent. The entire charge for the suite was twenty-eight dollars per night.

In the morning, Roberts called to say that he, too, was in the hotel, in a corner suite with the Mounties. The Customs agent added that the room adjoining Peroff's suite contained an electronics team of Mounties who had set up a complete wiretapping operation. The common wall had been turned literally into a microphone, and Peroff's telephone was bugged as well. All conversations held in his suite would be overheard and recorded on tape.

A short while later Peroff took the elevator down two floors and walked over to the corner suite where Roberts and the Mounties were waiting. Among them was the boss of narcotics for Canada, who had been waging his own personal war against Conrad Bouchard for several years. Peroff poured some coffee for himself and took a seat in the room, answering questions until about noon. He was told to call Bouchard and "let him do the talking" to see where the discussion led.

From the Mounties' suite he dialed the number for Bouchard's personal phone at the two-family house which he still shared with Lou Greco's widow. A gruff voice answered and Peroff identified himself. In a few moments, Bouchard came on the line.

"Frank?"

"Hi, Connie."

"You in Montreal?"

"Right," Peroff said.

"Good, good! Glad you made it!"

"Well, I had to disappear for a few days, you know?"

"Listen," Bouchard replied, "I don't like this phone I'm on. Don't say where you are yet. Just call me at another number that I'm going to give you. In half an hour."

Peroff jotted it down. Bouchard also gave him a code number as some sort of identification. The new number was for a message service.

"He was really excited to hear my voice," Peroff said. "But he's nervous as a bitch."

"Yeah, well, we got that bastard running around like a chicken."

Peroff was struck all over again by the thought of how drastic a change had taken place in Bouchard's life. Since the death of Lou Greco and then his own narcotics arrest and the six months in jail, Bouchard must have become a different man. Now he was out on bond, besieged by lawyers wanting their fees and pressured by the Mounties. He was even a target for other underworld figures who hated him. In the past, with Lou Greco, it had been another story. As the right arm of the legendary junk man and Mafia boss, Bouchard had brought in almost a ton of pure heroin, putting the deals together in rapid succession. Now he faced the prospect of going to prison forever.

The Mounties explained that Bouchard's trial was still being delayed by inefficient administration in the Canadian courts. It was now thirteen months since Bouchard had been arrested on conspiracy charges in the heroin-smuggling case. His defense was that he had been caught on circumstantial evidence only, so it was just possible that he could walk away free.

"So Connie has been walking around for eight months," a Mountie said. "He's still up to his neck in junk. But the more we can cripple him with legal fees, the more risks he'll have to take. We'll force him into a mistake."

"Well," Peroff said, "Connie and I just did paper deals, you know? A lot of counterfeit, mostly stolen stock. But junk is a bad word, to me. It's like taking a gun and shooting somebody."

"Let's put it this way, Frank. Connie Bouchard has killed an awful lot of people. And as long as he faces going to the can, he's a ruthless bastard. He doesn't care about killing people, smuggling dope, whatever. What he does is everyday shit to him—it means nothing. He's an animal, a hunted rat who would knife his own partners for money. He belongs in a cage."

Thirty minutes later Peroff called Bouchard's message service, this time from his own suite, with Hal Roberts and two Mounties looking on. He gave his code and the number for the hotel. In a short while the phone rang and Bouchard was on the line.

"Where are you, Frank?"

"At the Sheraton Mount Royal."

"What? What are you doing there?"

"Why? What's the matter?"

"That's a bad place, Frank! The RCMP uses that place," Bouchard screamed, referring to the Royal Canadian Mounted Police. Peroff glanced at the two Mounties in his room. "You'll have to move," Bouchard went on. "But first we'll have to have a meeting. Stay there until you hear from my people, eh?"

When Peroff hung up he turned to Roberts and the Mounties. "The guy's mind is very bad," he told them. "He wants me to move to a different joint."

"Say no," a Mountie ordered. "Fight him on that. Try to stay in this place, Frank. Because we have all our electronics set up here, in the next room. But if he absolutely insists on switching you, tell him you'll go to the Bonaventure Hotel. Okay?"

Peroff said he would do his best. Roberts and the Mounties departed, leaving him alone to wait for Bouchard to make the next move. An hour later, the phone rang again. A "friend" of Bouchard said he was in the lobby and was coming up to use the bathroom. When the man appeared at the door, introducing himself as Maurice Dufrenne, Peroff realized that he had never met him before. Dufrenne was good-looking, not tall but powerful, with a massive chest and large belly and hands almost as big as Savotok's. Bouchard was probably paying him well to act as a bodyguard and, no doubt, as a hit man.

Dufrenne went into the bathroom, came out and wandered around the large suite, making no effort to hide the fact that he was checking for anything that might look suspicious. He even went to Peroff's suitcase, which was open, and started picking up shirts and other pieces of clothing, looking underneath. When he was satisfied, he turned to Peroff and said, "Come on."

Peroff followed him down to the lobby and outside the hotel. They got into a blue Cadillac and Dufrenne started driving across Montreal. It was snowing and the traffic was thick, so the car moved slowly. Peroff talked about the week he had spent in Paris, repeating the line he had given to Bouchard about how he'd escaped through Switzerland, and Dufrenne echoed Bouchard's theme that Savotok had operated in a stupid, careless manner. Meanwhile, as they chatted, Peroff kept a careful watch to see where they were heading. He was alone with a paid assassin, and it was still entirely possible that Bouchard suspected him. If so, his life was in extreme danger.

After forty minutes the car pulled up near a restaurant called the Red Roof. They were on the opposite side of the city. It was midafternoon, but the Red Roof was dark inside. They walked into the small bar section, which was even darker. Adjusting his eyes, Peroff saw that there were plush leather chairs around the small coffee tables. And seated alone at one of them, with a drink in his hand, was Conrad Bouchard.

Peroff walked over and immediately Bouchard stood up and embraced him. In that moment, before they sat down, Peroff saw how the man had changed. More than a year ago, the underworld leader had worn a furry mustache and hair over his ears. Now his face was clean-shaven. The hair was shorter and neater, but it had begun to recede. Bouchard had been almost handsome once, perhaps a decent nightclub singer. But now, at the age of forty-two, his youth had vanished. He looked fifteen years older and twenty-five pounds heavier than before. He was not wearing the kind of expensive, made-to-order suits he had worn in the past but, rather, a simple sports jacket. There was not quite the same appearance of wealth.

More striking, however, was the hard, bitter expression which now permeated Bouchard's face. The lines were deeper, no doubt formed by the constant pressure and worry. There was a hint of Spellman's frown, but no giggling. No laughter at all inside him, Peroff thought. If you didn't know who he was, you wouldn't have a clue—not until you look into his eyes. When you see his eyes, you know just what he is. There's death in those eyes. No feeling behind them.

The three men sat down in the dark lounge area and ordered a round of drinks. Bouchard was in an affable mood, obviously glad to see Peroff and anxious to renew their relationship. But first he wanted to hear more details about Paris, perhaps to eliminate the last of his suspicions, if he had any, about Peroff's involvement.

"As I mentioned," Peroff told him, "I went through the Alps, you know? I ended up trying to rent a car. I abandoned the thing and hitchhiked across the border. Took me four days to get back to Rome. I'm still worried, too. I could get grabbed tomorrow, Connie. I'm gonna grow this beard and maybe go on a diet. The whole bit. I never thought they were doing a junk deal, that's for damn sure. It was just an act of God that I got away."

"You know," Bouchard said, "the word is that Abdul is the rat, but no one can prove it yet."

Peroff stared into Bouchard's sullen eyes, expressing no opinion on that last remark. It was clear, at last, that Bouchard had no real suspicions at all. The conversation turned to Chile, and Peroff reiterated the lie that he had turned a portion of the counterfeit bills into nearly nine million units of Chilean currency which already had gone down in value to about $70,000 in United States money. The rest of the bogus paper, he explained, was in a safe in the Carrera Sheraton in Santiago.

Bouchard nodded. "So it's sitting down there. What do you need to go get it for us?"

"Well, it takes a couple of guys. A pilot has to be able to go in there, and he's got to know that country, because he can't use the radio. He's got to fly into Chile in a prop jet."

"How much do you need?"

"Well, about twelve grand altogether. I've already spent five, and the pilot will want five more. And there'll be expenses for operating the plane."

"The gas and stuff we'll do on a card," Bouchard suggested, referring to a stolen credit card.

"Connie, do you really want to go to jail that bad? You know what I mean? There's certain times you take chances and certain times you don't!"

"Okay, okay," Bouchard replied. "What about the pilot?"

"I can call him now, if you like."

"Good!" Bouchard exclaimed. "We'll get the money, you know? We can work some deals, eh? I've got paper, good stock—everything, Frank. And you're the paper man, eh?"

Peroff laughed. "Yeah. Now, listen," he said, choosing his words with care. "For the plane, I have to physically go to Florida and arrange it. Because the problem is, there are damn few guys that are gonna give me the plane I want. I need a Navajo, a Piper Navajo. It's a turboprop. A half-million-dollar airplane. There's damn few people that are gonna let you take a plane like that out of the States, at the risk of never having it come back. So I gotta go see a couple of friends of mine and work that out."

"But meanwhile, you can arrange the pilot?"

"Yeah, I'll call him now. He's in Florida, unless he's working. The last time I talked to him, he had a job coming up."

Peroff stood up and went to a pay phone in the restaurant. Bouchard and Dufrenne came with him, standing at either side of him as he placed an actual call to Florida, to a real pilot whom he knew. By chance, the pilot's wife answered and said that her husband was on a flying job and therefore unavailable for three weeks.

"Well," Peroff said when he had hung up, "we can wait another three weeks, I guess."

Bouchard said, "We'll do some paper deals, eh?"

"Fine with me. I need the bread, baby."

Bouchard suddenly looked at his watch and said that he had to be somewhere immediately. He told Dufrenne to remain in the restaurant with Peroff until he returned.

"By the way," he asked, "why'd you pick the Sheraton Mount Royal?"

"Well," Peroff said, "I always stay in Sheratons. Like, for example, I told you it was a Sheraton in Chile."

"Oh, yeah. Well, when I come back we're gonna move you."

"Fine," Peroff said, now remembering the Mounties' instructions and adding, "How about if I go to the Bonaventure?"

Bouchard squinted his eyes in silence and looked at him with that hard, intense expression. "You know that's where I got arrested?"

"No," Peroff said, becoming dizzy, "I don't know."

There was an awkward moment during which Peroff wondered

how the Mounties, who supposedly knew so much about Bouchard, could have picked the two worst hotels in the city.

"That's where they busted me," Bouchard said. "It was the Bonaventure."

"Shit. You tell *me* where to go."

"When I come back, we'll go check you out and bring you somewhere else. I think it will be the Fountainbleau."

"Okay," Peroff said, thinking that just when he had eliminated all of Bouchard's suspicions, the Mounties' suggestion about the Bonaventure Hotel had rekindled them. On the other hand, Bouchard seemed to be nervous solely because of his own situation. He was a crazy mixture of personalities, one moment being so cautious and the next minute proposing any number of risky paper deals. The Mounties were correct in their assumption that he was "running around like a chicken," so desperate for defense money that he was forced to keep committing crimes. Still, there was no talk about narcotics.

Before leaving the Red Roof restaurant that afternoon, it suddenly occurred to Peroff that he was facing his first problem. What would happen, when they brought him back to the Mount Royal Hotel, if Bouchard and Dufrenne went to the cashier's desk and inspected the bill? Wouldn't they see the reduced rate and know something was wrong? After all, Dufrenne had seen the size of the room. Even if he wasn't the brightest of men, he would realize that twenty-eight dollars was far too low a price. How would Peroff explain it?

While Bouchard was gone, Peroff excused himself, telling Dufrenne he was going to the bathroom. In fact the men's room had a public telephone. He hesitated. What if Dufrenne walked in? Peroff went ahead, however, and was able to reach Hal Roberts at the consulate without being seen.

"They're going to check me out of the Mount Royal," he whispered into the phone. "He's making me move into the Fountainbleau."

"Damn!" Roberts exclaimed.

"Why didn't you tell me the Bonaventure is where he got caught?"

"Oh, yeah, that's right! Listen, the Fountainbleau is the best you can do? You can't keep it downtown?"

"Look, Hal, I don't even know where the Fountainbleau is!"

"Okay, okay."

"And listen," Peroff went on, "if they see me paying thirty bucks or something, I'll get a bullet in my ass right there! You tell the Mounties to make it around a hundred dollars. Otherwise I'm gonna have a lot of trouble. It could be stupid trouble."

"You're right," Roberts said. "I never thought of that."

"I'd better get off. Do something!"

It turned out to have been an important phone call. When Bouchard returned to the restaurant, they drove immediately across town to the Mount Royal. Bouchard waited in the lobby while Dufrenne went up to the suite with Peroff to help him pack. There was little choice, when someone like Bouchard told you to move. You moved.

At the cashier's desk, Peroff fumbled with his wallet as Bouchard and Dufrenne hovered next to him. He glanced at the bill quickly, but not fast enough. Bouchard snatched it out of his hand to examine it himself. Fortunately the Mounties had gotten it changed. The total amount for one night now came to ninety-three dollars. Both Bouchard and Dufrenne were impressed, to the point where the whole incident had an effect just the opposite of what it might have been. In fact, Bouchard even exclaimed that the bill was too high.

They threw his bags into Dufrenne's Cadillac and drove him back across Montreal to the Sheraton Fountainbleau. Bouchard checked him in personally and, this time, he felt free to go up to the room. Apparently Bouchard was comfortable at this hotel, because right away he picked up the phone and made several calls, conducting business in rapid French.

The Mounties, Peroff thought, were probably frantic. They would have to unhook all their electronics at the first hotel and find a way to install it again at this one. Bouchard and Dufrenne left at five o'clock, enabling Peroff to reach Hal Roberts by phone. Roberts said that the Mounties were already there, in the room next door to him.

"Dufrenne and I are going out to dinner," Peroff told him. "He'll be back here at about nine tonight, to pick me up."

"When you leave the room," Roberts said, "drop your key on the floor. In the hall."

Peroff did just that. Dufrenne showed up, eager to expose Peroff to one of Montreal's better restaurants. Bouchard, living under stringent bail restrictions, was required to be at home after nine and so would not be joining them. Leaving the hotel room, Peroff waited until Dufrenne walked ahead of him. Then he dropped the key, coughing loudly to conceal the sound. Now the Mounties in the adjoining room would be able to perform their new wiring task, and Peroff could get another key later at the desk.

But the troubles were not over. The next morning, Sunday, Roberts called and asked for a full account of the conversations that had taken place. After Peroff filled him in with every detail, Roberts announced that he would have to attend a meeting back at the Sheraton Mount Royal. Peroff balked, wondering what sense it made to risk sneaking across town, but Roberts insisted.

It seemed like a ridiculous request. As he rode by cab, Peroff wondered if Bouchard was having him watched. Or even if Bouchard called while he was out, it would require another fast line to explain where he'd been. Peroff told the cab driver to stop downtown and let him off. He hopped aboard a subway, went a short distance, got out and took another taxi the rest of the way. All for a meeting which turned out to be just as unproductive and useless as he had anticipated.

That afternoon, at the Fountainbleau again, Peroff was in his room waiting for Bouchard, who had promised to come over within the hour. At one point Peroff slowly opened his door, leaning into the hall. At the same time, a Mountie in the next room, wearing a white T-shirt, was opening his door as well. The two men peeked out, looked at each other, and both became so startled that they slammed their doors shut again. When Peroff realized that it must have been an electronics man for the Mounties, he opened his door a second time.

The Mountie did so, too, introducing himself as Pierre Boudreau, and they laughed over what had amounted to a slapstick comedy scene. Boudreau thanked him for leaving his key the night before and added, "We're all set again. I'll have two guys next door at all times. We can hear everything that goes on in your room, Frank. The phone, too. And if you ever have a problem, we'll be there. Don't worry—we listen. When you go to the bathroom, we can hear so well that we know whether you got diarrhea or not."

Bouchard showed up with Dufrenne later in the afternoon, and once again he started making calls as if he had found a safe office from which he could give orders and make new deals. Again he spoke in French, but this time all his words were being recorded in the adjoining room.

Without warning, Bouchard shouted and cursed into the phone, becoming extremely upset. He had completed one call and had begun to make another, but apparently the line had gone dead. Bouchard held up the phone, then slammed it down. Peroff got ready to face his accuser, to shout back and make denials, whatever, and meanwhile it was obvious that the Mountie's wiring job had been the cause of the problem.

"I'm gonna find out what this is," Bouchard said. "I'll be back."

He returned with two bellboys and said, "We checked it out. There's something wrong. It's in the hotel switchboard, but they can't clear it. At any rate, Frank, I've had you moved. Pack up again."

Peroff hurriedly threw clothing into his bags, handing them to the bellboys. They all marched out of the room and over to a new, eight-story addition at the rear of the Fountainbleau, where Peroff was resettled. That night, the Mounties installed—for the third time—their bugging equipment in the adjoining room.

Conrad Bouchard proved eager to show Peroff around the town. Most of the time, because of Bouchard's bail restrictions, Peroff wound up going out to dinner with Maurice Dufrenne, a connoisseur of good food in large amounts. But gradually Bouchard grew more restless and careless, breaking his rules and staying out late, getting drunk on a couple of occasions, which turned out to be the only times when he really laughed and seemed to enjoy himself. He could not hold his liquor well and was always on the lookout for women, but underneath he was in a constant state of controlled panic, worrying about the Mounties and facing the prospect of life in prison and scheming to find new, illegal ways of raising more money for his defense. He was desperate, but still an important figure with powerful underworld friends. And to each of these, in nightclub after nightclub, he introduced Frank Peroff as a comrade in crime.

He seemed completely relaxed with Peroff, inviting him into his home for long conversations and using Peroff's hotel room for hours at a time, conducting his business on the phone in what he assumed to be maximum privacy. Once he even fell asleep on Peroff's bed for an afternoon.

Meanwhile, Peroff was still required by Hal Roberts of U. S. Customs to sneak off each day and make his way back to the Sheraton Mount Royal, across town, for debriefing sessions. The necessity of these meetings was dubious and the actual effort to go there and back was filled with furtive antics and real tension. After being with Bouchard, Peroff would get to a "safe" public telephone and call Roberts, giving him a blow-by-blow description of what had gone on. Roberts would ask him to call back in an hour. When Peroff did so, Roberts invariably would say, "We have to hold another meeting," so then the journey would begin again.

Peroff would go to an underground shopping mall, where he would get on a subway train. He would go one stop and jump off, only to board another train back to the mall. Then he would meet Roberts either at a restaurant or take a taxicab to the Mount Royal, where most of the sessions took place. One time he got aboard a subway and felt he was being followed, so he passed right by the stop where Roberts was waiting for him. Generally he would take a cab, then a subway, sometimes walking off with the crowd only to step back in again before the doors closed, to see if anyone else did the same thing. Peroff took it upon himself to go through these diversionary maneuvers each day, just to be absolutely sure that he wasn't being followed.

Then there was the constant presence of the Mounties' electronics men in the adjoining room at the Fountainbleau. Whenever he returned alone to the hotel, Peroff would knock on their door first to inquire if anyone had been to his room. If he was still under suspicion, one sign of it would be if any of Bouchard's henchmen had gone to search his belongings. Did they give my room a toss? Are they looking for a tap? Did they *find* a tap? Before Peroff opened that door, he wanted to know if someone had been there in his absence. But the Mounties always answered, "Just the maids."

The electronics men had at least two tape recorders, one for the phone and another for the room itself. They could lie on their beds and listen to everything in Peroff's room. They would turn on their television set with the sound off, because they could listen to *his* sound. If they wanted the sound coordinated with the picture, they had to watch the same program as he did. Peroff would check in with them and ask, "What do you want to watch tonight?"

Early in the week, Peroff was asked to make contact with Albert Abdul, whom he had met in Paris. One evening Abdul came up to his room with his partner, both of them stoned on hash oil, and Peroff led off the conversation by giving his line about how he had just barely escaped arrest.

He told Abdul, "The least you and Savotok could have done was *told* me you were doing a junk deal. I almost got busted, man, for something I had nothing to do with!"

Abdul sobered somewhat from the effects of the drug he had taken. He apologized and proceeded to ask Peroff if he could get a plane with which to fly huge amounts of hash oil out of Pakistan. It was an unexpected proposal, and Peroff went into a long analysis of what kind of plane would be needed, but the agents who were listening apparently had little interest in it.

The following night, however, Peroff received a call from a man identifying himself as the Doctor, who had financed the heroin deal in Paris and had suffered the greatest loss. The Doctor wanted to hear, firsthand over the phone, what had happened leading up to the arrest of his people. Peroff replied that he had been in Paris on separate business and that he'd been lucky to get out of there when he did.

"I hear you have some money for me in Chile," the Doctor said.

"Yeah?"

"I'm entitled to that money."

"Well, you talk to Bouchard about that," Peroff said, and after a brief argument the conversation was over.

A renewed partnership with Conrad Bouchard grew slowly. It began with more talk about Chile. Peroff reiterated that he would have to go down to Florida to arrange, personally, the rental of an airplane with no money in advance. The fee of $5,000 would go to the pilot.

Bouchard asked, "Why don't *you* be the pilot?"

"No," Peroff said. "I can't do it. First, I don't know my way around down there without a radio. And if I *did* use a radio, it wouldn't work. You need a guy who knows every tree in that country just by looking out the window."

They were lounging in Peroff's hotel room, every word of their conversation being overheard and recorded next door. Bouchard asked, "What happened to all your planes?"

"Well," Peroff said, "I still use 'em once in a while, in Europe."

Another day, again in Peroff's room, Bouchard inched closer to a proposition involving narcotics. He asked, "How hard would it be to get another jet?"

"I don't know, Connie. I could look into it."

"We could both make a million dollars, Frank."

"Yeah, but I wouldn't do anything unless it made sense, you know? I mean, a jet plane is no toy."

Bouchard stood up, becoming intense. "If Savotok was half a man," he complained, "that guy wouldn't be in the can right now. If he had wanted to play straight, we could have avoided Paris and dealt right at the lab!" Now Bouchard sat down again, facing Peroff, his eyes glowing wtih sudden excitement. "For instance, Frank, if you and I were to do a deal, I'd have you right there in Marseilles, with the plane, dealing at the lab! I'd fix it for you!"

It had taken Peroff by surprise. First of all, he had come here only to learn, if he could, whether Bouchard was planning to send someone back to Paris to get the rest of the previous shipment, assuming there *was* more left. He had not expected to run into a situation whereby Bouchard would proposition him on an entirely new narcotics-smuggling scheme. It was the discussion of the plane, and Peroff's ability to fly it in and out of Europe and the United States, that was stirring Bouchard's imagination.

Peroff decided to turn him off completely. "Connie," he said, "you know I never fool with that stuff. Sure, I'm hurting for money, but there's no way I'd get involved in a deal like that. The only possible way would be if I got my end up front. And it would have to be astronomical. Otherwise, I don't even want to hear about it. Besides, I don't know anything about dope. You know how many times I've been propositioned. In fact, *you* propositioned me ten different times, Connie. And you know that I've never, never even considered it! No way am I going to do that."

His speech had been partially for the benefit of the listening agents. There was a limit to how much he could turn down without making them angry, but to what extent was he supposed to behave like an actual undercover agent?

There was no mention later on, by Roberts or the Mounties, of Bouchard's proposition to have him fly direct to a Marseilles heroin lab, so Peroff dismissed it from his mind. But the following day, all the agents became extremely excited when Bouchard phoned and announced, "We're gonna have dinner with Pepe. I'm coming over to get you."

This was a totally unexpected turn of events, beyond anyone's expectations. After Lou Greco's death, the reigning and undisputed leaders of the Montreal mob were Vincent "Vic" Cotroni and his brother, Giuseppe "Pepe" Cotroni. Greco had been in conflict with the Cotronis for some time, gaining his big advantage in narcotics when Pepe had gone to jail for several years. But now Pepe was out of prison and Greco was gone. On the one hand, it had made Bouchard's problems almost insurmountable. The Old Man, Vic Cotroni, known as "the godfather" for Montreal, could not stand even the sight of Conrad Bouchard. And the number-two man, Pepe, who supervised the narcotics operations, disliked him only slightly less, dealing with him at arm's length and with extreme distrust.

Yet Pepe had extended a certain degree of friendship to Bouchard after Greco's death. Bouchard was, after all, a powerful "French connection" who could be used by the main organization. The link to Pepe Controni had become Bouchard's hope for survival; it was his one remaining source of high-level Mafia power and credit for his junk deals. And an awesome source it was, judging by a U. S. Senate report issued several years earlier:

Giuseppe "Pepe" Cotroni
Head of the largest and most notorious narcotic syndicate on the North American Continent. A supplier of major Mafia traffickers in the United States. Has direct French-Corsican sources of supply. Is a terrorist and vicious hoodlum in the Montreal area.

Pepe was fifty-three now, while Vic Cotroni was ten years older, more in the background. Bouchard could approach Pepe with propositions; and, therefore, a private meeting with him could mean only one thing: he had gone to Cotroni with the possibility of using Peroff to fly heroin in a jet plane. It was Cotroni who could contract for a load of powder far in advance of making an actual payment. Like Greco in the past, he was able to make a deal solely on the basis of his personal credit. The lab in Marseilles would start production, which might take several weeks, and only when the heroin was ready would Cotroni have to send the money. Most likely Cotroni would use someone else's cash, and the payment could be made at the very moment that the drugs were picked up in Europe. For Bouchard, an association with someone of Cotroni's stature was crucial. Once Cotroni could be persuaded to make a contract with the lab, locating a financier would be relatively easy. Undoubtedly Bouchard had given Cotroni a sales pitch about Frank Peroff to the point where the Mafia boss was interested enough to propose having dinner with him.

Bouchard came to the hotel this time without Maurice Dufrenne. He led Peroff into his own car, another Cadillac, and they rode into a poor section of Montreal, where Cotroni had an office in a small, two-story building on the corner of a shabby street. Bouchard parked at the curb and told Peroff to wait.

After a few minutes, Peroff became restless and got out of the Cadillac. He stood on the sidewalk until Bouchard suddenly reappeared and said, "Get back in the car." Peroff obeyed, noticing that three well-dressed men were coming out of the same building. As he drove away, Bouchard said, "There's some people back there. I don't want them to see you. We're not going to dinner tonight."

Later, during his next debriefing session, Peroff learned that the Mounties had placed the entire episode under surveillance. Even though the meeting had failed to take place, the very fact that it almost had materialized was significant.

Before leaving Montreal, Peroff was treated to a rare insight into Bouchard's current state of mind. One afternoon they drove out of the city into a mountainous area near the Laurentians, an act which in itself was a defiance of Bouchard's bail restrictions, and they went to see a wealthy crook who kept a seaplane on the lake in front of his house. After introductions were made, the man announced that he was in possession of $1,700,000 worth of freshly stolen stock.

"It's Canadian debentures," he said. "All of it cold. We got it from an inside man in the company, and there's still six weeks before it gets hot."

Peroff was impressed. As a professional paper man, he knew that he could "turn" up to 60 percent of this stock in Europe within a week. Bouchard, of course, was initiating the paper deal so he could finance a narcotics package. Even if Peroff were to realize only 30 percent of the value of these stolen debentures, it would come to half a million dollars, enough to pay for all the heroin Bouchard might want.

"Give me forty-eight hours to check it out," Peroff said. "If it's like you say, maybe we can make some heavy money."

Bouchard's friend pulled two hundred thousand-dollar certificates from a briefcase and Peroff wrote down the serial numbers and other pertinent information.

"I'll check it out with a stock guy," he said. "Meanwhile," he added, turning to Bouchard, "don't go peddling this stuff in little pieces. Because there's a right way and a wrong way to do this."

Later on, Peroff had the Mounties check out the stock for him. While he was in their room at the Mount Royal the next day, the phone rang. One of the Mounties listened, hung up and reported, "We just busted a guy with some of that stock! They sent a guy into a local bank with eighty-five grand worth of it. He was trying to make a loan on it, using the stuff as collateral!"

Peroff was astounded. In more normal days, Bouchard never would have done something so foolish. The only smart move was that he had not gone to the bank himself, but had sent some flunky. Peroff went back to the Fountainbleau and reached him by phone. "Connie, your man lied," he said. "The stuff is no good. It's so hot that my guy wouldn't even talk to me on the phone! He hung up on me! Listen, Connie, this guy is a vice president of a big brokerage house, you know? He told me not to touch it with a ten-foot pole!"

"*Now* you tell me," Bouchard replied.

"Why, what's the matter?"

"Well," Bouchard answered, "we got a deal going. I haven't heard yet."

Apparently Bouchard didn't even know that his flunky had been arrested at the local bank. "I don't know what you did," Peroff lied,

121

"but I'm telling you, Connie, that stuff's no good. You might have trouble. That stock is on every bad list in the world."

Later, when Bouchard found out that his man had been arrested, his image of Peroff as a genius with hot stock was bolstered tenfold. In effect, Peroff had warned him in advance.

Bouchard came up to the hotel room with Maurice Dufrenne and explained that they had borrowed money from a loan shark in order to buy the stock. Now they not only owed the shark but had lost the eighty-five thousand dollars' worth of debentures, plus they would have to spend money for lawyers' fees to defend the flunky who had been arrested. On top of all his problems, Bouchard had taken a foolish risk and had gotten bogged down in even more trouble, making new enemies and bringing more heat upon himself.

Peroff relished the opportunity to say, in effect, I told you so. "That stuff isn't worth two, three points in Europe," he said. "I *warned* you, Connie! Didn't I tell you not to play games with small pieces? Now you've burned it, and we ain't gonna be able to do nothing! And whose fault is it? You couldn't wait? I asked you for forty-eight hours! You didn't want to listen? Well, you were stupid and greedy! You know why you did it? Because you think you know how! You tried to do it behind my back, and I wouldn't have known a thing. Well, Connie, that's all right, you do what you want!"

Bouchard was actually ashamed to the point of almost apologizing for his behavior. If Peroff had wanted an opportunity to reinforce his effectiveness as an undercover agent, he could not have asked for a more favorable series of events.

On Monday, February 27, ten days after he had arrived in Montreal, Peroff was told that he could go home the following morning. The mission was over. It had been unproductive, as far as Peroff knew, and the likelihood was that he would never see Conrad Bouchard again.

The final weekend of his stay had been unusual.

On Saturday, Dufrenne gave Peroff a personal demonstration of his ability as hoodlum. The three of them went for a ride in one of the Cadillacs and Dufrenne put on a pair of gloves. They rode to the home of another loan shark who had been giving them problems and Dufrenne got out, saying, "I'll be back in five minutes."

Peroff and Bouchard waited while the powerful bodyguard went inside and took care of his business. When Dufrenne returned he simply said, "I left him laying in a lump," and they rode off again.

On Sunday, Bouchard picked up Peroff at the hotel and announced that they were driving fifty miles outside Montreal to go snowmobiling at St. Marguerite. At first Peroff was apprehensive, but it turned out to be the one occasion when he thoroughly enjoyed himself. They rented snow suits, helmets and boots and rode the snowmobiles up winding trails into the woods. Peroff let out all his anxieties, pushing for speed and working up a healthy sweat before they came to a small shed where they drank hot liquor in plastic cups.

Bouchard was somewhat upset the next day when Peroff declared that he would have to leave. "I'll see you soon," Peroff lied. "I gotta go home and find out what kind of trouble I'm in over there. My wife's alone with the kids, you know? I'm going back to Rome, but I'll probably be there only a day or two. Then I'm gonna lie low for a little while."

The last time he saw Hal Roberts and the Mounties, on Tuesday, Peroff told them, "Sorry, fellas, that I couldn't get more for you. Nice knowing you guys. I've done my best, but I guess it's no use."

Bouchard and Dufrenne even came by that evening and drove him to the Montreal airport. Bouchard pressed him to return soon, reminding him of the Chilean money and mentioning possible stock deals they could do together. He even repeated his contention that a jet plane would solve all their financial worries. Peroff nodded, shook their hands, and boarded an Alitalia plane that would fly directly back to Rome.

Even the discomfort of the long, crowded night flight could not diminish Frank Peroff's relief that he had kept his undercover role a secret. The mission was over.

Stefano met him at the Rome airport at ten in the morning, European time, and the reunion with his family was even more emotional than the previous one. Peroff had called his wife from Montreal at least once a day, if only to let her know he was still alive and well, and now he explained that nothing substantial had happened in Canada. There was no more reason for the Government to threaten him with blackmail.

As before, he met secretly with Nunzio Galli and Sam Covelli of Customs, again in a car on the Via Veneto. Later in the week he made a few visits to the Embassy to answer more questions about his trip and also to ask about his expense money. There was still $6,000 due him for the passports he had purchased and now an additional $3,000 for the Montreal escapade. In addition, Peroff wanted to make sure his cover story would be issued soon, so he could be rid of Bouchard from his life.

At one of the debriefing sessions, however, he was introduced to an agent from the Bureau of Narcotics and Dangerous Drugs who asked him to repeat all his information again. Peroff started with the fact that Bouchard had mentioned no plans whatsoever to recover any heroin left over from the Paris deal.

"Any more discussion of junk?"

"Well, yeah," Peroff replied, recalling how Bouchard had mentioned the possibility of sending him to a Marseilles laboratory.

"Are you sure?"

"Yeah, but it was just talk. He just left it hanging. I mean, I sort of turned him down."

"Why didn't you tell any of this to the agents in Montreal?"

"I did," Peroff said. "First of all, Bouchard made that statement while he was being recorded at the hotel. And second, I told it to Hal Roberts of Customs."

"Ah, I see! I see!"

"What do you see?"

What the BNDD agent saw was the result of a difference in policy between his own bureau and U. S. Customs. The competition was one thing. Agents from one bureau did not trade information back and forth, as might be expected, but instead they allowed jealousies and rivalries to dominate and even hinder their work. Such pettiness was one reason for the general ineffectiveness of the Government in its attempts to contain narcotics smuggling. But in this case, the problem had been compounded by the fact that Customs and BNDD were looking for different types of information. Peroff's information about Marseilles laboratories had been worthless to Customs, since that agency's major concern was the actual finished product of heroin that came into the United States. But one of the prime functions of the Narcotics Bureau was the discovery and destruction of foreign labs. In fact, the BNDD had a mandate to pay informants the whopping sum of $250,000 for each lab that was confiscated with their help.

The Customs agent in Montreal, Roberts, had not even bothered to pass along his information to the Bureau of Narcotics. Apparently one organization had no interest in the possible success of the other, even though they were both fighting the same war against drugs. Peroff, who had understood none of these political matters, found himself staring in shock as the BNDD agent frantically sent coded messages to his colleagues in the States about the latest development.

During the first two weeks of March, Peroff was ordered to appear several more times at the Embassy in Rome, and was told to get ready for another trip to Montreal.

When he tried to resist, the same threats came back at him even more forcefully than before. The counterfeit money still hung over him, but also the agents could easily let Bouchard know that Peroff was an informer. "It's very easy for the truth to come out," they said. "Just a little slip."

Once again he tried to call Tom Glazer, the Secret Service boss in Paris, but could not make contact. "You're in hot water," Nunzio Galli confided to him. "They got you by the balls, Frank. They won't let go, either. You should never have called Glazer in the first place."

Galli, the oldtimer, had been one agent who had kept all his promises. While Peroff had been in Montreal, the Customs attaché had telephoned Ruth each day to see if there was anything she needed. He even shopped for the family at the commissary in the American Embassy, bringing cartons of canned goods to the villa.

Peroff listened intently whenever Galli spoke to him in confidence. He would have to return to Montreal, perhaps for a couple of weeks, to see if he could learn the location of the Marseilles lab. And in order to lure Bouchard into a deal, he would be provided with a Government-leased airplane, a million-dollar jet, complete with a pilot and an agent disguised as a radioman or copilot. If Bouchard did come up with a heroin-smuggling contract, Peroff would have to fly the plane by himself to France, lead the agents and French Nationals to the lab, and return to North America with at least some of the drugs on board. To keep his cover as an informer intact, the Americans or Canadians would arrest him and keep him in jail for a while. But then he would be released and, if a "working lab" in France had been seized, he would end up with a quarter of a million dollars.

Peroff had little faith in their promise of money. There was nothing in his experience to justify such belief or trust. If the threats against him—to withhold the cover story, to reveal his undercover role—had not been made, he would have declined to go ahead no matter how much of a reward they offered. Under the circumstances, however, he felt there was no choice but to go ahead.

"Whatever you do," Peroff said, "don't get a Lear Twenty-three. It's got the shortest range, and a minimum of electronics. I don't like it for crossing the Atlantic. The Twenty-four has added range, and a degree of additional safety, but that's still not too good." He asked Sam Covelli to request a Jet Commander or a Hawker 125 or a Sabre Liner. "If you *have* to get a Lear," he said, "get a Twenty-five. The others don't even have toilets."

He stood next to Covelli as the Customs agent dictated a Telex message to the States about the specifications for the plane. Peroff would fly from Rome to New York, and the special jet would be waiting for him in Washington, D. C. From there he would help fly it to Montreal.

On Tuesday, March 13, he was told that he would be leaving by the end of the week. At the same time, however, the agents informed him that Ruth and the children would have to go with him to New York. "Let's say a deal is put together right away," the agents explained. "In that case, the safety of your family becomes very important. But we can't protect them over here as well. We want them under U. S. jurisdiction while this is going on. We'll put your family up in a hotel in New York. So tell Ruth to pack."

V

By the time they were ready to board the plane on that Friday, the sixteenth of March, the Peroff family was loaded down with thirty pieces of luggage and, in a special cage, their white French poodle named Nasha. The plane made a brief stop at Orly Airport in Paris. Earlier in the week, Peroff had called his relatives in Florida and had learned that his nephew would be married soon up in New York City. There would be an opportunity for a quick reunion. From the Paris airport, he called the hotel in New York where his relatives were staying and spoke to his brother: "We're coming into Kennedy Airport. Bring Dad out there with you, so I can see him. Meet me outside the Customs section at Pan American."

It was past eight thirty in the evening when the plane touched down at Kennedy Airport. Peroff waited with Ruth and the children until everybody else had gotten off. When they finally emerged from the plane, five Customs agents greeted them, all busily shouting orders to each other and helping get the luggage together in one place in the corner. The Peroffs would not have to go through Customs in the normal fashion.

Amid the chaos, Peroff noticed someone staring at him, rather coldly, from the sidelines. The stranger was a black man of medium-light complexion, perhaps in his mid-thirties, wearing glasses and a dapper business suit and wing-tipped shoes. The man was sitting inconspicuously on a bench against the wall, near a drinking fountain, his chin resting on his fist. His eyes never wavered from Peroff's face.

Peroff kept glancing at him while the agents gathered up the

127

luggage. Several minutes went by; then, calmly, the man got off the bench and began walking over. He flashed a Federal badge and spoke in a formal, deliberately underplayed manner.

"Mr. Peroff?"

"Yeah."

"Soon as you get your things together, we're taking you to a hotel."

The black man was a Customs agent named Roy Gibson. His sole function at this stage was to act as Peroff's liaison in New York and to look out for the family. He knew nothing about the case itself.

"By the way, Frank, you'd better give me the gun."

"What gun?"

Gibson smiled for the first time. "Come on, Frank."

Peroff had told the agents in Rome that he planned to be "armed" during the upcoming trip to Montreal. It was clear that they had relayed the message to Gibson, who was still standing there with a slight, knowing smile. Peroff reluctantly walked over to the stack of suitcases and opened one, removing an Italian Beretta. He turned around and the agent was right next to him, with his hand out. Gibson took the weapon and stuck it under his belt.

"Listen," Peroff said, "I think my father and brother are waiting outside the Customs place. I'd like to see them alone for a few minutes."

"Sure."

"What'll I tell 'em?"

"Say you're a secret agent, that kind of thing," Gibson said, adding, "Here, take your gun back for now. Make it look good."

They went through a door to the other side of the Customs section and Peroff saw his father and brother.

"Come with me," he told them, and Gibson flashed his badge. The old man glanced at it, then saw the gun protruding from his son's waistband. They went toward Ruth and the children, and Peroff's father, in his mid-seventies, rushed over to hug them. He looked around at all the other agents and, in confusion, he began to weep.

Gibson gestured to Peroff. "You can take them into that room over there," he said, pointing to a small Customs office. "It'll be private. But make it short."

Peroff put an arm around his bewildered father and led him, with his brother, into the empty room.

"I don't understand," the father was saying. "Frank, what's going on here?"

"Things are happening, Dad. You may not hear from me for a while."

"Why? What—?"

"I can't explain just now."

"Are you in trouble?"

"No. No, I'm not."

"You're sure?"

It was an awkward moment. From an early age, Peroff's life had moved far beyond his father's comprehension. The hard-working tailor had been forced to rise early in the morning to get to his shop, often returning late at night. There had been a great deal of love, but little time for personal guidance. Now, as they stood facing each other in the small Customs office at Kennedy Airport, the situation was far too complicated for any real communication at all.

Peroff's mother had died a dozen years ago and his father had remarried. The brother, an insurance adjuster, stood there with his arms folded, disapproving of the entire scene. The last time Peroff had seen any relatives was several months ago, when he had brought them to Europe. He had always been circumspect about his life, but never so cryptic as now.

"Dad, just don't worry. It'll be all right. I'll try to explain some day, when we have more time."

Roy Gibson poked his head in the doorway, nodding to indicate that they should finish the conversation. The meeting had lasted no longer than ten minutes.

The agents had loaded all thirty pieces of luggage, with the poodle, into a caravan of waiting cars outside the airport building. Peroff, his wife, the children and the dog were ushered into the cars and the entire parade sped away from Kennedy Airport to the nearby Ramada Inn. They would stay there for the weekend before moving to a more permanent location in the city. During the brief ride, Peroff sat in the front seat of the lead car while Roy Gibson drove. The two exchanged only a few words, the black agent maintaining his cool, reserved manner at all times.

Two rooms were waiting for them at the Ramada Inn, arranged by the Customs agents. The Peroff family settled down for the night and Gibson left some phone numbers where he could be reached if needed.

On Monday morning Roy Gibson knocked at the door. The family packed up again for still another move. By nine o'clock the agents were driving them into Brooklyn, to an apartment hotel where Customs had set up living quarters.

"We'll drop your family off here," Gibson said as they pulled to a stop outside the building. "You're scheduled to be in Washington by one o'clock, for a meeting."

Peroff left the car to go up and inspect the apartment. Ruth and Roy Gibson followed while the children stayed in the cars with the other agents. The building was run down and shabby, almost a tenement, and the apartment itself was worse. It was bare and grubby and depressing.

"This stinks," Peroff said at last. "What the hell kind of a place is this, anyway?"

"Well," Gibson said, "you're right. It is lousy, Frank. This is the first time I've seen it, myself."

"Look, Roy, there's no way that I can take off and leave my family here. No way, man."

"You mean you refuse?"

"What do you think?"

"But Frank, we don't have much time."

After a brief discussion it was decided that they would continue into Manhattan and check in at the New York Hilton Hotel in midtown. Gibson went into the lobby first and registered the family under his own name. The agents helped bring all their luggage up to the pair of adjoining double rooms. Peroff said brief good-byes to his children, who had no idea of what their father was involved in or why all this was happening. He kissed Ruth, telling her not to worry, and left the Hilton with Gibson.

As they drove to La Guardia Airport, the two men still kept their distance from each other, saying nothing about the case. Gibson was not really involved in the mission and Peroff offered no inside information. At the gate for the Eastern Airlines shuttle, Peroff reminded the agent to watch after his wife and children while he was gone. Then he boarded the plane for the quick flight to Washington, D. C.

Once it had touched down at National Airport, Peroff glanced out the window and saw, as the pilot was taxiing toward the gate, a blue and white Learjet coming in for a landing. Peroff squinted to see more clearly and realized that it was a Lear Twenty-three, exactly the model that he had warned everyone against using.

Two Customs agents were waiting for him as he walked into the airport building. He asked them, "Is that my plane out there?"

"Yes. It just landed."

Peroff shook his head in disgust. The agents had arranged for a Lear Twenty-three with a management firm in West Palm Beach, Florida. It was not a million-dollar jet, but more in the range of $600,000. The Government would end up spending $6,000 to lease it for him. The whole experience was new to Customs and probably any other agency as well. It was not the usual thing, by any means, for an undercover man to be provided with his own airplane. Yet the mistake, Peroff knew, could be a crucial one. A Lear Twenty-three was simply not the right plane and, he told the agents, it might have to be replaced if Connie Bouchard came up with a smuggling deal.

They drove into downtown Washington, D. C., to a small hotel near headquarters for the Bureau of Customs. Peroff was checked in and soon a series of meetings began with agents from the United States and Canada. On hand were two Mounties including Jean Sourbier, whom he had met on the first trip to Montreal. Also present was Hal Roberts, the U. S. Customs attaché for Montreal, and several other Customs agents including the European desk officer. A few agents from the Bureau of Narcotics joined them in Sourbier's room after dinner. All the agents were staying in the same hotel, so the meeting lasted until past two o'clock in the morning with considerable imbibing throughout the night.

Peroff gave a short speech and obtained a commitment from them to have a better plane ready on twelve hours' notice. The plan of action was kept rather loose, since Peroff himself was the expert when it came to flying and also because he knew how to deal with Connie Bouchard.

"Whatever he may be," Peroff said, "Bouchard is no fool. And Cotroni is a genius. We're not playing with dummies."

He held back from making the observation that for every time a big narcotics seizure was made, there were more than fifty successful shipments of heroin. Men like Cotroni and Bouchard were shrewd criminals who had succeeded far more often than they had failed. If they hadn't, there would have been no drug problem in the United States in the first place.

It was agreed that Peroff would fly up to Montreal the following day, as a passenger in the Lear. The pilot from Palm Beach had been told very little about the possible danger involved. The co-pilot would be a young Customs agent from Homestead Air Force Base, heavily armed at all times. They both would behave as if Peroff was their boss.

"When you get to Montreal," an agent said, "just expose Bouchard to the plane. Lay it on him that you've leased it for a while and that you're ready to go ahead with whatever he has in mind. Take it from there, Frank. You'll be on your own."

The next morning most of the agents flew up to Montreal in advance, to prepare Peroff's room at the Martinique Hotel. Once again there would be a complete setup for monitoring his conversations, both on the phone and in the room. This time, all the Mounties and U. S. agents would be staying in the same hotel, to make it easier for Peroff to get to his sessions for debriefing.

He was driven out to National Airport that afternoon by the European desk officer for Customs, a man named Dan Massey. On the way Massey told him, "If a deal ever goes through, Frank, it's gonna go down in the States."

"What do you mean?"

"You heard me."

There was silence in the car as Peroff realized what the agent had meant. It had to do with more of the same rivalry, this time between the Americans and the Canadians. If Peroff took the Learjet to France and back, the Americans wanted him to land on their *own* soil so *they* could seize the heroin.

"Don't discuss this with the Horsemen," Massey added. "But as I said, it'll come down in the States. Preferably in New York or Jersey. This is not, under any circumstances, gonna wind up in Canada."

"Okay," Peroff said, amused at the outright admission that such competition and jealousy existed. If there was any glory to be gained, the Americans wanted it.

The Learjet was parked over at Page Airways at the airport.

Peroff got aboard with the pilot, Fred Davis; the young agent acted as radioman and copilot. Within minutes they were in the air, heading for Montreal. Peroff looked around the plane, inspecting the controls and the interior space. There was room for perhaps five persons in addition to the two pilots. There was a seat in back for two, with a pull-out card table, and two individual seats that swiveled around. The plane had a small bar and an icebox, and a hi-fi set with a tape deck, but no bathroom. Peroff still preferred using a Lear Twenty-four.

It was midafternoon when they landed in Montreal. The jet touched down on a runway separated from the commercial part of the airport, taxiing over and parking in front of the small building used by owners of private planes. Peroff got out and helped Fred Davis check the Lear and close it up. From there they took a cab directly to the Martinique Hotel, where Davis and the young agent would be staying. Peroff registered at the desk and went up to his own room. According to the plan discussed the night before, he picked up the phone and called Bouchard.

"You're here, Frank?"

"Right, Connie. At the Martinique."

"How's business?"

"Well, up and down. I'm hurting for bread, ya know?"

"Sure."

"Listen, I talked myself into a plane."

"You did?"

"Yeah, I think I'll be starting up again. With the jets."

"No kidding! You came here in a plane?"

"Uh-hunh."

"What kind?"

"A Lear."

"Really? A Learjet?"

"Yeah, a Twenty-three. I also have a Twenty-four, but it's out on charter, you know? I can get it on demand, though."

"But you've got a plane with you? Right now?"

"Yep. I can use it for three, four months. Until then, I won't need any heavy cash. I gota pay small amounts on the lease, but that's all."

"That's great, Frank!"

"I got a pilot with me, too. And a radioman."

"Listen, Frank, I'm coming over there!"

"When?"

"Right now! Can we go see it?"

"What?"

"The plane! Can I go have a look?"

"Sure, Connie, sure."

When Peroff hung up, he was almost startled at the thought of how excited Bouchard had sounded. He realized, suddenly, that the Mounties' electronics men in the adjoining room must have heard the whole conversation. There would be lots of intense communication among the agents. So far, the bait was working.

Peroff left his room and hurried to see the pilot, Fred Davis, who was staying on a different floor of the hotel. When he got there he asked for the keys to the Lear and to use Davis' phone. He called Hal Roberts of Customs, at his office in Montreal, and told him the news.

"Okay," Roberts said. "So Connie just wants to see it, eh?"

"Yeah. We're going in a short while."

"Look, Frank, just don't get in and fly that sonuvabitch away! You hear? Or else we'll roll a car in front of it!"

Peroff hung up, hoping that Bouchard had not arrived yet. He rushed back to his own room. Ten minutes later the mobster arrived with his bodyguard, Maurice Dufrenne, and the three of them drove out to the airport in Dufrenne's Cadillac.

"It's great to see you," Bouchard said. "What's new in Chile?"

"Well," Peroff replied, "that damn pilot in Florida took off on me again. He's got another job or something."

Bouchard noddded, his mind wandering off the subject. He asked, "Any more heat in Italy? From the Paris thing?"

"Well, I've been moving around, so I'm not sure."

"I really want to see this plane, Frank. It's available for travel?"

"Yeah, of course. You know, for transporting people, that kind of thing."

"Maybe," Bouchard said, "for me as well? Things are not too good here, with these trials, and I might have to disappear."

"Sure, Connie. Just let me know."

The Cadillac pulled into the airport grounds and Peroff gave directions to get to the plane. When they parked and got out,

Bouchard was amazed to discover that the Lear was sitting less than twenty yards away.

"Jesus Christ," he said. "It's that simple? I mean, nobody saw us!"

They walked over and Bouchard touched the side of the plane as if he were a small boy, full of awe and excitement. It was early evening but still light, so Peroff could give him a complete tour. Not any normal tour, however, because Bouchard's mind was focused entirely upon narcotics.

"You could put a lot of stuff in here?" he asked.

"Oh, yeah," Peroff said. "Listen, I could've carried dope a million times in the past."

"Let's see, Frank! Like where?"

"Well, watch this," Peroff said, bending down and unscrewing a square panel in the belly of the plane. "This is the electronics hatch," he added.

Bouchard bent down to look. "Hey," he exclaimed. "There's *room* in there!"

"Sure," Peroff said, watching Bouchard actually climb into the hatch with the electronics panel.

"Where else, Frank?"

Peroff brought him around to the front of the plane, to the cowling on the nose. Again using a screwdriver, he demonstrated the Lear's ability to conceal shipments of heroin, explaining, "There's electronics gear inside, see? Now, this gear doesn't get hot at all. And there's plenty of room to lay bags in here. Bendable bags, you know?"

Bouchard was ecstatic. "Where else?" he asked.

"Well, inside the plane, in the floor, you could put at least one layer, maybe two layers of bags."

"Holy shit," Bouchard muttered, his lips moving while he stood there calculating the pounds of narcotics that the Learjet could carry in secret. Peroff watched him, trying to avoid glancing around to see where the Mounties' hidden cameras were located. The entire episode was being recorded on videotape.

By the next morning Bouchard's excitement had become even greater. He called the room and announced, "Look, Frank, I got a meeting coming up. I'm having lunch with a guy, you know? And I'll be talking to you."

Peroff tried to make Bouchard almost beg him to stay in Montreal. "What do you mean?" Peroff asked. "Connie, I'm thinking of taking off. I got some business to do. I need bread, and—"

"No, don't leave! I got something happening! I'm having a meeting! Stay there!"

"Okay," Peroff said, wondering what sort of meeting it might be. Over the next few hours he received three more calls from Bouchard, who asked him questions and, apparently, was relaying the information back to a third party each time.

The questions were specific, having to do with the plane, about its size and ability, and the final query was directly concerned with heroin smuggling: "Could you go direct to France and back?"

"Jesus, Connie, you can't get in these things and just fly across the ocean! I'd have to go from Canada to Nova Scotia and Iceland! To make stops for fuel!"

"Oh! Okay, I'll get back to you."

At one o'clock in the afternoon, the phone rang again but this time it was Maurice Dufrenne on the line. He had instructions for Peroff to leave the Martinique Hotel, take a cab and proceed to Moishe's Steak House in Montreal. Peroff hung up and got in touch with the Mounties, who sounded more emotional than usual. (They gave him no details of their own surveillance and intelligence-gathering, which had indicated that at this moment Bouchard was inside Moishe's Steak House with the most important narcotics smuggler in Canada, Pepe Cotroni himself. The information amounted to a bombshell; it meant that if a heroin deal were to happen and result in a seizure, Controni could be grabbed on conspiracy charges.) Peroff was told to wait twenty minutes before leaving the hotel.

It was a fifteen-minute cab ride to Moishe's. The front door was on the sidewalk level, but immediately inside was a flight of stairs up to the restaurant. Peroff was reminded of several Jewish eating places on Second Avenue in New York City. He scanned the crowded room and saw that Bouchard was seated facing Dufrenne, across a table that was far back on the left side of the restaurant.

Two other men were with them, also facing each other. As Peroff approached their table, Bouchard was already rising to his feet, a curious eagerness in his eyes, and he gestured to one of the men, saying, "This is Pepe."

For a moment Peroff's reactions were numb. He found himself staring down at a man whom he had never seen, not even in a photograph, yet Pepe Cotroni was, to him, a living legend. Even though he had known Cotroni's younger brother Frank and the powerful Lou Greco, meeting Giuseppe Cotroni was different. In the world of crime, Vic and Pepe were regarded as gods.

Cotroni was a short man, under five-seven, but he must have weighed one-seventy-five. He was three-fourths bald and was dressed in a conservative blue-gray suit. He said, "Good to meet you," and Peroff took a seat at the table, his back to the wall, with Cotroni on his right and the fourth man on his left.

The underworld boss was fifty-three, a native of Calabria, Italy. The man with him was his personal bodyguard, a Sicilian with thick black hair combed straight back. Seated between the two of them, Peroff waited for someone to open the conversation. Bouchard and Dufrenne were at the far end of the table, virtually forced into conversation only with each other. Yet Bouchard took it upon himself to initiate the discussion by declaring loudly, "Frank has been living in Italy! In Rome!"

"Ah," Cotroni said, smiling, and all of a sudden he and the bodyguard were draping their arms around Peroff, asking him about the Old Country and pumping him with questions. It turned out that Cotroni was from a village in Calabria which Peroff himself had visited, so the discussion warmed even further. They talked about the size of the grapes in Italy and about the taste of the olives, and Peroff began to relax, realizing that luck had provided him and Cotroni with a common bond of sorts. He could see that Bouchard, while making small talk with Dufrenne, was watching everything with considerable anxiety, his stake in the outcome of the meeting undoubtedly quite high.

What had become clear so far was the fact that Bouchard had been discussing the Lear with Cotroni for the past three or four hours. That explained his phone calls and the quick questions. It was obvious that Bouchard had gone to Cotroni with considerable excitement about the prospect of using Frank Peroff and his jet planes for narcotics smuggling. Cotroni apparently had become interested enough to ask to see Peroff for himself.

"Parle Italiano bene?" Cotroni was asking.

"Eh," Peroff said, gesturing with his hands.

"Okay," Cotroni replied. "Parle solo Italiano. I don't want Frenchie to understand," he added in Italian, referring to Bouchard. "Use your head," he went on, still in his native tongue. "Connie isn't what he was before."

Peroff nodded in agreement. Henceforth they would converse only in Italian, because of Cotroni's clear lack of trust in Conrad Bouchard. It was an ironic twist for Peroff, to suddenly be favored over the French Canadian, and he smiled at Bouchard's expression of consternation over his inability to follow what was being said. For the remainder of the meeting, Bouchard repeatedly glanced over to see by Pepe's expression if things were going well.

"We have already eaten," Cotroni said in Italian. "But you must eat, too. I will order for you. First you will eat, then we will talk business."

The underworld boss called over a waiter and proceeded to order a huge steak for Peroff, with pasta. During the meal, Cotroni kept his questions on a light, social level. From Pepe's remarks, Peroff gathered that once again Bouchard had given a long, untrue story about how they had known each other for at least ten years and had even spent time together in prison. It was just another manifestation of Bouchard's desperate struggle to survive. For any heroin deal requiring heavy financial backing, he would need Cotroni's guarantee of credit, so that whoever put up the money was assured of protection from loss. To lure Cotroni into such a deal, Bouchard had described Peroff as one of his most trusted friends from the past.

"You knew Louis?" said Cotroni, referring to Greco.

"Yeah. Very well."

"I see. Conrad mentioned it."

When Peroff was finished eating, Cotroni turned to the subject of the jet plane. Still speaking in Italian, he went through a long list of questions as if he were conducting a test. It seemed to Peroff that Cotroni might not have believed what Bouchard had told him, and that he wanted to hear it for himself.

"How would you go about it?" he began. "Through what countries?"

"Well," Peroff said, using the best Italian that he could muster, "it would be a flight that would come from Marseilles or probably Cannes. From there I'd fly to England, maybe, and actually leave Europe from Shannon Airport in Ireland. I'd go to Iceland, then to Newfoundland, and make a quick refueling stop in either New York or some other coastal city. Just a stop. Then go direct down to Freeport in the Bahamas. And back up again."

"Why do you do that?"

"Because that's my doorway into the States. I'd come back in through a Customs substation, which is cool, or maybe I wouldn't even stop. Come in over Florida and just fly up to Philly or Jersey or even New York. That general area. Maybe into White Plains, New York."

"Would you bring it up to Canada?"

"No," Peroff said, remembering the U. S. agent's instructions.

"No? Why not?"

"Well, I really haven't made that many trips into Canada that way. Frankly, I'm not too sure of my way around. On this kind of thing, what you're talking about, I'd be worried. Coming into the States is one thing—that's my bag. But crossing that second border, into here, then I'm afraid."

"I see. You have warehouses in the States?"

"Well, I got a friend in Jersey, in the industrial-park business. I don't know if he's got any warehouses, but I'm sure he could steer me to some."

"We would want you to arrange a place that only you know about."

"Yeah, that can be done."

"Well, Frank, that's good. Very good. Bouchard says there's plenty of places to put that stuff in your plane."

"Yeah, that's true. But I'm not too crazy about it."

"What, the plane?"

"Well, see, the one I've got here isn't the best kind to do what, uh, we're talking about. A Jet Commander would be my preference. It has a compartment that I could fill with gas bottles, you know, to store the stuff."

"Is a Commander available?"

139

"I don't know. They're very hard to get your hands on, without throwing up a lot of bread. Otherwise I'd have one now."

"But the plane you *do* have is okay?"

"Yeah, but I also have the use of a Lear Twenty-four, see, that's better for crossing to Europe."

"Good, good," Cotroni said, now turning to more technical matters involving the refueling stops and the range of the various Lear models, and he even expressed a keen interest in the different altitudes at which the plane would have to fly. He questioned Peroff intensely about his method of flying into the States undetected, and, by the end, Cotroni seemed more than satisfied that he was talking to an expert smuggler. At last he cocked his head slightly and asked, in a friendly manner, "Have you ever fooled with this before? In any shape or form?"

It was as specific a reference to heroin as any that Cotroni would use during the entire lunch meeting. "Absolutely not," Peroff told him.

"Why not? I'm just curious."

"Well, I never needed money bad enough. Or nobody ever offered me the right amount. And," Peroff went on, staring at him intently, "nobody has yet, either."

There was a pause, and at that moment the check arrived. Bouchard made a halfhearted attempt to make believe that he would pick it up, but Cotroni grabbed it. As they all rose from the table, the conversation returned to the subject of Italy—the beauties of the country, the warmth of the people, the taste of the food. They were still on the topic when they emerged on the sidewalk in front of the restaurant.

Cotroni smiled at Peroff and said, "I am glad to know you. If I wanted to make a personal trip, down south, would you take me?"

The reference was to either the Bahamas or, perhaps, somewhere in Central or South America. Peroff said, "Yes, of course. Just let Connie know."

"Thank you."

They continued chatting for several more minutes. Whatever the test had been, Peroff judged it as a success. As they shook hands, he noticed a bakery truck parked just a few feet away, at the curb, and he saw in a fleeting second that a camera was inside, pointed at the group. His stomach churning into knots, he turned back to Cotroni.

"I like you," the Mafia boss was saying, and then he stepped into a Cadillac while his Sicilian bodyguard held the door.

On the way back to the Martinique Hotel, Peroff sat in the rear seat of Bouchard's car while the French Canadian drove and Maurice Dufrenne stared straight ahead in the front passenger seat. They rode in almost total silence while Bouchard was driving and thinking, almost talking out loud and arguing with himself, as if his mind was leaping forward with plans and schemes. Once, when a red light turned to green, he failed to go through the intersection until several horns started to blow.

Outside the hotel, Bouchard turned to Peroff and said, "I'll call you in about an hour and a half. You gonna be in the room?"

"Either there or in the bar."

"Good. You'll hear from me soon," Bouchard added, undoubtedly planning to call Cotroni right away to learn the Mafia leader's reaction to the meeting and just what the hell he and Peroff had said.

Inside the hotel Peroff was immediately summoned to meet with Hal Roberts, the Customs attaché, and the Mounties, who were in the process of spreading out hundreds of photographs. They asked him to point out Cotroni and his Sicilian bodyguard from among the pictures, and Peroff took only a few seconds to do so. He was told that two Mounties had gone into Moishe's and had sat near their table during the entire meeting; and, in fact, there had been a videotape camera inside the bread truck.

Peroff returned to his own room and received Bouchard's phone call at about three o'clock that afternoon. "Can we take a trip in the plane?" Bouchard asked.

"When?"

"Now."

"Where do you want to go, Connie?"

"Quebec City."

Peroff hesitated, wondering what the agents would say about it. "Let me check the winds, the weather and all that," he replied, "and I'll call you right back."

"Okay, good."

There was little question that another phase of Cotroni's test was being put into motion. Peroff called Hal Roberts, who obtained clearance for the trip and told him to go along with whatever Bouchard wanted to do. The Mounties' secret surveillance would be heavy, both here in Montreal and at the other end, in Quebec City.

Now Peroff telephoned Bouchard and told him, "It's okay, Connie, but give me an hour to flight-plan it and have it checked. An hour and we're off."

He went to see Fred Davis, the pilot, and told him to hurry out to the airport with the agent. By now, Davis had learned a lot more about the danger involved and had become so badly frightened that Peroff wondered if he was in any condition to fly at all.

"Just stay cool," Peroff said. "Play it as though I'm the owner of that plane and you guys work for me—period."

"Who'll be on board?"

"Don't even bother about that."

Within forty-five minutes, Bouchard was at the hotel with Dufrenne. At the airport, Davis and the "radioman" were all set to go. Somehow Davis had buried his fears and had pulled himself together, because now he seemed completely at ease, playing the role exactly as Peroff had requested.

Impressed, Bouchard climbed into the plane with Dufrenne and made himself at home. The pair sat in swivel seats, both men trying to conceal their nervousness. Neither had flown in a private jet before, and Bouchard seemed especially worried about what would happen next.

"Hey, Boss," said Davis. "I need some help with the flight plan."

Peroff went forward to assist him and Bouchard followed, again like a small boy, this time as if he were about to ride on a huge roller coaster for the first time in his life. He said, "What the fuck will this feel like, you know? I mean, Frank, I'm not scared, but—"

"Now, Connie, just take it easy. Don't get upset. You have to remember, see, that taking off in a private jet is really *different*."

"Yah?"

"Oh, yeah, it's not like a commercial jet, not at all. It's like getting into a rocket ship."

"It is?"

"Sure, 'cause it's overpowered. It's so much more vertical."

"Vertical?"

"The attitude, you know?"

"Attitude?"

"As soon as we get up and the pilot takes a fast check on his pressure, and the air speed builds to a certain point, *zoom!*"

"Zoom?"

"Well, see, the whole idea in a Lear is to get up to forty-one thousand feet, as fast as you can."

"Oh, I see," Bouchard said, hardly seeing a thing.

"Connie, don't get overly concerned. You'll feel 'G' forces here like you don't in a regular plane."

"What's 'G' forces?"

"Well, when we take off, you're gonna get really pressed back in your seat, you know? Because it's different!"

"Shit, I mean—"

"Look, why don't you and Maurice go sit in the back, there, okay? It's the best place, because those seats don't *give* at all."

Bouchard and Dufrenne moved to the rear and sat down next to each other. They strapped themselves in and Peroff went to the seat near the door. The plane was in position, and within seconds it was taking off. As Peroff had warned, the plane seemed to be climbing almost straight up as if it were headed to the moon. Bouchard's head was back against the wall and he shouted, "Holy shit! Jesus! Whoo!" At the same time, Dufrenne was trying to pull himself forward so he could see out the window, but the force of the plane's movement was too great. Peroff held his laughter inside while the underworld leader and his bodyguard struggled to regain an appearance of outward confidence and lack of concern.

During the whole thirty-five minute trip, Bouchard was moving all around the plane, going up to see the pilots and looking out the window, exclaiming about how wild the experience was, and at one point Peroff showed him the oxygen mask.

"This'll give you a high," Peroff told him. "You go out and get drunk and the next morning you throw that thing on, and it'll knock your hangover right out."

Bouchard put on the mask, breathing in the oxygen as if he were a comic version of an astronaut. Soon the young Customs agent, playing his own role, came back and took orders for drinks.

It was early evening when the Learjet approached the airport in Quebec City and Bouchard declared, "I've never seen a landing from the pilot's view. Can I go up and watch?"

"Sure, Connie. Come on."

They went forward and stood behind the pilot, who said, "We'll be on the ground in a few minutes."

"*What?*" Bouchard exclaimed, peering out the front window. "We're not at the airport! What's going on?"

"Connie," said Peroff. "Do you see those lights way over there? To the left?"

"Yeah, yeah. What about 'em?"

"Well, you count to twenty, Connie. At twenty, we're gonna make a nice, easy turn. When we get done turning, and you feel the plane straighten back up again, those lights are gonna be right in front of us."

"You're kidding! How do you know that's gonna happen?"

"Because there's a procedure. You can't just turn around and say, 'Hey, there's the airport, I'm gonna land.' You do it according to a certain method."

Bouchard started counting to twenty. At the same time he refused to sit down and strap himself in a seat. He wanted to stand and watch the entire landing. He counted slowly, watching the lights in the distance, glancing nervously at the pilot, and when he reached twenty the plane began its turn. When it leveled out again, the runway was straight ahead, glittering in the darkening twilight.

"Unbelievable," Bouchard whispered.

The landing was smooth despite a snow-covered airfield. When Bouchard jumped from the plane he walked all around it, checking to make sure there had been no damage. For a moment it seemed as if he might lean his face up to the Lear and reward it with an affectionate kiss.

They spent less than three hours in Quebec City, from the time they took a cab into the downtown section and back again. The pilot and the agent stayed behind at the small airport while Peroff joined Bouchard and Dufrenne. They went to a colorful, Mexican-style restaurant-nightclub complete with beautiful barmaids in skimpy costumes and waiters wearing sombreros. Bouchard met alone with several men who had been involved in his previous heroin deals and Peroff sat at the bar with Dufrenne, trying to watch from a distance.

On the trip back to Montreal, Bouchard took over as if the plane were his own, as if he had made a thousand flights in the past. He settled into a chair with his feet up, lighting a cigar and ordering drinks, relishing the role of a wealthy owner of a private jet. It had been such a brief trip, with so little purpose, that Peroff was more convinced than ever that the entire flight had been ordered by Cotroni as a test.

By now it was past eleven o'clock at night. At the Montreal airport Bouchard hopped off the plane and declared that he wanted to inspect the facilities set up for noncommercial pilots. Inside the building, Peroff showed him the flight-plan center and the coffee room, plus an area with a number of telephones, and led him into a modern, plush conference room used by owners of private planes. The room was empty, so Bouchard sat down at the long table, again with his feet up, playing the role, and spent the next half-hour on the phone, calling friends and conversing in French.

Just as they were leaving the conference room, Peroff spotted a police car outside, pulling up near the building with its toplight spinning in the darkness. "Connie," he whispered, "it's the law! Get in the bathroom!"

Bouchard's face went pale. He had just broken the rules of his bail restrictions by leaving Montreal, an offense which could have him sent back to prison. In a panic he followed Peroff's instructions while Maurice Dufrenne, forgetting his role as bodyguard, ran ahead and actually beat him through the men's room door.

Peroff stayed in the main section, leaning against the wall. It seemed unbelievable—two Mounties, despite the fact that *other* Mounties were keeping the entire scene under surveillance, walked in and sat down with cups of coffee. Peroff waited, watching them start up a meaningless conversation. What are they trying to do, he wondered, ruin everything? What if they make a mistake and Bouchard finds out about me?

After a while he walked into the bathroom. Bouchard and Dufrenne were standing there, almost trembling. "Well," Peroff said, "I *think* it's all right. It's the RCMP, but—"

"Shit!" Bouchard whispered.

145

"Connie, so far it's all right! They're having a cup of coffee."

"Yeah? Why'd they come into the fucking airport with their fucking light spinning around?"

"Don't worry, Connie! For Chrissake, it's a rule! The flashing light *has* to be on when they're in an airport!"

"I don't know," Bouchard said, removing a pair of phony horn-rimmed glasses from his jacket. He put them on his face as a disguise.

"*Stay* here a while," Peroff whispered loudly. "Just cool it—let me go watch 'em some more. Stay put."

He left the bathroom. The two Mounties were still sipping their coffee and talking. One of the phones rang and the young woman in charge of the flight center announced, "Officer Le Mouel? It's for you."

The Mountie took the phone, listened a while, nodding his head, and after a few minutes Peroff became even more concerned. Was some plan of action under way? Why hadn't he been told? Or was it a monumental mixup? Were these Mounties unaware of the fact that Bouchard was being watched? And were they hoping to arrest him for leaving Montreal? If these guys are here on a coffee break, why are they getting phone calls? What's happening?

He hurried back into the bathroom, where Bouchard was about to climb out the window. "Connie, look," he said, "I tell you what we're gonna do. I don't know how long they'll be here, but—"

"What are they doing?"

"They got their coffee, and now the guy's on the phone."

"What!" Bouchard whispered. "On the phone!"

"Listen, Connie, we can't gamble. Put the glasses back on. Okay. Now, you get between me and Maurice. And we'll just walk out, real fast."

"I don't know," Bouchard said, putting his glasses back on and stepping into line behind Dufrenne.

"All right," Peroff urged. "Let's go."

Bumping against each other in single file, they emerged from the bathroom looking like the Three Stooges. At the same time the Mounties left their coffee cups and headed for a side door. Peroff watched them go outside and get into their car. By the time he and Bouchard and Dufrenne reached the front door, the two officers were riding out of the airport grounds.

In Dufrenne's Cadillac on the way back to town, Bouchard

calmed down and convinced himself that the whole incident had been a needless cause for panic. "They were just in there for a cup of coffee," he said. "Don't you think so, Frank?"

Peroff decided not to help him. "I don't know, Connie. Jeez, I *wish* I knew."

"Nah, Frank, they weren't in there looking for me. No way, no sweat."

"I hope you're right, babe."

"It was all bullshit, Frank. Anyhow, this is just great! Fantastic!"

"What do you mean?"

"The plane," Bouchard said. "The plane."

That night, at his debriefing session in the Martinique Hotel, Peroff learned that Jean Sourbier, the Mountie, had made the call to the pair of officers at the airport. They had stopped in only for a coffee break, without any knowledge that they were walking into a scene that was under intense surveillance. Sourbier had told Officer Le Mouel, "Get the hell out of there! Fast!"

There were more photographs for Peroff to examine. The Mounties had capured Cotroni on film earlier in the day, and they already had pictures of Bouchard in Quebec City, entering and leaving the Mexican nightclub with Peroff and Dufrenne. There was obvious excitement over the fact that Cotroni had become involved, but still no specific heroin deal was in the works. Such a deal would take time. In the first place, Cotroni would have to choose a financier, on the theory that he gave his guarantee of credit but never, if possible, his own cash. Then, depending on the size of the heroin package, it would take a few or several weeks for a Marseilles laboratory to process the order.

In any case, Peroff's services with the jet would not be needed for a considerable period. So he planned to leave Canada right away. He would rejoin his family at the New York Hilton and maintain phone contact with Bouchard until the plane was requested.

Bouchard called the next morning and unexpectedly asked him to remain in Montreal for a few more days. He added, "We might take another little trip," but offered no explanation. Weary and wishing he could be with Ruth and the children, Peroff agreed to stay on.

In the early afternoon he was picked up by Dufrenne, who took him to an automobile garage which was used by Bouchard as a meeting place. Dufrenne owned the garage and was usually there when he wasn't acting as a bodyguard or henchman. That evening they went to Bouchard's house for dinner. They ate roast beef cooked by Bouchard's new bride of a few weeks, a woman with striking red hair and huge physical proportions to the point where Peroff found her extremely unattractive. Still, she was quite hospitable and polite. When they turned on the television after dinner, she switched the channel from a French-speaking station to one with English, for Peroff's benefit, and in general the evening was pleasant. The only sour note occurred when Bouchard's wife became angry at Dufrenne for eating not just the dinner but half the food in the kitchen as well. Bouchard got drunk and bitter, raving at how the world was closing in on him, and soon afterward Peroff left.

In the morning Bouchard sounded like a new man, revived and hopeful again, asking over the phone, "How much trouble would it be to fly to Detroit?"

"With you?"

"Yeah."

"I don't know, Connie. You're a hot man. Leaving Montreal is one thing, but crossing into the States? I'm not so sure. I mean, what about your bail restrictions?"

Bouchard explained that he wanted to meet with members of the Detroit mob. Bouchard apparently "owed" Detroit racketeers a lot of money which had been lost more than a year ago, at the time of his arrest, when the Mounties had seized ten million dollars' worth of narcotics.

"They got hurt for a lot of bread," Bouchard went on, "so I gotta deal with 'em again. The guy in Detroit is a buyer from us, see, and they want to make a meet. I'd rather deal in New York, but we owe these guys."

If they were moving toward a specific deal, Bouchard was being too cryptic about it at this point for Peroff to grasp the total picture. It was possible, however, that a planning stage had begun. On any smuggling operation from Europe to North America, the Montreal mob usually lined up its buyers—members of organized crime in the United States—well in advance.

"It's too risky carrying you through customs," Peroff said. "Why not tell your friends to meet you in Windsor, across the river?"

"Yeah, that might be good."

"Let me do some weather checks, Connie. I'm sure we can fly over to Windsor without any problem."

"Okay. I'll call back."

Peroff had to make several phone calls in order to get clearance for the flight from the U. S. Government. Hal Roberts of Customs finally gave him the go-ahead, however, and the Mounties again made preparations for surveillance.

"We can leave at about noon," Peroff told Bouchard at last.

"Good. Listen, Frank, you go out to the plane ahead of me, okay? Bring it real close to the parking lot. I'll be there at exactly twelve-fifteen. Exactly! I want to get on board without anybody seeing me. So be ready."

"Fine, Connie."

An hour later, at five minutes past noon, Peroff was in the Lear-jet, waiting near the edge of the airport parking lot. He told the pilot to start up the plane's engines and, at exactly twelve-fifteen, Bouchard's Cadillac made its appearance. Bouchard stepped out of the car, took no more than ten steps, and climbed into the plane. He was clutching a brown briefcase. Behind him came Maurice Dufrenne and a third man whom Peroff had never met.

"This is Victor Fauci," Bouchard said.

The man had to be another bodyguard. Victor Fauci was even bigger than Peroff, about six feet two and heavier than two hundred fifty pounds, all muscle, with a stare that was more menacing than any Peroff had seen. He did not know, at this moment, that Fauci had been Lou Greco's personal hit man, responsible for the shooting of more than fifty victims. Dufrenne was an expert with his hands, but Fauci was a professional killer.

The plane moved out to the runway but was delayed by the control tower because of heavy overcast and strong winds. While they waited for flight clearance, Peroff was aware that Fauci was still looking him over, sizing him up; and for the first time he felt a genuine pang of fear. Anything was possible, with Bouchard. With Dufrenne and Fauci, he could commandeer the whole plane and direct the pilot to fly anywhere. He could make an easy escape from Canada, if he chose. Why else, Peroff wondered, would Connie be acting with such caution? Why arrange the time for "exactly" twelve-fifteen and bring two bodyguards with him? Was the U. S. Government about to finance the escape of Conrad Bouchard in a Learjet?

"When are we taking off?" Bouchard asked.

"Soon, Connie."

Bouchard began roaming around the plane, playing the role for the benefit of Victor Fauci, who was about to experience *his* first ride in a private jet. "Don't worry about a thing," Bouchard told him, as if he himself had flown in Lears a thousand times. "When we take off, Victor, it'll be like a rocket. Ya know? But don't let it bother you. Wait'll you see what it's like! It's great!"

Still acting the part, Bouchard opened up the card table as a demonstration. Peroff told him, "Wait, Connie, until we take off. Soon as we're up, okay?"

"Sure," Bouchard said. "I was just showing Victor, here, how it's done." Now he yelled to the pilots, "Hey, everything all right? How long are we gonna be?"

"A few minutes, sir!"

"Okay, good! Soon as we're up, how about some drinks?"

"Yes, sir!"

By this time, Peroff could hardly keep from laughing. After only one flight to Quebec City and back, Bouchard had become the expert, even to the point of giving instructions to the pilots. When the plane was about to take off, he ran back and took his seat in the rear, making sure that no one else got it. He told Peroff to sit down next to him and gave orders to Dufrenne and Fauci to strap themselves into the swivel chairs, facing forward.

"Here we go," Bouchard said. "Don't worry, Victor. The attitude's gonna be stiff, ya know? It'll be vertical! Zoom! You'll feel the 'G' forces and stuff, but stay cool!"

After the takeoff, Bouchard leaped up and brought Fauci forward to show him the pilots' controls.

"Now, this thing here," he said, "it tells you how high you are, see? Maybe we can get you the oxygen mask, Victor. Good for a hangover. Okay, men, time for drinks!"

Now he was moving back into the passenger section, his transformation into the boss having become complete. He opened the table again and found a deck of cards, announcing that the four of them—Dufrenne, Fauci, Peroff and himself—were going to play

Hearts. The pilot, Fred Davis, came back and personally fixed the liquor.

The flight took an hour and fifteen minutes. Toward the end, Bouchard sat up in the copilot's seat, watching everything with utter fascination. Dufrenne and Fauci continued to play cards, oblivious of whatever else was going on. About seven minutes before landing, Peroff took over the copilot's seat and helped Davis with the controls while Bouchard looked over his shoulder.

They left the pilots at the airport and took a cab. Bouchard, sitting up front with the brown briefcase on his lap, gave the driver specific directions. They went to an intersection in downtown Windsor, got out, and proceeded into a luncheonette. Peroff followed them to a table near the back and the four men took off their overcoats. But Bouchard suddenly jumped to his feet, put his own coat back on, grabbed the briefcase and ran outside.

"Where is he going?" Peroff asked.

"He'll be back," Fauci said.

Peroff watched through the window of the restaurant, catching a glimpse of Bouchard getting into a different taxicab and disappearing. He settled back, with the two bodyguards on either side of him, and stared at the menu.

"What are we doing?" he asked.

"We're sitting here for a reason," Fauci said. "People want to get a look at you. They want to see *you*, but they don't want you to see them."

It was early evening by the time Bouchard returned to the luncheonette. Peroff had sat with the two hit men for at least three hours, eating steak and listening to their stories about life in prison. When Bouchard burst through the door he had a worried look on his face, as if he thought he were being followed. He motioned for them to get up and said, "Come on, let's go! Let's go!" Peroff had no idea what was happening. Not until much later would he find out that Bouchard had just delivered five kilos of heroin to the Detroit mob. He had brought the drugs in the brown briefcase.

They all got into a waiting cab and Bouchard told the driver to head for the airport. The briefcase was on his lap again, but this time it contained close to $150,000 in cash, some $30,000 of which was to be Bouchard's cut. (At this point, Peroff had no knowledge of the briefcase's contents.) Bouchard was pleased but extremely nervous, clutching the bag and swiveling his head back and forth to look out the window.

At the airport Bouchard was in a virtual frenzy, directing Peroff and Dufrenne and Fauci to hurry into the plane. When they were in the air, on their way back to Montreal, he drank heavily and tried to relax, without too much success. Peroff had never seen him so afraid.

As the Learjet was landing in the darkness, Bouchard went forward and shouted, "Listen, Frank, maybe just let me off at the end of the runway! What do you think?"

"Connie, learn something—just sit here and don't worry about a thing. Calm down."

But as soon as the plane touched down Bouchard exclaimed, "Let me off! I think I should get off now!"

"Connie, if we have trouble you'll *know* it."

"Just get this plane close to the parking lot!"

"Okay, Connie! Relax!"

The jet taxied over to within several feet of where the Cadillac was parked. Maurice Dufrenne got out first and ran over with the briefcase. He opened up the trunk and tossed the bag inside.

Bouchard was already in the back seat, ready to leave. Peroff and the others climbed in with him. Dufrenne took the wheel and literally roared away from the airport grounds, speeding into downtown Montreal. For the next two and a half hours, they rode in and out of the city streets, at high speeds, at times parking a while and then pulling out, obviously making sure they were not being tailed. As the furious, incomprehensible driving went on and on, Peroff thought he might lose all patience. The car went in a crazy pattern, up one side street and down another, back and forth, making him dizzy and almost nauseous.

Near eleven o'clock, the Cadillac pulled up in front of Bouchard's home. "Come on inside with me," Bouchard told him. "Maurice will take you back to your hotel in about an hour."

He followed Bouchard into the house while Dufrenne and Fauci drove off again in the Cadillac, which still carried the briefcase in its trunk. Bouchard turned on the television set and fixed some drinks. He sat in an easy chair and took off his shoes. Peroff glanced at him, watching him nod his head. Bouchard was smiling to himself, mumbling under his breath.

If he only knew, Peroff thought, that the Mounties had kept the entire trip under surveillance, in Windsor as well. Unseen agents had filmed them once again but they, too, had missed the significance of the briefcase. In fact, Peroff learned, Conrad Bouchard had delivered the five kilos of heroin, and the money on the return flight, right under their noses and at the full expense of the U. S. Government.

There was still no deal, no definite or specific conspiracy by Bouchard to smuggle heroin from Europe to North America in a private jet leased by Frank Peroff. There were the usual debriefings that night and the following morning in the Martinique Hotel, but Peroff could get little information about the agents' thoughts or plans. They showed him photographs of Bouchard meeting with Detroit mobsters in Windsor, during the period when Peroff was in the luncheonette with Dufrenne and Fauci.

"You'll be taking off today," Hal Roberts said. "The Lear will land at Newark Airport and Roy Gibson will meet you there."

Peroff made one last call to Bouchard, saying, "I have to leave, Connie, but I'll be in touch. I've got a charter for the jet. I'm going back down to Florida and then I'm cutting out. You'll hear from me soon."

When he boarded the Lear that afternoon, Peroff sat alone in the back, trying to piece together what had gone on. It was Friday, the twenty-third of March. Two and a half months had gone by since he had made contact with Tom Glazer of the Secret Service. Since then he had delivered more than $400,000 worth of counterfeit American money. He had gone to Paris, where he had spent ten days as an undercover man, resulting in the arrest of Herman Savotok, Irving Spellman, Jules Handel and five Frenchmen. There had been the seizure of twenty-five kilos of heroin. He had returned to Rome and had allowed himself to be pressured into that first trip to Montreal, when Bouchard had mentioned the possibility of getting to a Marseilles lab. Then he had allowed his entire family to be uprooted from Rome, his children taken out of school and thrown into a hotel in New York. He had just completed his second trip to see Bouchard.

So what had happened? There had been the meeting with Pepe Cotroni, the czar of drugs. There had been the trips to Quebec City and to Windsor. But there was still no deal.

He closed his eyes as the plane headed toward Newark, New Jersey. His life in Rome seemed so far away, as if it had come to an abrupt halt at the moment he had met Bouchard's henchman, Angie, entirely by accident on the Via Veneto. How long was he supposed to allow himself to keep on with this? When could he return to Italy and pick up the pieces of his life? There were no answers, not yet

VI

The Learjet landed at Newark Airport in the evening. It was cold and windy and Peroff had to go through Customs procedures in the noncommercial section, on the field itself. Without revealing his role as an unofficial agent for Customs, he opened his bag on the ground and allowed it to be searched. There was a delay before Roy Gibson showed up to greet him. When Gibson arrived, the plane took off again, without Peroff, and continued down to Florida.

Gibson drove him across the George Washington Bridge, into New York City. "As soon as we get to the hotel," he said, "we have to call Dan Massey."

"What for?"

"He'll have instructions."

Massey was the European desk officer for Customs whom Peroff had met in Washington, prior to the Montreal trip which had just ended.

At the New York Hilton, Gibson went with him up to the pair of double rooms where Ruth, the children and the poodle had been living in virtual isolation. There were four double beds, two bathrooms and little else. The family had become tired of ordering room service for every meal, but otherwise their spirits were reasonably high. The only problem had been some complaints by the hotel manager, who was confused by the fact that Ruth had signed for room service both as Mrs. Gibson and, on occasion, as Mrs. Peroff.

Gibson sat down with them for a while, sipping a vodka collins, and he made the call to Washington. It was the first time that Gibson had become any more than superficially involved in the case.

He spoke with Dan Massey for several minutes, then handed the phone to Peroff.

"How'd it go, Frank?"

"Okay, I guess. Actually there's nothing. There's no deal with Connie, so far."

"I heard you met with Pepe."

"Yeah, but they made no propositions. I guess I'll be going back to Rome with my family."

Massey ignored the last remark, which had been more of a question, a plea, than a statement. "Listen, Frank, I'm leaving the country for a while. Take the weekend off. On Monday, Roy will pick you up and take you to Customs headquarters."

"Here in New York?"

"Yeah. I want him to debrief you, from the minute you left Washington until you got to Newark. Everything that happened in Montreal. No matter what they've done up there, I want it all on tape."

When the conversation was over, Gibson stayed for about fifteen minutes longer, shedding some of his cold, professional manner. Peroff was beginning to like the Customs agent.

"Have a good weekend," Gibson said as he was leaving the hotel room. "Just give a call if there's any problem."

"You're fucking-A right I will," Peroff said, smiling, and Gibson's face broke into a wide grin.

The debriefing sessions went on for two days. Gibson brought Peroff into the Customs office on Varick Street in Manhattan, taking him through the loading-dock entrance to avoid even the chance that he might be seen. They went up a back stairway and into a special room, where Gibson locked the door. The room was full of boxes containing confiscated passports, and there were piles of old suitcases with false bottoms which had been used by smugglers of heroin and cocaine.

Gibson's questioning was meticulous and thorough. After the two long days, his file was voluminous. He used a tape recorder and took notes as well, combing Peroff's memory for every detail of his recent stay in Montreal. When the last session was over on Tuesday night, the Customs agent was well versed on all aspects of the case.

But no new developments followed. The waiting and temporary living at the Hilton continued through that week and into April, without any concrete plans for Peroff at all. Soon it would be a month since the family had arrived in New York; the hotel bill was climbing to $2,000 and the manager was demanding some payment; and Peroff himself was becoming worried and restless.

He called Gibson and asked for help with the hotel situation. "This guy's getting cuckoo downstairs," he said, referring to the manager. "You'd better come over here and take care of him."

Peroff's own financial situation, moreover, had deteriorated over the past few months. His expenses in Rome, Naples, London, Paris, Montreal and now New York all added up to a considerable amount of cash from his own pocket. Ever since the trip to London and Paris, he had been carrying cash in a satchel, doling it out for airplane flights and hotel rooms and meals, not to mention the passports and driver's licenses he had purchased for Nunzio Galli. Even though he had been partially reimbursed, the Government still owed him about $12,000. Peroff's main concern, however, was not the $12,000 but the status of his fragile business affairs in Europe. He had spent $150,000 in cash for his hospital project in Italy, but the option would dissolve without further payments. Other projects would be in jeopardy soon as well.

"Roy," he said, "please tell your bosses that I have to make a trip to Rome. A quick trip, while we have a lull on our hands."

"For how long?"

"Just a week. Or two, if possible. Listen, I'm about to lose all my options—I'm dying! I'd like the twelve grand, too, but I'm about to lose a hospital deal and I need to do some maneuvering on my yacht, or they'll repossess it."

"Well, I'll see, but—"

"And Roy, I want to get Ruth out of the hotel, here, because this manager is driving us crazy! It'll be a goddamn month, Roy! These kids have been living in two rooms! Three kids! Jeez, man, our whole lives are in your hands!"

"Well, what do you want? I mean, for the kids?"

"I want them in a home, dammit, or an apartment. Something like that."

"Okay, Frank. I'll speak to my people."

The next day Peroff was summoned again to the Varick Street

office of U. S. Customs, where he met several senior agents. When they refused to let him return briefly to Rome, Peroff exploded with anger.

"All right," he shouted, "then you guys can shove your heroin deal up your ass! I'm not gonna do any more! I want out! I go up to Montreal and risk my life, and my family is held hostage here in New York, and we're losing everything we own in Europe! I mean, what do you think I am? I'm a human being!"

"But Frank—"

"And you guys don't even *have* a deal! There *is* no deal with Connie Bouchard! What is this? The whole thing is stupid!"

"You don't understand, Frank—it's important."

"Then give me the money that you owe me, and then let me go to Italy for just one week!"

"Let us discuss it among ourselves, okay? We'll be in touch with you."

When he left the meeting, Peroff felt that at least he had unburdened himself of some of his feelings. In his room at the Hilton, he picked up the phone and tried to call Jack Anderson, the newspaper columnist, in Washington, D. C. When a reporter in Anderson's office came on the line, Peroff hung up. He had no intention of telling the outside world anything, but the mere fact of placing the call had calmed his anger. In his former life as a manipulating, wheeling-and-dealing crook, making phone calls had been as natural as breathing. On impulse he dialed for information, got the number of the White House and put in a second call. He asked for the Press Office and made contact with a secretary for Ronald Ziegler, the spokesman for President Nixon.

"My name is Frank Peroff," he said.

"What can we do for you?"

"Nothing at the moment. But if things don't go right, you may be hearing from me in the future."

"What's this about?"

Again, Peroff hung up.

The following afternoon Roy Gibson showed up at the Hilton as an emissary from his bosses at U. S. Customs. In his hand was a letter in which several "conditions" had been set forth regarding

Peroff's existence, the first one stating, "You may not leave the United States." Gibson read through the statement, sipped his drink and waited for a reaction.

Peroff had hardly listened past the opening condition. If he couldn't go back to Rome, even for three days, then everything he had tried to build up over there would crumble. "What if I just pack up my family and leave tonight?" he asked.

"I don't know, Frank, but I think they'd grab your passport before you could get on the plane."

"You know," Peroff told him, "I happen to be a con man, at least I have been. And one thing I can't stand is being conned myself."

"What are you going to do?"

"Do I have a choice?"

Gibson thought a moment. "Not really," he said. "I'm supposed to tell you—take it or leave it."

"Well, I *leave* it."

There was a silence while Gibson stared at his drink. Ruth was also in the room, apprehensive but saying nothing.

"Let me have the letter," Peroff went on. "I'd sure as hell like to show Jack Anderson. Even the White House. Is this how they treat somebody who works for the Government? Give me the letter, Roy."

Gibson shook his head, smiling sadly. "No," he said, "but my *official* visit is over." He put the letter back in his pocket. "Now maybe we can talk on a personal level."

"Go ahead."

"Well, the big boss in Washington is the Commissioner," he said, referring to Vernon Acree of Customs. "It's possible that you could call him. But I'm not gonna be here whenever you do whatever you're gonna do. And I'll deny that this conversation ever took place."

Peroff stared at him. Gibson was being a loyal company man, but he was also trying to help as a friend. At last Peroff said, "You recommend that I call Acree?"

"Look, Frank, it's up to you. Far as I'm concerned, you and I never even discussed it."

Gibson got up to leave and Peroff waited until he had reached the door. "Roy," he said. "Thanks. I mean it." But Gibson merely smiled, trying to preserve the cool detachment that was so much a part of his manner.

Ten minutes later Peroff made up his mind. He called the Customs headquarters in Washington, D. C., and asked for Commissioner Acree's office. Within seconds, Acree himself came on the line and Peroff was so stunned that he had to take a few moments to collect his thoughts.

"Listen," he said, "I'm Frank Peroff. I'm the guy who was involved in that bust in Paris."

"Oh, yeah. Right."

"Well, now I'm in New York. About three weeks ago I came back from Montreal. I was up there with a Learjet that your guys leased for me, and—"

"*What?*"

"An airplane. They leased it for me. I—"

"Wait a minute. Why don't you take it from the beginning?"

"You mean you don't know about all this?"

"Tell me about it."

Over the next several minutes it became clear that Acree had known nothing of Peroff's work aside from what had taken place in Paris. Peroff went over his experience quickly, adding that he had tried to call Jack Anderson.

"What were you going to tell him?"

"Well," Peroff bluffed, "I was going to say exactly how you people treat somebody who gets forced into this kind of situation. You bankrupt me, you won't let me go back to Rome, you won't even pay my expenses—I'm paralyzed!"

"Mr. Peroff, I suggest that you come here tomorrow. Fly down here and we'll resolve this thing."

"Okay, I will."

"Good. Be at my office at ten in the morning."

Peroff took an early shuttle flight from La Guardia Airport to Washington, D. C. He spent nearly two hours alone with Commissioner Acree, giving him the entire story of Bouchard, the jet plane, the meeting with Cotroni and the current situation in which he felt stranded in New York with his family.

"All I want is what I've spent," he said. "So far I'm still twelve grand in the hole. And if I can just have one week in Europe, I can salvage up to eighty percent of my investments."

"Did you actually talk to Jack Anderson or tell him anything?"

"Absolutely not. I said that to shock you a little bit."

Acree muttered something.

"I even called the White House."

"You did? What'd you say?"

"I just told 'em my name and said that I might be calling back some day."

"Well," Acree said, "I don't care what you did, so long as it stays in the house."

It took Peroff a moment to realize that "in the house" meant within the confines of the Government. Acree seemed willing to help, asking him to return to the office after lunch. At the second meeting, Peroff was told to fly back to New York that night and call again the following morning. He did so and received instructions to make another trip to Washington the day after that.

By now it was mid-April. Time was running out for Peroff's European business ventures. His family was growing restless and weary at the Hilton Hotel. Yet nothing had been solved in terms of his role or what the Government wanted him to do. He was determined to force a conclusion, a decision, one way or the other.

At the next meeting in Washington, Acree was not present. Instead, an assistant commissioner, Walter Ryan, took Peroff into his office and they sat down to work out how much money was due him. Peroff tried to make an itemized list of all his costs, but Ryan wanted receipts for everything. Of the $12,000 that Peroff claimed he had spent, Ryan offered $7,900 until more bills or receipts were found.

Later in the day, another meeting was held, again in Ryan's office, but now Roy Gibson suddenly appeared. He had flown down from New York and had just arrived. Also on hand was Pete Murphy, the Customs boss whom Peroff had met in Paris, sitting there like an apparition from the past. Two other Customs officials joined the meeting which, to Peroff, seemed to be organized in the manner of a trial. Ryan was the judge, seated behind the desk; and Peroff was in the witness chair, facing Gibson, Murphy and the others as if they were the jury.

A three-hour argument ensued, with Peroff confronting a narrow list of choices for himself. If he walked out, which he was free to do, they would not pay the $7,900 promised him. And, much more important, they would nullify his passport and thereby prevent him from returning to Europe anyhow.

"After this *next* trip," he was told, "we'll try to work it so you can go back to Rome for a week."

"What next trip?"

"Well, we want you to go back up to Montreal. First of all, the BNDD is out of this. And the focus has changed. We're not interested in the lab anymore. But there *is* a deal in the works."

"There is?"

"Yep, and it's gonna happen with Cotroni. That's why we're going ahead with this."

"You're kidding."

"No, we've got information from other sources. It's a question of time, but a deal is gonna be formulated. We know."

"What happened to my quarter of a million? My reward for the lab?"

"There ain't gonna be no quarter of a million, Frank. There's a possible hundred grand for you if it's a hundred kees. And fifty grand if we grab Cotroni. Also more per head, but it depends on the importance of the people arrested."

Again it seemed more like glib talk than an actual guarantee of any money. If they'd let me return to Europe, he thought, I'd walk out on the spot.

"Also, Frank, we want Ruth away from New York. We want to make sure this thing goes right. If you're worrying about her, it'll interfere with your performance. We want you alone, in a hotel room somewhere."

"But what *about* my family?"

"We'll send them down to Puerto Rico. They'll be put into an apartment or something like that. One of our agents down there will look after them."

"And when do I go to Montreal?"

"Right away. Soon as your family gets to Puerto Rico."

"So it's a 'go' situation? For real?"

"You bet. And from this point on, if we go forth, Roy is your control agent. Do you agree?"

"What the hell choice do I have?"

The whole situation had become bewildering to him, perhaps because it had changed so fast. One moment it had seemed as if nothing was happening, but now the operation was in full swing again. He was going to Montreal, to resume the relationship with Bouchard. There was information that Pepe Cotroni was formulating a heroin deal.

As he rode by himself on the plane back to New York, Peroff tried to sort out the new developments. How much danger would there be if Cotroni was the arranger and guarantor behind the scenes of a deal? Plenty. Ruth and the kids would have to be shuttled down to San Juan, Puerto Rico, too far away for Peroff's liking. If he became involved in an actual deal, his family would be Bouchard's first target. The French Canadian would want to hold them hostage, if he could find them, until the deal was completed. The stakes would be that high.

During the past three weeks at the Hilton, Peroff had called Bouchard at least ten times. The conversations had been extremely cordial, but never once had a proposition been offered. Peroff would open by saying he was "down south" somewhere, leaving it to Bouchard's imagination as to the exact location. Once he said he was calling from Costa Rica, another time he mentioned that he was in the Bahamas. The last conversation, just four days ago, had gone like this:

PEROFF: "Hi, Connie."
BOUCHARD: "Where are you?"
PEROFF: "Down south."
BOUCHARD: "Is your family there?"
PEROFF: "Nah, Ruth's in Europe. She took the kids and went to Spain."
BOUCHARD: "How's business?"
PEROFF: "Well, I got money problems. Anything happening? You know if anybody wants to fly?"
BOUCHARD: "Well, maybe. Why don't you come up here?"
PEROFF: "Hey, I gotta try to make a living, babe. Money don't grow on trees. But I think I'm gonna go up to the States for a while. Gonna try to work some deals with the planes. Try to build that up a little bit, because I think I may be too hot over in Europe. Maybe I'll bring Ruth back down to Miami in a month or so."

BOUCHARD: "You've been to Europe, too?"

PEROFF: "Yeah, I've made a couple of quick trips. Back and forth."

BOUCHARD: "Well, come up here whenever you can."

All his conversations had been recorded, by himself, on a tape-cassette machine given to him by Customs, using a simple wire with a rubber suction cup (an induction coil) for the phone. And the recorded cassettes had been turned over to Roy Gibson each time they had been completed. None of the information had suggested that a heroin deal was in the works, so the agents must have had an independent source, probably the Mounties. At the final meeting in Ryan's office, Pete Murphy had done most of the talking about Cotroni. If what Murphy was saying turned out to be true, the implications could be overwhelming.

Roy Gibson had already calmed down the manager of the New York Hilton. The next day he also made sure that Peroff received his $7,900, personally arranging for a Customs check to be drawn on a secret fund account and cashed by a senior officer in New York. A day later he helped the Peroff family check out of the hotel and they all went to Kennedy Airport. Ruth and the children were put on a plane that afternoon. Peroff told her not to worry and Gibson assured them that an apartment would be set up in San Juan. Peroff himself then checked into the International Hotel, near the airport, to wait for his imminent trip up to Montreal.

He was awakened at three o'clock in the morning, in his hotel room, by the telephone. Before he could turn on the light and adjust his mind to the sudden interruption, he heard Ruth's voice on the line. She was calling from Puerto Rico, on the brink of tears, complaining that the family's living quarters in San Juan were so miserable that she couldn't sleep. They had been met by a Customs agent named Luis Cruz, who had taken them to a building in a depressing section of San Juan. The apartment itself was awful. It had no curtains, no towels or sheets, no carpets, no kitchen utensils worth mentioning; and the hallways were filled with young people using drugs. Planes roared overhead every several minutes and, Ruth added, across the street was where they held the cockfights.

"All right," Peroff said, rubbing his eyes. "I'll figure something out."

When he hung up he was furious. He was too far away from his family to help them, alone in a hotel room awaiting instructions to fly up to Canada as an undercover man. Unable to sleep, he got dressed and went down to the lobby of the International Hotel and found a copy of *The New York Times*. He searched the classified section and found, to his surprise, an advertisement for a three-bedroom condominium in Puerto Rico, right on the beach, available for rent. The owner lived in Connecticut.

At eight o'clock in the morning he reached the owner, a woman, by phone from the hotel. She described the condominium in detail, adding that it would cost $500 per month, the same price that Agent Cruz was paying for the horrible apartment where his family was. He called Ruth and told her, "I think I got something. I'm working it out. I'm doing the best I can."

Over the next three days he made a number of calls to Roy Gibson and Luis Cruz, arguing with them over the living quarters for Ruth and the children, cursing at them and letting loose his rage. The worst aspect was having so little control and being unable to fly down to San Juan to help. Near the end of the week, Gibson showed up at the hotel and Peroff greeted him with a scowl, assuming that it was time for him to board a plane to Montreal while the situation was still unresolved.

"Well," Gibson said, "there's a little delay. Go on down to Puerto Rico. Get your wife straightened out."

"What's the delay?"

"It can't be helped. Why don't you just go down to San Juan, and do whatever you want. When you get it in your mind where you want to put her and all, we'll work it out. And just wait down there until we're ready."

"How long?"

"Probably about a week," Gibson said, adding that the delay had something to do with the Mounties' ability to provide the proper surveillance. Apparently they were involved in a separate case in Montreal, so they were momentarily short of manpower.

That afternoon Peroff flew down to Puerto Rico, angry over the fact that his week at the International Hotel had been unnecessary. He joined his family and tried to straighten out the apartment situation, cursing at Luis Cruz so vehemently that the agent called Washington demanding an apology from Peroff.

"You'd better keep your gun loaded," Peroff warned him, "because you're gonna need it! I'm gonna kill you!"

Eventually Gibson called and pleaded with Peroff, saying, "Try to settle this thing, Frank. You don't have to apologize, but let's get it straightened out."

"He owes *me* an apology," Peroff roared. "Treating my family like that? Who does he think he is?"

It took two weeks for the battle to end. Peroff and his family remained in the dingy apartment during that time until the new quarters were available. He rented a station wagon for Ruth and bought a television set for the children, trying to make the situation tolerable. At last he was able to sublease the condominium apartment, wiring three months' rent to the owner in Connecticut. The new quarters were beautiful, with a large terrace overlooking the ocean. On the first of May, Peroff realized that his children were missing the entire spring session of school, an irretrievable loss of time for them, no matter how nice it was to have this "vacation" in Puerto Rico.

A day later Roy Gibson called from New York to say that Peroff's trip to Montreal, his third, was on. "I'm going up there right away," Gibson said. "I'll meet you at the Martinique Hotel."

"Wait a minute," Peroff said. "I told Connie that I've made four or five trips to Europe and back. And Bouchard is a cautious guy. He might want to look at my passport, to see if I've been telling the truth. I ought to cover myself."

"Okay, Frank. Make a stop at Kennedy Airport. Go see the head of Customs there, and I'll make sure he's expecting you. He'll have your passport fixed."

So Peroff left his family again, flying from San Juan up to Kennedy Airport in New York. He went to the Customs official whom Gibson had mentioned, and together they worked out fictitious dates showing when Peroff had come back into the United States. Four stamps were placed in his passport, validating the reentries. An hour later, Peroff was on an Air Canada flight to Montreal.

* * *

Roy Gibson's room at the Martinique Hotel was on the top floor. Peroff met him there with Hal Roberts and the plan, as usual, was kept vague and loose. It was another "fishing trip" to see if Bouchard would come up with a deal. Once again the Mounties had bugged Peroff's own room from next door, so that all conversations could be recorded and analyzed.

When Bouchard came up to Peroff's room with Maurice Dufrenne and Victor Fauci, the bodyguards, he was in an extremely good mood, in much better spirits than before. During Peroff's two weeks in Puerto Rico, there had been several calls to the French Canadian, all recorded and given over to Customs, in which Bouchard had talked of escaping from Canada.

"If my trial goes against me," Bouchard had said, "I'm gonna take off. Maybe I'll use your plane, eh?"

After discussing it with various agents by phone, Peroff had called Bouchard again with a specific plan of escape which the Government had approved. Whenever Bouchard wanted, Peroff would bring the Lear to Montreal and fly him down to the Virgin Islands. The Government actually was hoping that Bouchard would utilize the plan, because it would enable Peroff to deal directly with Cotroni from then on.

But now the situation had changed. Bouchard had hired a public relations man in Montreal to get his own side of the previous narcotics case into the newspapers. While the trial was still being delayed, the papers were carrying stories to the effect that the Mountie responsible for Bouchard's arrest was, in fact, a personal friend of narcotics smugglers. Also there was talk that the Canadian entrapment laws might be eliminated, in which case Bouchard would go free on the basis that *he* had been entrapped, by the Mounties.

"I'm gonna win," Bouchard said when he came into Peroff's room. "It's all going in my favor, Frank."

"Good, Connie. That's great."

There was no more talk by Bouchard of escaping. Bolstered by the recent publicity campaign against the Mounties, with new hope that the case would go his way, Bouchard was free to think up new schemes and crimes.

"Did you bring the plane?" he asked.

"No, I came commercial this time."

"Where is it?"

"Still down in Florida. In Palm Beach. I got it working out on charter, you know? I mean, I can't hang onto a Lear unless it starts paying for itself."

"Oh," said Bouchard. "That's right."

"So what's new, Connie?"

Bouchard's eyes suddenly gleamed. "Well," he said, "we've got a hash deal in the works. Hash oil."

"Really?"

"Unlimited amounts, Frank."

"Yeah?"

"Two tons at least. It's all in Pakistan."

"No kidding!"

"And, you know, we can make as many trips as we want. Not just one! We can go as fast as you can bring it. Back and forth."

It was the beginning of a deal, at last. Not involving heroin, but still a huge amount of narcotics. The hash oil would be carried in large tins the size of coffee cans. For flying it into North America, Peroff would receive nearly $200,000, depending upon the number of trips he made.

For the next four days, Peroff went back and forth from Bouchard to the agents. After each meeting with Bouchard, he would sit down with Roy Gibson and go over every detail. Gibson, a meticulous investigator, would use a tape recorder while he questioned him thoroughly. On several occasions Bouchard used Peroff's hotel phone, conversing in French, so the Mounties had not only the discussions in the room but the telephone material as well.

After a period of confusion among the United States and Canadian agents, Peroff was told to agree to the deal.

The discussions continued, with Bouchard calling four or five times each day to go over new details. He told Peroff that he was conferring with Cotroni on the deal and, in fact, the Mounties confirmed it. The Mounties also revealed that from Bouchard's phone conversations in French they had picked up more specific information. The hash, they said, was only going to be the "top layer" of narcotics. The rest would be morphine base, which was used to produce heroin. Cotroni, they had learned, was planning to set up his own laboratory in Canada. Meanwhile, Bouchard apparently was trying to keep this a secret from Peroff and thereby limit his slice of the money.

"Typical of Connie," Peroff observed.

When he was ready to leave Montreal, the agents' excitement was evident. It was a "go" situation involving the first actual proposals by Bouchard, and the expectations were high. If the "hash oil"—or morphine base, as the Mounties believed—was ready, then the operation could take place within a week. Bouchard, Cotroni and virtually the heart of the Montreal mob, responsible for so much of the narcotics in the United States, could be destroyed.

Roy Gibson took a night flight out of Montreal. The next morning, Peroff telephoned Bouchard from his hotel room. "I'm going to New York," he said. "But I'll call you this afternoon."

When he arrived at La Guardia, Gibson picked him up and they drove into Manhattan, to the Lexington Hotel at Forty-eighth Street, where Gibson had arranged a room. They made sure the tape recorder was set up for the call. Peroff dialed Bouchard's home number and the French Canadian answered.

"I'm all set, Connie," he said. "Whenever you need the plane, let me know. I'll call you every day if you like."

"Forget about that other stuff," Bouchard said, and Peroff waited with a queasy feeling in his stomach. So it was no deal? All over? But Bouchard added, "They've agreed to deal in powder."

It was as if a huge bell had sounded. Peroff glanced over at Roy Gibson, who was monitoring the call and trying to show as little reaction as possible. The message was clear: "powder" meant heroin.

VII

From New York, Peroff flew back down to Puerto Rico and rejoined his family in the condominium apartment overlooking the beach and the ocean. He kept in constant telephone contact with Roy Gibson in Manhattan and Bouchard in Montreal, still recording each conversation with the French Canadian. Bouchard would say, "Things are working," and Gibson inevitably would ask, "What's new?"

Commencement of a firm heroin deal, even in the earliest stages, marked a kind of watershed for Peroff, as if he were passing through an invisible line. Once he was on the other side of that line, there was no chance of turning back. Now he faced the prospect of waiting until at least the end of June or early July, simply because it would take that long, about two months, for any large amount of heroin to be processed in Marseilles. He would not be allowed to return to Italy during that time, so it was certain that his business ventures in Europe would collapse and leave him bankrupt. In Rome, Nunzio Galli would arrange to put all of the Peroff family's furniture and other belongings into storage.

There was no question that when the operation ended, Peroff would become one of the most hunted men in the world. The Government would provide him with money and protection, but his entire life-style, including that of Ruth and the children, would be changed forever.

It plagued Peroff to think that he had been maneuvered and pressured this far. He would stay awake late at night, pondering and scheming, trying to weigh all the tiny decisions he had made, all the steps which had added up to a long series of concessions and finally to the complete erosion of control over his own actions. He would try to apply the formula which he had used so well in the past, on the other side of the law: was the profit equal to the risk? Well, perhaps. He would have to try to make it so. Having crossed the invisible line, he was now committed to making the Government's operation work, so that in the end he, too, would benefit. He had crossed the line, leaving the criminal world behind and becoming a full-fledged undercover agent in the process. He would have to perform as one with all the talent that he possessed. Everything depended upon it.

Toward the middle of May, Peroff was summoned to New York City. In the presence of Roy Gibson, he sat in a room at the Statler Hilton Hotel and answered questions posed by a number of federal agents, on a wide variety of subjects mainly involving white-collar crime. Soon afterward, back in San Juan, he received a call from Gibson and was told that the Government wanted him to make his fourth trip to Canada. Apparently the Mounties were sending back information that, according to their sources, a major deal involving Pepe Cotroni was, in fact, being put together. The agents were impatient and wanted to make sure that Peroff's involvement was secure.

This time Peroff was instructed to check into the Seaway Hotel in Montreal, a few blocks from the Mounties' headquarters, and Roy Gibson took another room on a separate floor. When Peroff called Bouchard, the French Canadian reiterated that "everything's fine, we're moving along," but he also sounded nervous, as if a new problem had arisen.

"I'm coming over in a few minutes," Bouchard said. "Wait for me at the front door of the lobby."

Peroff quickly called Gibson at his room in the hotel and told him, "I'm not sure what's going on, Roy."

"Did he give you a clue?"

"Nope. He just said to meet him downstairs."

In the lobby, Peroff went to the front door and stood there wondering what Bouchard's tone of voice had meant. He had no doubt that plainclothes Mounties would be following, but that was no insurance against any major trouble.

Within a few minutes he saw Bouchard's blue Cadillac drive up to the door. Bouchard was behind the wheel. The rear door opened and Maurice Dufrenne stepped out, nodding to Peroff and indicating that he should get in back. He did so, realizing that Victor Fauci was on the opposite side of the seat. The door slammed and Bouchard drove off and Peroff was sandwiched between the two huge bodyguards. The car was speeding through the streets of Montreal and both Dufrenne and Fauci were unusually silent.

Bouchard spoke first, as he drove. "How're you doing, Frank?"

"Fine. What are we doing?"

"Oh, we're going to a meeting. With Savotok's people."

Savotok's people? Peroff thought back to Paris, to the scenes with Herman Savotok and Irv Spellman and Jules Handel. They were all in prison in France. Bouchard's reference to "Savotok's people" either meant his relatives or the mysterious Doctor, who ran a separate underworld organization here in Montreal.

Peroff tried to get comfortable as he sat with Dufrenne and Fauci on either side of him. He felt a sharp, twisting pain in his stomach as he tried to anticipate the meeting, if there really was one. Maybe they've found some proof linking me to the Paris bust. Is it possible that they know I'm working undercover? It occurred to Peroff that maybe the Doctor and his associates had gone to Bouchard with the evidence, and that Bouchard was now bringing him to a showdown at which he would have to defend himself.

The car ride seemed endless. Peroff had the sinking feeling that this was one of those freak accidents for which everyone is unprepared. Where the hell are we going? Are the Mounties really following us? Or are they sitting back at the Seaway Hotel with egg on their faces?

There was no doubt that "Savotok's people" were angry over what had happened in Paris. Maybe they went to Bouchard and said, "Look, Connie, everything went wrong. Now, as payment, you deliver Peroff." Deliver me, he thought, or wipe me out by himself, with the help of these two monsters. Oh, shit, this is what I've hoped would never happen. Are we going up to the Laurentians? Someplace like that? Where they can kill me? Am I covered? I'd better pray that the Mounties are around, somewhere, or . . .

The Cadillac took a turn toward the waterfront. Dufrenne and Fauci were professional killers, but they wouldn't take a chance like that right here, not in a populated area. Would they? Maybe this is just a stop before we make the final trip. . . .

Now the car pulled up outside a restaurant. For the first time in fifteen minutes, Bouchard spoke up. "There's some people in here," he said, pointing toward the drab-looking restaurant. "And they're looking to kill you."

Outside the car, Bouchard continued, "There's a war. Savotok's nephew is in there. Also some guys that don't want to introduce themselves. We gotta straighten them out."

"On what?"

"You know, Frank."

"No. What?"

"Chile," said Bouchard, and Peroff's nerves began to loosen. "There's a lot of questions, Frank. About the money. The Chile money. They want their part of that deal, you know?"

At least, Peroff thought, it's got nothing to do with Paris. Not yet, anyway.

He followed them into the restaurant. Seated alone at one of the tables was a man in his late twenties.

"This is Savotok's nephew," Bouchard said.

The restaurant was dark, even though it was midafternoon, and the place was empty aside from two other men at a neaby table. One of them, Peroff assumed, was the Doctor.

They sat down, Peroff facing the nephew. Bouchard, flanked by Dufrenne and Fauci, took a chair so he could watch the confrontation from a slight distance.

Savotok's nephew began in a low tone of voice, staring at Peroff with obvious hatred: "You owe us money."

"I don't owe nobody any money. Except Connie, here."

"You owe *us* money."

"Listen, my deal is with Connie."

"Right now you're a dead man. You know that?"

"Don't get excited," Peroff said. "Look, everything is based on when I can get that money out of Chile. And besides, the damn *value* of it is getting worse and worse! Don't you know the situation down there? The value is dropping down to nothing! You have to understand—I've *already* got some expenses sunk into this.

173

And it's gonna cost so much more to go *get* the stuff. I'm gonna have to use somebody *else* to help me get it, and he'll have to be paid, and what I'll have left is bullshit! On top of that, we gotta split it—me and Connie. And then you divide it up your way, with him. By the time we're done, you're ending up with only *eight grand* or something! Because of the low price, right now, on Chile money!"

"Wait a minute," the nephew said, raising his voice. "We've decided that this is gonna be a *three*-way split. You, Connie and us."

"Bullshit! That ain't the deal I made! I ain't gonna do it!"

Maurice Dufrenne suddenly interrupted, saying, "Wait Frank, you—"

"Hey," Peroff yelled, "you shut up! I didn't make no deals with you! Keep out of this!"

Underneath, Peroff realized that he was frightened, perhaps more terrified than he'd ever been in his life. These men, all of them, were professional killers, not just hoodlums but experts at violence. There was no choice but to take the offensive and keep it, to the point of screaming, giving nobody else a chance to gain the upper hand. If necessary, Peroff thought, I'll turn into a wild animal, a monster, to keep them off their guard.

"Calm down," Bouchard said.

"And *you* stay out of this, too!" Peroff shouted. "In another minute, Connie, *you and I* are gonna do battle!"

"Why? Why?"

"Because you're a fuck! Whose side are you on, here? Don't put *me* into the middle of this shit! If you guys had come up with the bread at the right time, we'd have gotten that Chile money a long time ago! But now it's a big risk, with very little to gain!"

Savotok's nephew decided to approach the topic from a new angle. "Listen," he said, "we have some diplomats in Chile who will do whatever we want. They can bring that money out for us. All you have to do is tell us where it is. You can draw us a map."

It was time, Peroff thought, to do something dramatic and crude. "I'll tell you what I think of that idea," he said, getting to his feet. He stood there and calmly pulled down the zipper of his pants. "Now," he said, "do you want it here or outside?"

Bouchard burst into laughter, holding his sides, while the young man fumed at Peroff's threat to urinate on him. So the offensive was working. From this point on, Peroff remained standing.

"I ain't trusting my money to no diplomats," he said. "I tell you what I *will* do, though. When the time is right, when *I* think it's right, you have your man down there and I'll have the stuff delivered to him. Your share, that is. And you get it out *your* way. But you're never gonna see *my* money."

"What about the rest of the counterfeit?"

Peroff thought a moment. He had told Bouchard that the balance of the counterfeit bills was in a hotel safe in Santiago. But it was best, now, to kill that part of the fantasy forever.

"A friend of mine took it out of the safe," Peroff said. "But when he got to New York, he was shot. He got killed for it."

Part of the story had a factual basis. Not the part about the counterfeit money, but the other half concerning the shooting. Two months ago, Peroff had read in the newspapers that a friend, the husband of a South American ambassador, had been murdered on a street in New York City. Peroff had kept a clipping about it, for an occasion just like this one, so now he fished it from his wallet and threw it down on the table.

"That's the guy," he said.

It took almost an hour for Peroff to keep making up details about the circumstances surrounding the dead man's involvement with the counterfeit money; and after that, he went through a long, meticulous explanation of why the Chile money's value had dropped so low. Occasionally Peroff glanced over at the two other men, who were sitting and watching as if at any moment one of them might pull out a gun. At one point a phone call came into the restaurant for Maurice Dufrenne, who left soon afterward with Victor Fauci, much to Peroff's relief. But there was still an atmosphere of tension, so he remained standing and ready, if necessary, to lift up a chair as a weapon.

"The point is," said the nephew, "my uncle is in jail."

"Well, go tell your friends! I mean, you guys put him in the can—get him out! Jesus, man, don't tell me! *I* wasn't part of that deal, I didn't know—they almost got me in there *with* 'em. I don't want to hear any shit about Savotok! He didn't do right by me! He didn't tell me that I was risking my ass being there in Paris with him. He may be your uncle and all that crap, but—"

"Wait a minute!" the young man shouted, now standing up to face him. "Why *weren't* you busted in Paris? Why didn't they arrest *you?* Eh? Why didn't they follow you and try to sink you with 'em?"

Peroff noticed that Bouchard was looking at him with keen interest. The men at the other table, too, were staring, waiting for an answer.

"Well," he said, "they almost *did* get me. I had to sneak out of Paris and go through the fucking Alps!"

"Yeah, but why the hell weren't they on your ass when the bust went down? How'd you get away?"

"Look, I don't know. Maybe the French cops didn't know I was there!"

Savotok's nephew smiled for the first time in the entire argument. He bent down and opened a briefcase, took out some photographs and dropped them on the table. Peroff looked down and realized that he was in almost every one of them. The pictures showed him in Paris with Savotok and Spellman and Handel.

"They knew you were there, all right," the nephew said. "My uncle's attorney got these from the French police. The *cops* took these pictures. Your face is all *over,* man. So don't tell me they didn't know you were there! They did! And why didn't they bust you? Why?"

Peroff looked away from the young man's face. He glanced at Bouchard, then at the two silent observers. They were all waiting, but he could think of nothing to say.

At last Peroff told the nephew, "I didn't even realize there *was* a junk deal, until Connie told me four days after I left Paris. Maybe I was smart enough to smell trouble. But don't even *talk* to me about that deal. I've been a hot man ever since, in Europe. I'm forced to break my ass for bread, now, because of that thing. Don't tell me to apologize for not getting busted for something I had no part in!"

It was a standoff. If the Doctor had forced Bouchard to call this meeting, in hopes of getting some payment for his loss, he would have to accept the disappointment. Either that or it was time for Savotok's nephew to pull a gun.

"Come on," Bouchard said. "We'd better go."

Peroff followed him out of the restaurant to the street, where a taxicab was waiting. When they got inside, Bouchard told the driver to take them to the Seaway Hotel. Now all the fear was gone, but the energy was still there, in the form of anger and fury. He had never really hated Connie Bouchard until this moment. But now Peroff knew, from direct experience, just how vicious a man he was. To cover his own ass, Bouchard simply delivers *me* to his enemies instead! And he tells them, in effect, kill *Peroff* if you want!

"I really meant it in there," he said. "I swear, Connie, you are a real fuck. Whose side are you on? What were you trying to do? Put me in the jackpot?"

"Look, I knew it was a bad scene. But only you could have told these guys the right answers."

"Bullshit!"

"Look," Bouchard said, "*I* don't want to get in a war! *I* don't want to get shot over the goddamn Chile money!"

"Connie, why the fuck did you send the counterfeit to me in the first place?"

The cab pulled up in front of the Seaway Hotel. Bouchard said, "Listen, I'll come in with you. We'll have a drink and discuss the other deal."

They went through the lobby and into the hotel bar, but a few minutes later they were interrupted when a man entered the bar, recognized Bouchard and walked over to their table. He was dressed in a white suit and red tie, a flamboyant man who reached down and hugged Bouchard, kissing him on both cheeks. Bouchard introduced him as Artie and explained that they were old friends. Artie sat down, joining them for drinks, and announced to Peroff that he was the food and beverage manager for the hotel. It took only seconds for Peroff to realize the possible trouble. How much did Artie know about the Mounties' use of this hotel? What would happen if Bouchard tells him I'm staying here? Will he become suspicious?

"Did you hear what happened?" Artie was saying. "The day before yesterday?"

"No," Bouchard said. "What happened?"

"Well, did you read about that guy that robbed the bank?"

"I think so."

"Wait'll you hear this, Connie. The guy robs the bank and he checks in here! And the place is full of RCMP guys! All of a sudden they come in, and I'm the only one on duty here. And they got warrants, you know, and the bank robber's sleeping up in his room! I go up with the Horsemen and I open the guy's door with my pass key. I went right in with 'em! Guns, the whole bit. If I only knew! Shit, Connie, I would've snuck in there and hit him myself!"

"Did he have the money that he robbed?"

"*Did* he! They took a hundred-something grand off the guy! It was all there in his bag. If I only knew! *I'd* have wiped him out."

Bouchard slammed his fist on the table at the thought that he himself could have robbed the bank robber. "Why didn't you *tell* me?" he demanded.

"I didn't know! How would I know the bank robber was up there?"

"Jesus Christ," said Bouchard, who was already concluding that he had lost money.

While the two were commiserating, Peroff wondered which way the conversation would turn next.

"Anyway," Artie was saying, "this hotel is used by the RCMP all the time. They're always all over the place."

"Listen," Peroff said, his throat sticking, "I'm taking off, Connie."

"All right. Call me."

Peroff wandered out of the bar, hurrying when he reached the lobby, and went up to Roy Gibson's room. When he was inside he told Gibson, "Hey, let's get the hell out of here."

He explained about the food and beverage manager, adding that the entire day had been a horrible experience. "Okay," Gibson said. "Don't go to your room. Stay here. I'll be back." Gibson went downstairs. Peroff waited for an hour, thinking that it would be best, from now on, to deal with Bouchard strictly by telephone. The stakes had become too high for anything to go wrong.

Gibson came back to the room and reported, "Connie was already gone when I got down there. But I saw his friend, Artie. I struck up a conversation with him. We had a few drinks, you know, and it looks pretty cool. No sweat."

"He didn't suspect you?"

"Nah, I conned him. Besides," Gibson added with a sly grin, "there's no such thing as black Mounties."

They agreed to cut short the trip. Gibson would fly down to New York that night and Peroff would follow the next day, after calling Bouchard to let him know his plans.

When Peroff arrived at the Montreal airport, he was still suffering from his fears of the previous day. His main concern was to leave as quickly as possible, before there could be any more confrontations or dangerous situations. He hurried through the airport crowd with his bag, heading for the Customs section, but when he got there he heard a voice saying, "Hey, I know you!"

Peroff found himself staring at a U. S. Customs official whom he had met briefly on his first trip to Montreal, back in February. It was the same official who had questioned him while he was waiting for the long-delayed arrival of Hal Roberts. At that time, Peroff had started growing a beard; but he had shaved it off a few weeks ago, in San Juan.

"Don't I know you?" the official asked.

Peroff closed his eyes, reached up and rubbed his forehead. The last thing he needed was another scene. What if one of Bouchard's men is here, watching me?

"Weren't you up here a while back?"

Peroff looked around, hardly able to believe what was taking place. He whispered, "Yeah."

"What business are you in?"

Peroff stared at him, squinting hard.

"What are you doing here? Why are you in Montreal?"

Taking a deep breath, Peroff simply opened his bag for the official to inspect its contents. The crowd behind him was becoming impatient and, worse, curious.

"I asked you a question, sir!"

Again in a whisper, Peroff said, "Hal Roberts, you dumb ass— remember? Hal Roberts!"

The official looked at him strangely; then it clicked. *"Oh!"* he shouted. *"Oh, yeah! Okay, that's all right!"* He leaned his face toward Peroff's and added, now in a confidential tone, "Sorry about this."

Peroff took his bag and hurried to the plane.

* * *

179

Through the end of May and the first half of June, Peroff's calls to Bouchard from Puerto Rico were cause for both encouragement and frustration. On the one hand, Bouchard confirmed that Pepe Cotroni was formulating and arranging the heroin deal. An order had been placed in France. Production in the lab was under way. On the other hand, Bouchard himself was facing so many problems that his own participation in the deal was uncertain. First, he would have to be in Europe *with* Peroff when the shipment was picked up. In order to do that, he needed two or three weeks without having to appear in court for his ongoing cases and trials. The main concern was his previous narcotics charge, the one for which he was out on bail.

"Nothing can happen for a while," he said. "I'll have to go through these fucking court appearances, you know? They want me there at least once a week, so I can't get free."

"Maybe I should go to Europe *alone*, Connie."

"Nah, I gotta be there with you. They *want* me to do the deal," he said, referring to Cotroni's people, "but now all of a sudden they say they *don't* want me to do it unless there's enough time. For the trip, you know? There's a real problem. I got a meeting, but we'll have to see about it."

The same conversation was repeated during several calls, until Bouchard suddenly reported that Cotroni's people had given him their final, negative word. "I can't go," Bouchard said. "Not until I get a break up here. They want to wait until this thing is over," he added, referring to his trial. "But I'll beat the rap."

It was the seventeenth of June. Peroff's whole existence had been reduced to the apartment in San Juan and his conversations on the phone to Bouchard in Montreal and Roy Gibson in New York. How long would Bouchard's court problems go on? The only answer was for the Canadian Government to obtain a postponement for him, perhaps by making a secret arrangement with the judge.

Peroff called Gibson and told him, "Roy, if they don't *do something* up there, this is never going to happen! I'll end up staying here forever."

"I'll see what I can do, Frank."

One of Peroff's concerns about the timing was his children. They had missed school since mid-March. Their term would have ended

180

right about now. He hoped they could start again, somewhere, in September.

For a week there was no change. On the twenty-fourth of June, Peroff made his usual call to Bouchard but got his wife on the phone. She sounded ecstatic, yelling, "Three months! October! Three months!"

"What's three months?"

"A postponement!" she said. "Actually three and a *half* months!"

Peroff hung up, bewildered. He had asked Gibson to see if the Government could arrange a *one*-month postponement for Bouchard. Any longer delay might make him suspicious. Perhaps his wife had misunderstood.

But that night he reached Bouchard and heard the same news. "They've postponed my case! Frank, they gave me over three months! It's a 'go' situation! The deal is on!"

When he got off the phone, Peroff was excited but worried. He called Gibson immediately and said, "Well, you fixed it. The bastard got his postponement and the deal is on. But you know, Roy, you guys ain't done *nothing* right."

"What's the trouble now?"

"Well, shit, I asked you to get him a month! All of a sudden he's got *three!* I mean, we don't *need* that much time! Connie's got a suspicious mind, and don't you think he's gonna ask himself *why* he got so long? When do you guys ever use your brains?"

"Relax, Frank. Either you've got a deal going or you don't. Keep me informed."

Now the proportions of the deal began to emerge. Bouchard would drop a detail here, a fragment of information there, passing on what he was learning from Cotroni. It soon became clear that this operation was one of the most important in the history of narcotics law enforcement.

Cotroni's involvement as the key organizer was enough to make it a high-priority case. But the order placed with the heroin lab in Marseilles was for a staggering one hundred kilos. At a wholesale price of $3,500 per kilo, a total of $350,000 would have to be paid to the French suppliers. Also needed was about $50,000 for the plane and other expenses, so that the sum of $400,000 was to be used to underwrite the deal. According to Bouchard, Cotroni had already sent one of his men from Montreal to Europe with an initial $100,000, which had been put up as a deposit. The additional $300,000 would come from an outside financier who, of course, would receive Cotroni's personal guarantee of credit, which was an absolute form of insurance against any loss.

A few days later Bouchard announced that another fifty kilos had been added to the deal, but under a separate financial agreement. As long as Cotroni was arranging the full payment for the original hundred kilos, no further cash in advance was required. The extra fifty kilos would be given to Cotroni on credit. When the Montreal mob sold it to Mafia traffickers in the United States (for $27,000 per kilo, or $1,350,000 for fifty kilos), Cotroni would split the return, plus the lab cost, equally with the Frenchmen.

For his own services with the Learjet, Peroff negotiated a handsome percentage. He behaved on the phone exactly as he would have done if he were still a crook. After some haggling, Bouchard promised him $200,000 per fifty kilos or $600,000 altogether, plus expenses. Peroff would fly to Europe and pick up the entire load of heroin in Rome, where he could land and take off with little trouble. He would bring it back, all three hundred and thirty pounds, to the Philadelphia-New Jersey area. The heroin would be stored in a warehouse and sold to leaders of organized crime in Detroit and New York City. Negotiations with both mobs had been completed.

Of course, when Peroff actually landed in the States there would be a veritable army of federal agents on hand to greet the plane. The Canadians would have Cotroni and Bouchard on conspiracy charges. And the Americans would move against the Detroit and New York mobsters, whose names were known to Peroff and the agents, not to mention the actual seizure of one hundred and fifty kilos of pure uncut heroin. Such a confiscation would be phenomenal. The eventual street value was over $300 million. Never had any government agency in the world grabbed a shipment of deadly narcotics even close to that amount.

During the last week of June, from his apartment in San Juan, Peroff was on the phone with Bouchard as often as three times a day. As the excitement grew, so did the tension. In Montreal, Bouchard was meeting almost daily with Cotroni and his associates, referring to them as "the guys" and becoming extremely cryptic when he reported new details. Now he seldom used Pepe's name on the phone.

Peroff could feel the hardness in Bouchard's tone of voice as arrangements for the huge heroin shipment were accelerated. The stakes were extremely high, in terms of both profit and danger. And, knowing how Bouchard's mind worked, Peroff already anticipated the next step. In circumstances so important, the underworld wanted insurance against any outsider like Peroff trying to steal the heroin for himself. Bouchard would send his henchmen to "put the grab" on Peroff's family, if he could, until the shipment was picked up and safely delivered.

There was no question that Bouchard was trying to find out just where Peroff was located. Whenever he asked directly, Peroff would simply reply, "Down south." Then Bouchard would ask about the weather, obviously pressing for more information, but Peroff would always give an evasive answer, never even suggesting that he was in Puerto Rico.

He had given Bouchard a story that he had taken his family to Miami while he himself was "doing business" in South America and the Bahamas. On a hunch, he called a mob-connected friend in Florida and inquired as to whether anyone had been looking for him.

"As a matter of fact," the friend said, "Connie Bouchard has been asking around for you. He's made several calls to people, you know? I know three guys he's talked to here in Miami."

"What did he say?"

"Well, at the end of one conversation with *me* he said, 'Oh, by the way, have you seen Peroff? Is his family down there? I'm trying to reach him.' That kind of thing."

"That son of a bitch," Peroff said, shuddering at the thought of mobsters like Victor Fauci and Maurice Dufrenne kidnapping his children and holding them hostage. They were the kind of men he had avoided in the past. Now he was experiencing their tactics firsthand, realizing the mob's vicious disregard of human life in a new, personal way. Almost without knowing it, he had come to despise Conrad Bouchard and everything for which he stood. The hatred had grown into an obsession.

In a call toward the end of June, Bouchard reported that "the guys" were making final plans. "How's the machine?" he asked, referring to the Learjet, and Peroff assured him that it was ready. In the back of his mind, he knew that the Government could have it available within twenty-four hours.

At the same time, while he was relaying all the information to Roy Gibson in New York, the bureaucracy of the Government was undergoing a change. "It's nothing to worry about," Gibson told him, but the agencies' reorganization was a factor to be dealt with nonetheless. On the first of July a new federal Drug Enforcement Administration (DEA) would go into effect, absorbing the Bureau of Narcotics completely and taking five hundred Customs agents as well. Among those to be transferred from Customs to DEA were Luis Cruz here in San Juan, Hal Roberts in Montreal and Roy Gibson in New York.

"So I'll have a new boss in a few days," Gibson said. "His name is Mike Reilly. He's already on top of our case, Frank. I've filled him in."

"Listen," Peroff said, "there's a money problem again. I'm running out of bread, Roy. My phone bill alone is already over three grand."

"You're kidding!"

"The hell I am. You try coming down to Puerto Rico and making calls to Montreal and New York every day! And Roy, the other expenses are high. Ruth and the kids have to eat down here, you know? Tell Customs—"

"Okay! I got the message!"

That afternoon, the Customs Bureau shut off Peroff's telephone. According to Luis Cruz, the local agent, the Bureau was officially getting out of the case and, therefore, the new DEA would have to install the service again.

"It's just a bureaucratic thing," Cruz explained.

Meanwhile, Peroff was able to use the phone of a neighbor on the same floor of the apartment building. The neighbor was from the United States, here in Puerto Rico as an employee of a traffic-engineering firm. When Peroff first went down the hall and asked to use the phone, the neighbor's wife agreed and, after overhearing bits of the conversation, assumed that he was a secret agent. Peroff said nothing to erase her assumption and she asked no further questions.

From the phone in the neighbor's kitchen, Peroff got in touch with Roy Gibson on July first and the new boss, Mike Reilly, came on the line. Reilly had been transferred from the now-defunct Narcotics Bureau to the DEA in New York where he acted as the link between the federal agency and the Mounties in Montreal. Peroff answered hundreds of his questions, explaining that Bouchard would be giving instructions for the plane within a week or two, perhaps sooner.

"Keep us posted," Reilly said.

A few days later, Peroff gave about twenty hours' worth of tape-recorded cassettes to Luis Cruz, who was now a DEA agent and anxious to be more a part of the case. It was a complete record of the conversations with Bouchard until this point.

On July fourth he received word from Montreal that a crucial meeting was to be held the following night. "We may get the go-ahead," Bouchard added. So it was about to happen. For Peroff, the long waiting period down here in Puerto Rico would come to an abrupt end. At any moment he would be called upon to make his first—and last—flight in a plane loaded down with heroin.

The next twenty-four hours seemed unbearably long. On Thursday night, the fifth, he went to the neighbor's apartment and tried to reach Bouchard but the line was busy. He kept calling every fifteen minutes, always with the same result. At last he gave up, totally frustrated, and returned to his own apartment.

But he started all over again on Friday, the sixth of July, reaching Bouchard's message service and asking the operator to relay word that he was trying to get through to the home number. All day he went back and forth from his own apartment to the one down the hall until, at about five o'clock, Bouchard suddenly answered his phone.

"Hallo!" came the familiar voice.

"Jesus Christ, I've been trying to get you for I don't know *how* long!"

"I've been busy. I got your message."

"Did you? What happened last night?"

"Trouble with the phones down there?"

"No," Peroff shouted. "I've been calling you, and your phone's been busy! I've—"

"Oh, yeah, my phone's been busy for a while, yeah. Where are you?"

"I'm down south."

"Yeah?"

"Yeah."

"Nice weather down there?"

"Yeah, not bad."

"Yeah?"

"You got good news?" Peroff asked.

"Well, uh, I had a meeting last night. And, uh, the guys are gonna meet all together Saturday, you know? To make a decision, you know?"

"Why, they—"

"So, uh, then we'll know. I told them I was ready and everything, you know?"

"Yeah. Do you think—"

"So, uh, Saturday I'll have a sure answer, you know? *Everybody's* gonna be there at the meeting."

"You want *me* to be there?"

"And, uh, you know this guy down there, down south, uh, Vesco? Vesco?"

"Yeah. I *read* about him."

"You heard of him?"

"Yeah, sure," Peroff said. This was the third time in the past two weeks that Bouchard had dropped that name. Once he had asked, "Did you ever run into Vesco? When you lived down in the Bahamas?" And a second time he had said, "Have you ever been to where Vesco's living? Down there in Costa?" The reference was to Robert L. Vesco, the famous "fugitive financier" who had fled the States earlier in the year. According to the papers, Vesco was now living in Costa Rica.

If Peroff remembered the figures, Vesco had been accused by the Securities and Exchange Commission of looting foreign mutual funds of a preposterous sum in the area of $224 million. In terms of white-collar crime, Peroff himself had never even come close to pulling off a swindle that large. It was probably the biggest single fraud case in history.

Also, not long ago, Vesco had been indicted for having tried to block a federal investigation into his affairs. It was said that a year ago he had entered into a conspiracy with former Attorney General John Mitchell and former Commerce Secretary Maurice Stans. The allegation was that he had given $200,000 in cash, secretly, to President Nixon's reelection campaign, with the understanding that they would use their influence to block the investigation of him.

But what the hell did Connie Bouchard have to do with Robert Vesco? Playing along, Peroff said, "I've seen him quite a few times."

"Yah? You ever talk with him?"

"Well," Peroff said, "let me tell you, I know a couple of his *people*, you know?"

"Well, let's say that I would, uh—let's say that I'd have, uh, a very close friend of his, you know?"

"Yeah?"

"Um, that you could go and see—and ask him for any fucking amount of money on his behalf, you know?"

It took three long seconds for Peroff to reply. At last he managed to say, "What do you mean?"

"Well, I'll let you know, I'll explain to you, uh, after the Saturday meeting. Tomorrow night."

Peroff was stunned, almost in shock. He was standing there in the kitchen of his neighbor's apartment in Puerto Rico. Ruth and the neighbor's wife were in the living room, seated so they could see the blank expression on his face. Robert Vesco was the financier for the heroin deal?

"You mean," Peroff said in a weak voice, "he'll put up some bread?"

"Yah."

"You're kidding."

"He'll put up a lot of bread."

Again there was a pause. Bouchard was hesitating, undoubtedly wondering how much more he should say over the phone. And Peroff was trying to get hold of himself and collect his thoughts. First the case involves Pepe Cotroni, "head of the largest and most notorious narcotic syndicate on the North American Continent." Then it becomes a deal for one hundred and fifty kilos, which would be the biggest seizure ever made, by far. And now it's being underwritten by the most famous fugitive in recent memory?

"Yeah?" Peroff asked.

"Yah," Bouchard said.

"Because," Bouchard went on, "there's a guy from Montreal in his organization. His name is LeBlanc, you know?"

"Yeah," Peroff said, realizing that Bouchard meant Norman Le-Blanc, a French-Canadian accountant who had become Vesco's most trusted associate.

"And, uh—"

"I don't know who the guy is, but I mean, you know—"

"He's a guy from Montreal," Bouchard went on. "His righthand man."

"Yeah?"

"This guy made a fraud here for a hundred and ten million, you know?"

"Uh-hunh."

"He's a righthand man of Vesco, you know?"

"Uh—"

"And one of the guys at the meeting is like a father to LeBlanc, you see?"

"Right."

"And any amount of money, I think, will come from there. So you might have to go direct down there to get the bread, you know what I mean?"

Peroff could hardly control his excitement. "One of the guys" in Montreal who was "like a father" to Norman LeBlanc was probably Pepe Cotroni himself. And Bouchard was saying that he, Peroff, would have to fly down to Costa Rica to pick up the money.

"I was just there!" Peroff exclaimed.

"Yeah? When was that?"

"Just a couple of weeks ago! Don't you remember I told you?"

"Oh, you were there—that's right."

It had been one of the many lies Peroff had told him concerning his whereabouts. Now he found himself babbling, his voice almost speaking by itself. "You see, you gotta understand—there's a couple of other guys—"

"All I'll have to do," Bouchard began.

"There's a couple of other guys that used to live in Freeport!"

"Yah?"

"That moved there," Peroff added, referring to Costa Rica but hardly knowing what he was saying or why. "You understand?"

"Yah."

"And *I* was just down there, doing some little, uh, business there!"

"Yeah," Bouchard said.

"Shit."

"Yeah. Listen!"

"Yeah?"

"Uh, one of the guys at the meeting, there, I will be able *only then* to give you his name, you see?"

"Right."

"And then with *this name,* uh, I'll give you another phone number where you can reach me, you know?"

"Right."

"Because on this phone here, I don't want to take a chance to give out that name, you understand?"

"Right, right."

"So I'll give you, when you phone me like, uh, Sunday morning—I'll give you the name exactly. And if we have to go through there, we'll go through there."

"Right."

"So you will go to Vesco or LeBlanc. I think it will be LeBlanc."

"Okay."

"And, uh, you tell him to phone this guy's name I'm going to give you, understand? In Montreal."

"Yep."

"And he'll give you whatever, uh, we need. Understand?"

"Yep."

"Okay. So don't, uh, you know—we won't talk over the phone."

"In other words, what he'll give me is what *I* need? Or for the whole thing?"

"Yah, yah, yah. Everything."

"Everything?"

"What we need."

"I see."

"Understand?"

"Yep."

"So give me a ring about ten o'clock Sunday night."

"All right," Peroff said.

"Okay?"

"All right," he repeated.

"All right, good-bye."

"Good-bye."

* * *

His heart pounding, Peroff rewound the tape machine to make sure it had been working. It was on the counter of his neighbor's kitchen, without question the most important conversation he had recorded. He stopped the tape, pressed the "Play" button and, yes, it was all there, starting with Bouchard's greeting and his own voice: "Jesus Christ, I've been trying to get you for I don't know *how* long!"

He stepped into the living room, where Ruth and the neighbor's wife were sitting in silence looking at him. "Your face—" Ruth said. "What's the matter?"

"I'll explain it to you later," he replied. The neighbor's wife merely looked perplexed, still under the impression that a James Bond-type agent was hard at work right here in her own apartment.

Now Peroff called New York, trying to reach Roy Gibson at the DEA office. Instead he found himself talking to the boss, Mike Reilly, who reported that Gibson had left for the weekend.

"Well," Peroff said, "do you want to hear the biggest riot in the world?"

"Lay it on me, Frank."

"Bouchard just told me that Vesco—Robert Vesco!—is gonna finance this thing!"

"Hunh?"

"Look, I almost don't believe it myself. Let me play it for you— I got it right here, on the tape."

"Go ahead," Reilly answered.

Peroff switched on the recorder and held the phone close to it as the tape began to play. It was as if he were going through the whole shock all over again. Bouchard was cryptic as usual, not wanting to speak Pepe's name aloud but caring little about the others. *"I had a meeting last night,"* he had said, which was probably when he first heard, for sure, that Vesco and LeBlanc were actually going to finance the deal.

"And, uh, you know this guy down there, down south, uh, Vesco? Vesco? . . . Let's say that I'd have, uh, a very close friend of his, you know? . . . Um, that you could go and see—and ask him for any fucking amount of money on his behalf, you know? . . . He'll put up a lot of bread . . . And one of the guys at the meeting is like a father to LeBlanc, you see? . . . And any amount of money,

190

I think, will come from there. So you might have to go direct down there to get the bread . . . You will go to Vesco or LeBlanc. I think it will be LeBlanc . . . And he'll give you whatever, uh, we need . . . Everything . . ."

When the taped conversation was over, Mike Reilly asked him to play it again. Peroff did so and afterward Reilly said, "One more time, Frank—I'm gonna record it here, at my end."

During the third playback, Peroff figured that this new development would produce a number of complications. All sorts of federal agencies, grand juries, investigators and so forth were seeking Vesco's extradition to the United States. Now they would all have to get involved in the case. If they were going to get him back in the States for any reason, this would be it. Well, he thought, there's no turning back now.

"It's interesting, Frank."

"Where do we go from here?"

"Roy'll call you later."

The next day Peroff held two more phone conversations with Bouchard, who mentioned Vesco and LeBlanc by name during both discussions, and the explosive information was duly recorded at Peroff's end. Not until the following morning, Sunday, did he hear from Roy Gibson, who indicated that he already knew about the latest development.

"I hear we have a new situation," Gibson said.

"It's a son of a bitch, ain't it?"

"Listen, Frank, I'm on a special assignment in New York. I'm calling you from the street, so I can't talk long. What's his name, Luis Cruz—he'll pick you up tonight."

As planned, Cruz showed up and drove him down to the local DEA office. Peroff brought a brown paper bag containing some empty cassettes, plus his recorder. The machine was set up and Cruz connected a monitoring wire so he could listen to the conversation at the same time that it was being taped.

At first there was confusion on the line and Bouchard said, "Something wrong with your phone? You're very far!"

"I am," Peroff replied. "I'm calling from—from a long way."

"Yeah? How's business?"

"I'm breaking my ass, man. For food money!"

191

"Yeah?"

"You ain't kidding!"

"How's the machine?" Bouchard asked, meaning the airplane.

"Same situation. It could be available."

"Yeah? Good!"

"Everything look okay?"

"Yes," Bouchard replied. "I told you—I told you I had a meeting. I had that meeting. I just came in, maybe half an hour ago. And I mentioned to you a name there, a French name? And the place where you've been about a month and a half ago?"

"Hunh?"

"Costa, down there? Costa?"

"Right," Peroff said.

"Remember the name I mentioned to you? A French name?"

"Yeah," Peroff said. "Not the American name, right? The French one," he continued, aware that Bouchard now wanted to avoid mentioning Vesco or LeBlanc by name. But it was clear that the "French name" was Leblanc and that "Costa" was Costa Rica.

"Right," Bouchard said. "Well, he's a partner with the other one. You understand? And apparently *this week* you'll have to go see this guy. As soon as I get the okay, you know? Somebody is coming back from there—tomorrow or the day after, you know? And he'll have a password for you. Understand? And he'll let you have three, you know? Three hundred. With that password. It should be enough to pay for everything. Get that three hundred and go where, uh—"

Translated, Bouchard meant that one of Cotroni's people—if not Pepe himself—was now in Costa Rica with LeBlanc and Vesco. This man was returning to Montreal tomorrow or the next day with a password for Peroff to use in Costa Rica when he picked up the money—$300,000!—for the French suppliers in Europe.

The question was, where would Peroff and Bouchard meet? At first, Bouchard suggested that he would fly down to Costa Rica and meet Peroff there. Then they could go together in the Learjet, with the money, to Europe. But this plan was changed. Instead, Peroff would fly to Costa Rica by himself, pick up the money and go on to Rome alone. Meanwhile Bouchard would board a commercial flight from Montreal, using a fake passport. The two men would meet in Europe.

But Luis Cruz scribbled a note and passed it to Peroff. *"Make sure he goes with you to Europe."*

So Peroff told Bouchard, "The best thing is, when I go down there, I'll pick up the three and then come up to where you are. Because I got to go up there anyway, to get to our final destination. I'll have to go north, you know? So when I get up there, then you can come *with* me, Connie."

The conversation went back and forth, with Luis Cruz frantically writing instructions and waving his arms, until Peroff coughed, put his hand over the phone and whispered, "Get the fuck *off* me!"

There was a discussion of Bouchard's need for a new passport. Would Peroff arrange for a fake one? In turn Peroff decided to ask for some money for the plane's operating costs. He figured that as long as the Government was stalling on his expense payments, he might as well try to get some from the underworld.

"If I go down there to Costa," he told Bouchard, "and this guy gives me the three, can I take some of it? To get the machine straightened out?"

"Well, I think so."

"How much can I take?"

"I don't know. How much do you need?"

"Well, can I take twenty?" Peroff asked. If he really did get $20,000, under the pretense of using it for his lease on the airplane, he would send it right to Ruth here in Puerto Rico.

Bouchard gave a little sarcastic laugh over the phone.

"Maybe a bit less," Peroff went on. "But no more than twenty."

Bouchard started complaining about his trial costs. It was time, Peroff thought, to see if he harbored any suspicions about the three-month postponement he'd been granted. "Why," he asked, "did they postpone it for so long?"

"Well, because there's a lack of judges for the summer," Bouchard said, apparently having no thought whatsoever that the Government might have postponed his case on purpose. "Some are retired, some are on vacation. Some are sick, too," he added.

"I see."

"Okay, so listen—let me talk with those people as soon as this gentleman comes back tomorrow or the day after, right? In the meantime, uh—"

"Those people at the meeting, did they say this deal is on?"

"Right."

"Okay, that's all I want to hear."

"Oh, it's perfect. And the gentleman that is in Costa now, uh, he's coming back tomorrow or the day after. Understand?"

"Right."

"He's going to bring back the password, for you to give down there."

"Okay."

"You'll pick up the dough, because I told them you have the machine to go there."

"Yep."

"It'll be in hundreds, I guess."

"Hunh?"

"The three—it'll all be in hundreds," Bouchard repeated.

"No problem."

Once again they discussed the passport for Bouchard and where they would meet each other. Peroff said he would get the $300,000 and fly up to Montreal and, at that point, he would "fix" the passport so the French Canadian would have no trouble.

"Then you come *with* me," Peroff added. "Never mind going over there commercial. You gotta trust me, that I know my business."

"That's what I've said all the way. Because otherwise there wouldn't be a deal."

"See, if you go with me, you'll come out a lot better. Because I know how to do it. I made my living like that"—flying people in and out of countries—"for a long, long time, babe. So when it comes to that part, you do what *I* tell you. When it comes to *your* part, then I'll do what *you* tell me."

"Okay," Bouchard said. "So I'm gonna get news from these people tomorrow."

"I'll call you again tomorrow night."

"All right."

Peroff said good-bye, but Bouchard added, "What *time* is it where you are now?"

He's still trying to find where I am, Peroff thought. He just doesn't give up. "An hour different from you," he replied. "An hour later."

194

"Yeah?"

"Right. It's midnight here."

"Yah? How's the weather?"

"Uh, not bad. A lot of rain," Peroff lied.

When he got off the phone, he felt as if he might grab Luis Cruz's throat and choke him. The constant note-scribbling and interference had made the entire conversation seem mixed up and jumbled in his mind. They were still in the local DEA office in San Juan when Cruz declared, "My orders are to take that cassette from you."

"No, no," Peroff said, more out of anger than calculation. "I'll give it to Roy Gibson when I see him."

"I've *got* to have it," Cruz demanded. "Please, Frank."

Peroff already had dropped the cassette into his brown paper bag. It was the fourth crucial conversation having to do with Vesco, LeBlanc, Costa Rica and all the rest. He had given Cruz the second and third recordings, having kept the first; and now, out of instinct, he decided that this fourth one was just too important to give over. So he reached into the bag and pulled out a blank cassette instead.

"Here," he said. "You win."

Agent Cruz took the unused tape and placed it inside an envelope. In triumph, believing that he would receive credit for a job well done, he mailed it to Roy Gibson in New York. Then he drove Frank Peroff, who still had the real cassette, back to his condominium apartment.

VIII

This week, Bouchard had said.

Stay calm, Peroff told himself. We'll wipe out the Cotronis, Bouchard, the Marseilles lab, the Detroit and New York mobs—and Robert Vesco. There'll be two pilots on the Learjet with me, the way we did it up in Canada. Probably both of them agents this time, heavily armed. I'll go down to Costa Rica—this week! —and the three hundred grand will either be there or it won't. Unbelievable. Why would Vesco want to finance junk? Maybe he's hurting for ready cash. Who the hell cares? All I have to do is go there. Bouchard figured I'd probably heard of Vesco, yeah, but not LeBlanc. But LeBlanc is the key, here. A French Canadian, from Montreal, now in Costa Rica with Vesco. The key is LeBlanc's relationship with Cotroni. Jeez, there's gonna be a million feds in on this thing. All this Watergate crap going on, hell, and this Mitchell-Stans trial, holy shit! Wasn't it Vesco who said that he had "the missing link" to Watergate? Whatever the hell that means. Maybe they'll extradite him on this fucking thing and oh, man, I'm right in the middle of it. Steady, steady . . .

Now using public phone booths to make his calls, he spoke several times on Monday with Roy Gibson, pleading for reassurance, demanding reimbursement from Customs for expenses, waiting to hear news of what the DEA was planning—and Gibson was underplaying things as usual, keeping that cool distance in his voice.

"Well," Gibson said, "there's a lot of research going on down in Washington. A lot of discussion. Stay loose, Frank. We'll be in touch."

That night Peroff called Bouchard and learned that the "gentleman from Montreal" was still in Costa Rica making final arrangements for the $300,000. Bouchard hesitated, then quickly mentioned Pepe Cotroni by name, referring to him as the "father figure" to Norman LeBlanc. According to Bouchard, Cotroni was the "mastermind" behind the heroin deal. The Mafia leader and LeBlanc had been long-time associates, Bouchard went on, and they were still close friends. LeBlanc was with Vesco in Costa Rica, and it was even possible that Cotroni himself would make a trip down there "this week" to personally assure the financiers that his credit guarantee had been given in good faith.

Bouchard warned, however, that Vesco and LeBlanc were not to be told about the extra fifty-kilo deal. They were being given the impression that the total shipment was only one hundred kilos. They would receive $50,000 "back off the top" and, therefore, the investment by them was actually $250,000, for which they would receive $1,400,000 from Montreal—their half of what Cotroni would get from the sale of a hundred kilos.

It wasn't such a bad return on their money, not at all, but still they were being cheated out of the profits from the additional fifty kilos. The latter represented a secret arrangement between Cotroni and the French suppliers. Peroff held back from remarking, out of amusement, that if he were Robert Vesco he'd be pissed off as hell.

Stay loose, Gibson had said.

On Tuesday, the tenth of July, the neighbor's wife down the hall came to say that there was a phone call for "Richard Santos" —the alias that Peroff was using at times in Puerto Rico, so Bouchard couldn't trace him—and he hurried to the phone. It was Roy Gibson in New York, saying that his boss, Mike Reilly, was on the other extension.

"How're you doing?" Reilly asked.

Peroff described the latest Bouchard conversation, about Cotroni, and waited for his instruction.

"Well, we want you to go ahead, you know? To Costa Rica."

It sounded almost ridiculous. What other course of action was even possible? Here we are, Peroff thought, sitting on a bombshell. By now the FBI was probably in on this. Also the Securities and Exchange Commission, no doubt. And maybe the Watergate special prosecutor, Archibald Cox. Also the U. S. Attorney's Office in New York, where Vesco was indicted with Mitchell and Stans. The whole *world* must be involved—and Reilly makes the big announcement that we're going ahead. So what else is new?

But Peroff suppressed his thoughts and said, "Good."

Reilly continued, "We're considering, uh, you going down there on a commercial flight."

Peroff wondered if he had heard him correctly. The guy must be joking, he thought. "What?"

"We want you to take a commercial flight."

Peroff laughed and said, "For what?"

"To get the money."

"Are you kidding?"

There was dead silence at the other end. Roy Gibson, on his extension, said nothing.

"I'm being serious," Reilly said at last. "What's the problem?"

"What's the—are you out of your mind? What do you *mean,* what's the problem?"

"We'll protect you."

"What? How the hell are you gonna protect me in Costa Rica? I mean, Vesco nearly *owns* that country. What are you *talking* about?"

"You can do it, Frank."

"Wait a minute, hold on! My only *value* in this deal, my whole *function,* is knowing how to fly in and out of places with that jet! I mean, this deal *started* on that basis. The Learjet is what brought the whole damn thing about! I can't turn around and tell Bouchard that I'm flying commercial! He'd laugh me off the fucking phone!"

"Frank, I *know* you can do it."

"No, hey, it's impossible! Who's gonna give me three hundred grand in a suitcase, if I'm boarding a regular flight? I'd have to fly back up to the States, and—"

"We'll make sure there's no problem in walking it through."

"Yeah," Peroff screamed, "but how do I explain it to *them?* Do I say to Vesco, 'Don't worry, man, the cops are on my side,' or what? I mean, Jesus, you're driving me crazy! Do you *want* me to end up a dead man?"

"Frank, we want to avoid the possibility of losing a jet plane down there, and—"

"What about *me*, you son of a bitch? It's my neck you're playing with!"

"Frank, we'll *protect* you."

"But they're not gonna give me the money that way!"

"Well," Reilly said, "do you refuse?"

"You're asking me to commit suicide!"

Off the phone, he realized that he was almost crying from the frustration. It just made no sense, none at all, and yet the guy was serious, he meant it! He must be a damn fool, Peroff thought. Why's he worried about losing the Lear? We'd have two agents aboard! Oh, man, this thing just has to go through. We gotta start living again, all of us, Ruth and the kids—we're living like damn hermits, hiding under false names all over the place. And if the whole case came to a stop, what then? Bouchard would still be on my ass about the Chile money and all, and the Doctor and that crowd, too. Connie is an animal and I want him put away, for the rest of his life! Why is Reilly trying to get *me* killed? We've gone this far—I can't let it die. . . .

Sweating and nearly hysterical, Peroff called the DEA office in New York and again reached Reilly. In a calm voice, holding himself back, he said, "Okay, Mike. Look, I *want* to pursue this. I'm the *last* one who wants to kill this case. I tell you what—*I'll* go out and get a jet. How's that? I'll get one, somehow, and you just supply the two guys, the agents."

"Frank, are you saying that you refuse to go down there on a commercial flight? Is that your answer?"

Peroff waited before making a reply. There was a trap, here. He had no idea of why, but he was being set up, forced into a position whereby *he* was the one sabotaging the case. Okay, Peroff thought, I'll call his bluff. "I agree," he said. "I *agree* to go down to Costa Rica on a commercial plane."

"You do?"

"Yep. But on just one condition."

"What's that?"

199

"Well, very simple. You just bring another agency into this. If the DEA wants me to put my life on the line, let the FBI get involved, too. Or I'll even give you a choice. You can pick from the FBI or the SEC or the Senate Rackets Committee."

"But why?"

"Because I want someone *else* to know what's going on."

"I don't understand, Frank."

"Well, you should! I'm not willing to put my ass on the line with only *you* knowing about it! Because I don't think you know what the hell you're doing! I don't trust you! I think you're trying to get me killed! I don't know why, but—"

"Frank, what reason would we have—"

"You tell *me* the answer! Go ahead! I mean, either you're trying to kill me or you're the biggest incompetent I've ever met! One or the other!"

"Well, we *can't* bring another agency into this."

"No? Why not? What if we went to the Senate? To the Rackets Committee? I mean, wouldn't they be interested?"

"Frank, we can't do that."

"Well," Peroff went on, bluffing, "what if I told you I've *already* called the Senate?"

There was a cold silence at the other end. "If you did that," Reilly said at last, "you're a walking dead man."

Was it a threat? Where was the danger, from the Senate or from Reilly himself? "Well," Peroff replied, "I haven't called anyone. I can't understand why nobody else can get involved, that's all. Why can't *you* call the Senate?"

"We just can't."

"I don't know why not," Peroff said, now on the verge of delirium. "My wife and I struggle and go through this, for months! You guys break my back and force me to do this. When I agree, I do my fucking best! Now I finally get it to where it's coming down any day, to where it's *within reach,* and all of a sudden you tell me to go commit suicide! What am I supposed to do?"

"Frank, I'm gonna hang up."

"What do you think, that I'm not a man? You think I'm a piece of shit? That you can shovel me around and it don't mean nothing? Well, I'm a man! You can't *do* this to a human being!

You break my ass and give me a stiff neck, and then you expect me to sit here and take it? I've never done that for anybody. What gives *you* the right? Who's *your* boss? Reilly? Reilly! Answer me!"

Over the next several days, Peroff spoke on the phone again with Mike Reilly at least ten times, trying to convince the DEA boss that it was both illogical and too risky to fly commercially to Costa Rica. *"You'll pick up the dough,"* Bouchard had said, *"because I told them you have the machine to go there."* Peroff also spoke to Roy Gibson, who was even more laconic than usual, offering neither consolation nor explanation.

Peroff impulsively brought up the Senate again. "What would happen," he asked, "if I called the Rackets Committee?"

"That wouldn't be wise," Gibson said. "Your life wouldn't be worth two cents."

"What do you mean by that?"

"Well," Gibson said, "you just don't want to do that. It would cause problems, Frank. You don't know what a problem *is,* compared to the headaches that might cause."

It seemed, to Peroff, that the agent was offering a word of honest advice rather than issuing any personal threat or warning. It was true, after all, that going to the Senate could have extremely dangerous consequences. He could end up a major witness in Congressional hearings, an informer, in which case a thousand other crooks might place him on their most-wanted lists.

"Listen, Roy, we've got a *time* crisis at this point. I mean, Connie is gonna be getting final word on the deal—then I'll get my orders! Soon, Roy! And what am I supposed to say? Look, we've gotta have a meeting!"

"Maybe you should be here in New York."

"Sure, fine. I mean, we'll discuss the situation and resolve it. It's that simple, really, a foolish proposal by this boss of yours, and—"

"Okay," Gibson said. "I'll get back to you."

A day later it was agreed that Peroff would fly to New York for conferences with DEA officials. He told Gibson, "I've got to bring my family with me, Roy. The lease on this apartment is running out. And Customs owes me around fifteen grand, by now."

"You'll have to leave your family there," Gibson said. "Come to New York alone."

"Roy, I can't do that! I won't! The lease is just about gone! And besides, man, Bouchard has been *looking* for my family. He'd put the grab on 'em, if he could. I want them protected, Roy! Until this deal is finished!"

Gibson hung up and reported back to him later, "It's okay, Frank. Bring your wife and kids."

So it was settled. Gibson had even asked some questions about the Learjet, about whether both pilots could be federal agents, and of course the answer was yes. So maybe they're coming to their senses, Peroff thought. We'll talk it all over in New York, and work everything out.

They were ready to leave Puerto Rico on Thursday afternoon, the seventeenth of July. While the family was packing, Peroff called Bouchard and stalled him a bit, saying that he was waiting for a mechanical part to be replaced in the Lear. Bouchard no longer spoke of a password, but mentioned that arrangements were being made for Peroff to receive exact instructions as to what he should do when he landed in San José, Costa Rica.

Luis Cruz, the local agent, showed up to say that he had orders to drive them to the plane. Peroff gave him the cassette which contained his fifth crucial conversation with Bouchard, the one in which the French Canadian referred specifically to Pepe Co-troni. Of the five "Vesco tapes" recorded by Peroff, he had given over three to Luis Cruz, who was sending them to New York, and had kept two for himself.

At the apartment, Peroff gave Cruz some kitchen utensils and also sold him a television set for fifty dollars. The agent had brought airline tickets for the entire family. The Peroffs, plus thirty pieces of luggage and the dog, arrived at the San Juan airport by midafternoon. When they were inside the terminal building, Cruz hurried to check them in and expedite their boarding. Meanwhile, Peroff went to the ITT office in the airport and placed a call to the DEA's New York headquarters. Roy Gibson answered.

"Well," Peroff said, "we're about to get on the plane."

"What do you mean, *we?*"

"Well, Ruth and the kids, we—"

"You were supposed to come here by yourself!"

Before Peroff could speak, Mike Reilly came on the line. *"What is this?"* Reilly shouted. *"You're supposed to come by yourself! We're putting you up alone here in Manhattan! For two days! What's this with your family?"*

"You, uh, we—"

"We never talked about your family! I've had enough of you, Peroff!"

"Wait a minute, now, I—"

But Reilly was screaming and cursing, to the point where Peroff wondered if he had only imagined his previous discussions on the phone. Yet Cruz, a DEA agent, had come with airline tickets for Ruth and the kids, under instructions! Peroff was stunned by Reilly's long outburst, so much so that he could not find the words to make a reply.

"Go to hell," Reilly was saying. Then the DEA boss hung up on him.

During the flight, Peroff tried to imagine what sort of man Mike Reilly was. He'd never met him in person, but it was hard for him to remember anyone whom he might have hated more. Is the guy crazy? What does he have against me? Well, we're all on board this plane, whether he likes it or not. For Christ's sake, Cruz took us to the airport on orders!

Somehow, he thought, I've got to bring everybody to their senses. Get all the facts into focus. Any reasonable man would agree that the Learjet is essential. Without that plane, Connie would never have come up with a deal in the first place. Why eliminate it now, when I'm just days away from needing it? What do they think, that I'll *steal* the thing? With two federal agents aboard? Do they think I'd do something that foolish, when my own family is under their protection? What do they think my motives are? Money? How can I make any money if the deal doesn't happen? And don't they *want* it to happen? Of course they do. They're just misguided, uneducated, stupid—but surely we all want the thing to happen!

When the plane landed at Kennedy Airport in New York, the Peroff family waited until all other passengers had gotten off.

Eventually Peroff let Ruth and the children go first. He followed a short distance behind, wondering what might happen now.

Roy Gibson was standing with another agent inside the terminal building, appearing somewhat nervous and forcing a smile. The black agent was extremely well dressed as usual, looking as sharp as he had when Peroff had first met him at this same airport.

"I've got some money for you," Gibson said.

"Fifteen grand?"

"No. Eleven hundred."

"Well, that figures."

"It's in cash," Gibson replied. "You have to sign a receipt for it."

Peroff glanced at the piece of paper that Gibson was holding. The document indicated that he should sign beneath the words "Paid in Full."

"You expect me to agree?" he asked.

"Unless you sign, you can't get the money."

"It's less than a tenth of what I'm in the hole for!"

"Well, look, Frank—if you want this bread, you have to sign."

Peroff stared at him, trying to read Gibson's mind. How does he really feel about this? What the hell is going on here? It's just not understandable! But he suppressed his reactions, hoping to avoid any traps. The important thing, at the moment, was not his expense money but the narcotics case.

"I'll sign it," he said, "but I'm doing it under protest. And you," he added, gesturing to the other agent, "can be my witness that I'm not in agreement."

The second agent nodded, and Gibson watched Peroff sign the receipt. He took it and handed over the $1,100 in cash. Then Gibson walked over to Ruth and spoke with her, being very polite, even joking.

Peroff wanted to race over and scream at him, remind him that he was faced with going to Costa Rica in a few days and that the situation had to be discussed, to get the air cleared, because it was a real bombshell and too important to be left up to any one man or even any single federal agency. But Gibson was making a deliberate effort to avoid all discussion of the case. Peroff waited, still mystified, until Gibson turned, with the other agent, and walked away. Without a word.

* * *

He looked over at Ruth and his two daughters and his little son, at all the luggage, at the crowd in this section of Kennedy Airport. His whole family was here. His control agent had just walked off without any communication.

"Ruth," he said in a low voice, "what are they trying to do to us?"

"I don't know. It's unbelievable."

"Wait here," he said, walking toward a pay phone. He took out some change and dialed for information in Washington, D. C. He got the number for the special Watergate prosecutor, Archibald Cox. It was just a chance, but maybe Cox would have the power to do something. Not make anything public, but get Reilly and the other DEA bosses to sit down with the SEC and the FBI and so forth. Cox himself wanted to question Vesco, about his relationship to the whole Watergate crowd.

He called the special prosecutor's office, but there was no answer. Hanging up, he tried to figure out his next steps. It was already evening, so the best idea was to get his family settled for the night.

They took a pair of cabs over to the Hilton Inn, not far from the airport, and checked into adjoining rooms. They ordered dinner for themselves and the children. Peroff tried to get some sleep but kept waking up in a cold sweat. At last he put on a robe, after midnight, and picked up that morning's *New York Times*. The main headline was a wild one: NIXON WIRED HIS PHONE, OFFICES TO RECORD ALL CONVERSATIONS; SENATORS WILL SEEK THE TAPES.

The story was incredible; apparently the President had been bugging his own conversations, so that now he was in possession of possible evidence against himself. If I were him, Peroff thought, I'd burn those tapes tonight! There was massive coverage of the Senate Watergate hearings. On page thirteen, Peroff saw an unrelated story with a photograph of John Bartels, the acting head of DEA. It was something about "mistaken raids on the homes of innocent families" by federal narcotics agents. Well, Peroff thought, Bartels is gonna have a few more headaches—from me.

On page twenty-six, he saw a photograph of J. Fred Buzhardt, a "Special Presidential Counsel." One of Nixon's lawyers, Peroff mused—in charge of handling dirty tricks. Well, okay, *I've* got one for him. I've got one he can *avoid*, that is, before it happens!

Three pages after was a story about the Mitchell-Stans case, scheduled to go to trial in September. It would take place in Federal Court, right here in New York City. "Mr. Vesco, the New Jersey financier who paid the secret $200,000 political contribution, was indicted with the other defendants on May 10, but he fled the country." How, Peroff wondered, are they going to prove that Mitchell and Stans are guilty if Vesco isn't here to testify? The prosecutors must be dying to get him back here.

Peroff set down the newspaper and started making notes on paper. Ruth woke up at about four in the morning and said, "Are you all right?"

"I just can't sleep."

"What are you doing?"

"Writing a little speech."

Before jotting down his thoughts, Peroff had called Bouchard in Montreal that night, from the room in the Hilton Inn, and he had tried to build up a story that there might be a delay in getting the Learjet ready for the trip. "Well," Bouchard, said, his voice becoming hard, "they want you to be in Costa Rica this weekend."

"This weekend?" Peroff asked, the growing importance of time, or lack of it, now clearer to him than ever.

"Yah. Look, don't let nothing go wrong. Those guys will be waiting."

"Okay," Peroff said, but suddenly he was filled with panic. Bouchard now knew where he was; the underworld gangster could reach out and put his hands on Peroff and his entire family at the Hilton Inn, with no trouble at all. And at this moment, Peroff thought, the agents have abandoned us!

Worse even was the new tone in Bouchard's voice. As a former associate of criminals all over the world, Peroff recognized that tone and its full implications. A man like Bouchard, despite his lack of formal education, no matter what his failings in terms of expertise, underwent a profound change of personality when the time drew near for "doing his action." When the deadline for a deal approached, Bouchard went into a kind of quiet frenzy, suffering an inner anxiety while, at the same time, his mind became much sharper than usual. Peroff could tell by the tone of voice that Bouchard's senses were keener, that the combination of fear and anticipation had put the familiar change of character into motion.

"Everything has to work like a clock," Bouchard was saying. "You can't fuck this up, Frank."

"No, no, I won't. Don't worry," Peroff said, realizing that any mistake on his part would be fatal. He's a different person, Peroff thought, and he knows exactly where I am. I'm a sitting duck here with Ruth and the kids, and Bouchard has too much at stake in this for me to make a false move. Cotroni's sitting up there in Montreal with a huge heroin shipment waiting in Europe, and Vesco's sitting in Costa Rica with $300,000 waiting for me—and Bouchard is holding it all together. I have to go *this weekend!*

"So what's the problem?" Bouchard asked.

"Well," Peroff lied, "the plane's down in Atlanta. It's an equipment problem," he went on, making up a story filled with details about the inner workings of Learjets. "But it shouldn't be much longer than a few days' delay," he added, thinking that somehow, if Mike Reilly and his superiors could be made to listen, the case might go forward on schedule.

"All right," Bouchard said. "As I say, they're expecting you down there, in, uh, Costa, this weekend. Final instructions will come for you, directly, this Friday night."

It was Tuesday night now, which left only three days. "How do I get the instructions?" Peroff asked.

"You're at the Hilton Inn, yes?"

"Uh-hunh."

"So that's near Kennedy Airport," Bouchard continued, adding that on Friday night Peroff should drive a short distance over to the International Hotel. In the lobby there, at five thirty, a call would come through for Peroff, by name, from someone in Costa Rica. Instructions would be given to him for when he landed in San José.

After only a few hours of sleep, Peroff awoke that morning—Wednesday, July 18—in a state of anxiety beyond anything in his previous experience. The time factor was so critical that he could think only of reaching out to the highest levels possible. There were two places to go, in his mind, where decisions could be made with the proper speed: the White House and the Justice Department.

Before nine o'clock he picked up the phone in his hotel room, with Ruth watching, and dialed information for Washington, D.C.

With the general number for the White House switchboard, he placed his first call.

"This is the White House," came a woman's voice.

"Mr. Buzhardt's office, please."

As special consultant to President Nixon, J. Fred Buzhardt was working on litigation involving the Watergate scandal. Surely he wouldn't want *another* Watergate on his hands.

"Hello," a man's voice responded at last. "Can I help you?"

Peroff nervously looked down at the notebook in which he had written out a long statement during the previous night. "Who am I speaking to?" he asked, and a verbal tug-of-war began, each man refusing to give his name. Eventually the man at the White House end identified himself as Peter Grant, an attorney and an assistant to Buzhardt.

"Who are *you?*" Grant said.

"Look, I have a statement. I want to read you something that I've written. I'm not quite finished with it, but I want to give you my ID number. It was assigned to me by Customs."

Peroff gave him the number—D-73-1 (N.Y.)—and added that his name could be checked easily. "I'm an undercover agent for DEA," he explained, "but Customs originally gave me the number. I've got a problem, but all I want is to *solve* it. I mean, I'm trying to *help* the Government, that's all."

Grant said he would have the ID number checked and added, "Call me back in two hours. Collect."

Even to wait two hours at this point was almost unbearable. "If the White House can lay on some pressure," he told Ruth, "it can get down the line to Reilly. This guy Grant, he can help put everything on the right track." What he wanted to say to Grant went something like this: "I'm sitting on the biggest narcotics case in history. It's a strong one, and it's all set to go. Here I'm getting final instructions on Friday night, and I have to go down to Costa Rica over the weekend! I don't want it to die! I'm not asking for any money—the thing is, my whole life has been ruined, right up to this moment. We've come a long way, and all of a sudden Vesco's name popped up and the DEA has gone crazy! They want me to kill myself, in effect—and they've left me alone, here, with only my own ingenuity to keep stalling Bouchard. I'm not some kook trying to talk to the President. But this case has changed from just a narcotics investigation to one that can become very political, very explosive. I'm asking the White House to get *involved* in it. And apply pressure! If nothing else, hold a meeting and listen to the facts!"

He also wanted to tell Grant, in detail, about the importance of keeping up a good story for Bouchard, if the delay had to last very long. Actually *no* delay could be explained or accepted at this point. "And I'm in a unique position," Peroff wanted to scream. "Because I'm the only one who can make this case go! The DEA can't put in any substitute for me. If I don't make this trip, the whole case is dead! You have to realize that these people in Costa Rica are absolutely not amateurs or fools. We have to get that into Reilly's head! Every move from here on has to be perfect, without error—or the case will die or I'll be killed. Please, please get everybody to sit down and talk. Fast!"

He rehearsed his statement, made more notes and watched the time going by far too slowly. Unable to wait any longer, he tried to call Commissioner Acree of Customs. Acree's secretary came on the line, and Peroff told her the full story of his urgent situation. Then he tried calling John Bartels, head of the DEA, to complain that the agents under Bartels were blocking the case, but he could not get through to him. He tried a number of other officials, telling his story all over again to one Customs agent and hoping to get someone, anyone, personally involved.

At last it was time to call Peter Grant at the White House again.

"Hello," he said. "It's me."

"Mr. Peroff? How are you, Frank?"

So it had worked; Grant had checked the ID number and had learned Peroff's name. At least, Peroff thought, he knows that I'm not just a crazy man.

"What's the problem you mentioned?" Grant asked.

Peroff proceeded to read his full statement from the pages of a notebook. It was quite formal, specific and far less emotional in tone than the way he was feeling. The statement mentioned "monetary and emotional grievances" against federal agencies, but Peroff wanted to assure the White House that money was not his chief goal. He did appeal for protection, however, noting that his family's safety was in growing jeopardy because the heroin deal was building to its climax.

"My past is not an honorable one," Peroff admitted, reading into the phone as Peter Grant listened. "However I have never been convicted of a major crime." As for his current dilemma, "I did not want to get into this situation. I did not volunteer. . . ."

After outlining his experience, mentioning "blackmail and coercion" as the main pressures used against him, Peroff listed the ingredients of what was at stake right now:

1. One hundred fifty kilos of heroin were involved.
2. The deal was based on the fact that Peroff himself would provide the transportation.
3. Involved also were "top people in the Mafia in the U. S. and Canada."
4. A "new development" (Vesco) had occurred which made the entire operation "one with a completely different tune."

Peroff then stated, "I do not have enough faith in the people that I have so far been associated with, to risk my life in the manner that they have asked me to. . . . Actions have occurred on the part of the DEA that convinced me that the Justice Department does not want to make this case with Vesco. It is my opinion that a high-level decision was made to sabotage further efforts. Because of this, I have told agents of the DEA my intentions to bring this to the attention of certain Senate committees, in particular the Jackson investigations subcommittee. I was told very clearly by a DEA agent that 'if I put myself out in front with Jackson, my life isn't worth two cents.' I am not a politician, so I do not know the ramifications of what would happen if Vesco were brought back. I do, however, know that efforts to bring him back have so far failed, and that if this heroin case proved out, there would be no question of being able to bring him back. . . . I feel that this cannot end like this, and I do intend to bring it out in the open. I have in my possession tapes and other evidence to substantiate my assertions. . . . I felt the White House should have knowledge of this, and I only hope you make your own investigation of this case. It compounds the Watergate situation, and my own feelings are only that I am very sad."

Peroff added: "This situation has nearly broken me. I feel degraded and tired. My wife has become ill over this period. I have three beautiful children who deserve a father and a mother in good health. I am now in New York. I would be happy to come to Washington and answer any questions you might have. I only hope I have made myself understood, and you take this in the way that it is intended. I love my country and I hope that one day I can live a normal life in it. . . . This statement is just the briefest summary of the situation. . . . I am prepared to let the facts speak for themselves."

When Peroff was finished, Grant asked a number of questions, including, "Where does it stand right now?"

Peroff told him of the call he was to receive from Costa Rica on Friday evening and stressed that he would be expected there, in a private Learjet, over the weekend. "The problem now is *time*," he added. "What I hope for is a meeting with all parties."

"What room are you in, there?"

"Six-three-six. The Hilton Inn, near Kennedy Airport."

"Let me do some checking," Grant said. "Call me back tomorrow."

In the afternoon, Peroff placed a call to the Justice Department, which was in the most unique position of any Government body. Justice was in charge of the DEA and, as well, prosecution of the Mitchell-Stans-Vesco case there in New York. Peroff called the U. S. Attorney's office in Manhattan and asked for someone in charge of the case. A man named John Wing came on the line, identifying himself as an assistant U. S. Attorney under Paul Curran. And, Wing said, he himself was leading the effort to convict Mitchell, Stans and—if extradition were possible—Robert Vesco.

Peroff and Wing conversed on the phone for at least an hour. Whereas Peter Grant at the White House had been noncommittal, Wing was openly excited and enthusiastic. The prosecuting attorney was also incredulous and angry, expressing dismay that such a case involving Vesco's possible involvement had not been brought to his attention.

"I can't believe," Wing said, "that there's a case like this and I don't know about it! It's impossible! *Why* don't I know about this?"

Peroff mentioned that he had spoken with someone in Buzhardt's office at the White House, and reiterated that his motive was not to expose any wrongdoing at the DEA but to get the case moving. "I can't stall Bouchard very long," he added. "A deal like this has a certain precision, and—"

"You're speaking of *Conrad* Bouchard? Right?"

"That's correct."

"And you have tapes of him mentioning Vesco and LeBlanc?"

"Two cassettes."

"Is there anything salvageable about this?"

"What do you mean?" Peroff replied. "It's all a 'go' situation!"

"All you have to do is go down to Costa Rica? And get the money?"

"Yeah. I get final orders Friday night! By phone! My damn tape recorder's just broken down, but someone from the Government could monitor that call for me. . . ."

Wing grew increasingly puzzled and agitated on the phone. He would not commit himself on the subject of whether this case, as it stood, was enough to have Vesco extradited, but he did speak of the possibility. While all attempts on fraud charges had failed, a narcotics allegation almost assured success. Treaties between the United States and Costa Rica or the Bahamas were explicit when it came to drugs.

"Would you like to hear the tapes I've got?" Peroff asked.

"Look, I'll be back to you on this. Mr. Peroff, would you be willing to meet me this Sunday, at my office? Or anywhere you like?"

"Well, sure, but don't you think it should be sooner? The time factor is crucial, and Sunday is awful late. I mean—"

"I'm going to get to the bottom of this," Wing declared. "Right away, when I get off this phone. And don't worry, we'll be talking before the meeting on Sunday."

Peroff gave him his room number at the Hilton Inn, and Wing in turn gave his direct-line phone number at the U. S. Attorney's office. This conversation, even more so than the one with the White House, lifted Peroff's hopes. Both calls had been successful, though. Higher authorities, with the motivation and power to act, to apply pressure, were aware of his desperate situation. The case was aboveboard, out of Mike Reilly's personal control.

"It worked," Peroff told his wife, who had been keeping the children quiet in the adjoining room. "Now we've got some people on *our* side."

That evening, he called Bouchard again to keep up his stalling act while making sure that the deal was still on.

"I may have to go down to Atlanta," he said. "To check the plane."

"Before you go to Costa," Bouchard said, "don't come to Montreal. Stay out of here, Frank. When you get the dough down there, they will tell you where I am. I think I will drive to another city in Canada, understand? And you can fly up here, with the dough, and meet me."

Bouchard added that someone in Costa Rica might join Peroff on the plane, for the ride up to Canada. The critical message was simply to stay out of Montreal completely, to avoid any surveillance there by the Mounties. When Peroff picked up Bouchard, probably in Quebec City, the flight to Europe would begin.

Thursday, the nineteenth of July.
Still alone in the Hilton Inn, pacing around his room, waiting, Peroff agonized over the way he'd been abandoned by Mike Reilly and Roy Gibson, at such a crucial time. "I know Roy believes in this case," he told Ruth. "But I can't understand why he'd just leave me in the lurch like this." If I just sat here, he wondered, what would happen? Would they let me rot? As if the whole thing had been a bad dream?

In the morning the phone rang and Ruth answered it. A woman was on the line, saying that she was calling from Buzhardt's office at the White House. Peroff took the phone.

"This is Mr. Buzhardt's personal secretary," the woman said. "I have Mr. Phelps for you."

The man named Phelps got on and asked a number of questions about Peroff's role as an informant, then declared, "I'll get back to you."

There were more calls that day, from Phelps again and also from another Buzhardt aide, a Mr. Meyers. Peroff himself placed several calls to the White House, invariably speaking first to Buzhardt's secretary. The response was always the same, a combination of further questioning and the instruction to wait for additional communication.

"We're checking on it," Phelps or Meyers would say. "We're working on it. Stay put."

Growing more anxious, Peroff tried three times to reach John Wing, who had not called back as promised. Each time the assistant U. S. Attorney's direct-line phone rang, but there was no answer.

Again at night, Peroff reached Bouchard in Montreal. The situation was the same, only more intense. Any mistake by Peroff that ruined the deal would be fatal to him.

Friday, the twentieth.

Ruth answered the phone and spoke to a man from Buzhardt's office. Peroff got on and was told that he was speaking to Buzhardt himself, plus a Mr. Andrews on another extension. Peroff remembered seeing Buzhardt on television, on a news program focusing on Watergate. The voice sounded exactly the same.

The man identifying himself as Buzhardt stayed on for about thirty minutes, asking questions about Peroff's role in Paris and wanting to discuss his meetings with Commissioner Acree of Customs. When that call was finished, Peroff waited again and received a second call, from the same man, and went through another round of interrogation. The result was the same: "Hold on. We'll be in touch again."

As that Friday afternoon wore on, Peroff thought he would collapse from the tension. So far no real help had been mobilized by his efforts, yet the time to receive his call from Costa Rica was drawing near. At about five o'clock he called Bouchard, who indicated that the long-distance instructions would come as scheduled.

"Be there," Bouchard said, his voice now that of a cunning, totally committed gangster. "And Frank, don't mention nothing about the fifty, you know?"

Peroff understood. It was a reference to the additional fifty kilos, which Cotroni was getting secretly and at no advance cost from the French suppliers.

A short while later, he and Ruth left the children in their room, with the door locked, and took a cab over to the nearby International Hotel. They went into the lobby and sat down to wait.

Peroff wondered if he might be insane, if he was just dreaming the whole affair and fantasizing about Bouchard and Costa Rica. His tape recorder had broken down, but even if it were working he would not have brought it along. Someone from the Montreal mob might be watching his every move.

Thirty minutes went by. Suddenly a clerk behind the counter called, "Mr. Frank Peroff? There's a phone call for Mr. Frank Peroff!"

"Yeah. That's me."

"You can take it on a house phone, right over there."

Peroff walked over and picked up one of the phones. An operator with a Spanish accent, sounding far away, told him it was a person-to-person call.

"I'm Peroff," he said.

"You may go ahead," the operator replied.

"Hi, Frank!"

It was a man's voice, sounding more like that of a New Yorker than someone from Central America.

"Hello," Peroff said. "What's *your* name?"

"None of your business."

"You really sound like a Spaniard. Nice weather down there?"

"Great. But it's expensive."

"Yeah, I'll bet."

"Listen, Frank, this is a go situation, here. Let me get the description, so we'll know you. You're about two-fifty pounds?"

"Yeah, that's right."

"Sunglasses?"

"Right."

"What kind of suit will you wear?"

Peroff thought a moment. "Blue plaid," he said.

"Fine, fine. You're coming down right away?"

He closed his eyes. God *damn* that Reilly and Gibson, he thought. After six months, it turns out to be *me* that has to stall! "Well," he said, "I've got just one little problem with this Lear. With the jet. It's to do with the instruments. I need a new piece put in. I imagine it'll take several days, no more. But listen, I'll call Connie when I'm ready. So you can keep in touch with him, you know, and—"

The caller from Costa Rica cut him off, saying that it upset him to hear that the Learjet was not ready to leave right away. He asked a number of specific questions about technical aspects of the problem, requiring Peroff to explain in great detail. At last the man said, "Call C.B. when you're all set to go. Tell him your e.t.a. and we'll meet you."

The burst of initials stood for Conrad Bouchard and "estimated time of arrival."

"Okay," Peroff said.

"And Frank, just make sure you got plenty of ice on board. For the bar, you know?"

"Sure will. You got a deal."

"When you land, we'll be there."

He could hardly eat or sleep that night. From his room at the Hilton Inn he made a call to Roy Gibson, without success. He tried again on Saturday morning and also placed a call to John Wing, to give him the good news; he too was unavailable.

Near noon the phone rang. It was Peter Grant, calling from Buzhardt's office at the White House. So far Peroff himself had placed ten calls to the White House and had received six in return.

"Well," Peroff said, "everything's set! All I have to do is call Bouchard and tell him when I'm leaving. I got final instructions from Costa Rica. All I need, now, is the plane. Have you got any news for me?"

"We're working on it," Grant said. "Things are moving."

"Do you want me down in Washington? I'll do whatever you want."

"No, no. Just stay where you are."

"For how long?"

"It's going to be taken care of, in a day or two. We'll get back to you. Sit tight."

For the rest of the day he went over everything in his mind, calculating what the timing would be. The White House and the U. S. Attorney's Office in Manhattan would be making their moves; no doubt a big round-table discussion would take place within a few days, early next week. It was ridiculous to think that everyone with whom he had spoken was part of some huge, interrelated conspiracy to sabotage the heroin case. Ridiculous, laughable, absurd.

Sit tight, the man had said.

All during Saturday night he sat by the phone waiting to hear from someone—Peter Grant, John Wing, anybody—and the follow-ing morning he realized that he'd slept only a couple of hours. He remained in his pajamas and robe, slumping in a chair to read the newspaper and sip coffee and smoke one cigarette after another. Ruth ordered breakfast for the children in the next room, and they ate in front of the TV set.

At noon, while Peroff sipped his second cup of coffee, there was a knock on the door. John Wing? Roy Gibson? Someone from the White House? Ruth went to answer it. She opened the door and stood facing three men. One was the hotel manager. From his chair across the room, Peroff recognized a certain look about the other two. They were cops.

"Is Frank Peroff here?"

"Who are you?" Ruth asked.

"New York City police. We're detectives here in the Borough of Queens," one of the men said as they both showed their badges. "Can we talk to him?"

Ruth allowed them inside the hotel room.

"Frank, did you ever live in Orange County, Florida?"

"Yeah."

The detective explained that Peroff had been charged with "ob-taining property by worthless checks" in Florida, the alleged fraud occurring back in the spring of 1972, a year and three months be-fore.

"Do you have any warrants?" Peroff asked.

"No, we don't need 'em. We got a phone call from the Orange County sheriff, who gave us this hotel as your address. They want us to hold you."

Peroff shook his head and managed a smile, telling the two de-tectives to sit down and make themselves at home while he went to shave. Not everything was clear to him, but the timing of this sudden development was too dramatic, too precise to be overlooked. There were only a few individuals or agencies with knowledge of his exact location: the White House and, no doubt, the Secret Service; the U. S. Attorney's Office in Manhattan; and also, without question, the Drug Enforcement Administration. The sheriff in Orange County, Florida, could not have known his whereabouts without some deliberate help.

But now he remembered that back in February, these same warrants had been brought to his attention. It was on the day of the Paris arrests, as he was leaving the American Embassy to return to Rome. Tony Mercado, the BNDD agent, had told him, "Frank, we just got word that there's a warrant for grand larceny on Ruth, issued in Florida—something to do with draperies. That's all we know. But there are also two warrants in Florida for you, both for bad checks. A couple of thousand dollars' worth."

Peroff had been mystified about all three warrants. The one for Ruth was especially inexplicable, because he himself had paid for all the draperies in their Florida home. "That one *has* to be wrong," he had told Mercado. "As far as the warrants against *me*, I just don't know."

"Well," the agent had said, "don't worry about it. They're local Justice of the Peace warrants. We'll take care of everything."

So he was not at all a fugitive from justice. In fact, he had forgotten about the warrants until this moment.

"You'd better get dressed," one of the detectives said.

"Just a minute. I want to call an agent of the Department of Justice, a DEA agent, and then I want you to speak to him."

The two detectives stared at him, bewildered, while he dialed Roy Gibson's special number. He had been unable to reach Gibson since his arrival at Kennedy Airport on Tuesday evening. Now on Sunday morning the DEA agent was available.

"Where've you been?" Peroff asked.

"Where are *you?*" Gibson replied.

"You son of a bitch, you know damn well that I'm at the Hilton Inn." There was silence at the other end. Peroff added, "You did this to me, didn't you?"

"Did what, Frank?"

"Oh, come on. There's two of New York's finest here. They're gonna lock my ass up! I mean, Roy, this *has* to be the dirtiest pool I ever heard of. You bastard, I'm gonna get you. I'm not joking, I'm gonna—"

"I didn't do anything!" Gibson protested.

"Sure you didn't. This is just a coincidence, right?"

"Don't panic," Gibson said. "Just go to the can and rest for a day or two."

"Oh, fuck you. I mean it, Roy. Listen, I got the orders! How about that?"

"For Costa Rica?"

"*From* Costa Rica, babe. I'm supposed to let Connie know when I'm leaving, and he'll alert them down there. It's all set!"

"Okay, cool down. Put one of the cops on."

Peroff stared at the phone for a moment, then handed it to the nearest detective. He went into the bathroom to shave. The detective on the phone was mostly listening and nodding his head, while Ruth spoke with the worried hotel manager, who wanted to make sure that the Peroffs would pay their bills. *This is incredible,* Peroff thought, now realizing that his children were in the next room, probably listening and wondering what was happening. How could this be? Connie Bouchard is waiting for my call, the people in Costa Rica are waiting, we're at the brink—and now I'm going to jail!

The detective had hung up. Apparently he was now somewhat aware of the situation because he muttered, "I'm really sorry we came here."

With deliberate irony, Peroff dressed in the same blue-plaid suit, with a bright yellow shirt, which he had planned to wear on the trip to Costa Rica.

He kissed Ruth and hugged the children, telling them not to worry, and left the Hilton Inn with the two detectives. They drove him to a central booking precinct house in Queens. It was early afternoon on this Sunday, the twenty-second of July, and Assistant U. S. Attorney John Wing was to have called by now. We were going to meet today, Peroff thought. We were going to discuss one of the most important cases in the world; but here I am, a prisoner.

He was fingerprinted, photographed and put into a cell in the station house. Each cell contained several men who had been arrested that same day. Among the prisoners, almost all of them black and poor, Peroff felt conspicuous in his expensive blue suit.

At the Queens Courthouse that night, Peroff stood before the judge for arraignment.

"Where's your lawyer?" the judge asked.

"I don't have one."

"Well, it's no bail. You'll remain in custody and come back here tomorrow."

It was near ten o'clock when he was taken back up to a large cell in the courthouse.

Peroff motioned to one of the jailers. "Pssst," he whispered. "Come here."

The jailer walked over. He was an elderly man, a bit cautious, and obviously perplexed by Peroff's manner. "What is it?" he asked.

"Listen," Peroff said in a low voice. "This is for real—something very big is happening, here. I have to make some urgent, confidential phone calls."

"Well, I—"

"I don't even want *you* to hear my conversations. I mean, the information is secret. You'll be better off if you don't know anything. See?"

The doubletalk went on for about twenty minutes, until the jailer agreed to let Peroff use the telephone. He took him out of the cell and brought him into his office. As he was closing the door, to give him some privacy, he asked, "How do you like your coffee?"

Peroff called Roy Gibson and reached him at home. "All right," he said. "I'm spending the night in jail. But listen, Roy, the whole deal with Costa Rica is go, it's firm. Now what the hell good is putting me in the can? Don't you *want* this case to happen?"

"Of course we do," Gibson said. "But we're gonna have to go through a lot of effort, Frank, to get you outa there. I mean, *if* we can get you out."

"Bouchard has been waiting for my call since Friday night! That's forty-eight hours already!"

"Don't worry, Frank! Listen, I'll call you tomorrow. Just don't reach out for a mob lawyer. Let it ride. Stay in jail."

"Have you talked to Ruth?"

"I'll be speaking to her in the morning. No sweat."

"Roy?"

"Yeah?"

"Try to *do* something, okay? Whatever's happening, it's wrong. I mean, let's be straight with each other."

"I'll do what I can, Frank."

At eleven o'clock that night, the prisoners were led through the mazelike corridors of the courthouse building into the adjoining Queens House of Detention. At the reception center for the jail, the handcuffs were removed before Peroff and the others were placed in temporary cells. Trusties—guards with special privileges —brought them glasses of Kool-Aid while they waited.

Once again Peroff had his photograph and fingerprints taken. He was told to undress so the physician could make a thorough exam, which included a quick anal search for hidden weapons or tools or drugs. All bandages were briefly removed from the prisoners' bodies, in case razor blades were concealed underneath.

"You'll be on the fourth floor," a guard said. "There was a riot up there last week. Still a lot of tension, so be careful."

The prison officers placed his wallet and other valuables inside a manila envelope. They gave him a sheet, blanket and pillow case, which he carried with him up to the cellblock. It was past one thirty in the morning, extremely dark inside the jail, and most of the prisoners were asleep.

"In here," the guard said.

Peroff stepped inside a cell which had a double-deck bed against one wall. The young man in the bottom bunk, a Puerto Rican, opened his eyes.

"Sorry to wake you up," Peroff said.

"That's okay," the cellmate answered, jumping out of the bed and removing his towels and toilet articles from the top bunk, where Peroff would sleep.

In the darkness Peroff tried to make his bed, which was an almost impossible task. He stuffed the blanket inside his pillow case, since there was no pillow. Then he undressed down to the yellow shirt and his shorts. When he climbed up on the bed he realized how tired and hot he was. By now he had sweated through all his clothing.

"When you wake up in the morning," said the young man in the bunk below him, "I got some toothpaste and stuff you can use."

"Thanks," Peroff said.

"What's your rap?"

"Bullshit, that's what."

"Same here."

"What are you in for?" Peroff asked him.

"Murder one."

With that, Peroff thought he might just roll off his bed. "No kidding," he said, on his back and realizing that he wasn't far from the ceiling.

"Yeah, it's a bum rap. I can't afford a good lawyer, so I'm in trouble."

"Shit," Peroff muttered.

"How long have you been here?"

"Look," Peroff said, "I'm tired as hell."

"Okay. Good night."

"Good night," Peroff said, but as the minutes and hours dragged on he found himself unable to sleep. The plastic-covered mattress crackled every time he moved, and the springs made loud twanging noises. He lay still, listening to the snores of the other prisoners, wondering if he would ever find out just why he was here.

It seemed as if he had just gotten to sleep. The light above him was blasting into his eyes and radios were on all over the cellblock, tuned to New York rock 'n' roll stations. Peroff groaned and turned on his side. Below, his cellmate was already getting dressed.

"How're you doing?" the young man said.

"Okay."

Peroff glanced down and noticed that the cell contained a small sink and a toilet bowl. His Puerto Rican companion was seated on the bowl, in full view, humming to the music. When the young man was fully dressed he went to the cell door and, to Peroff's surprise, simply opened it and walked out. Peroff was certain that the door had been locked the night before.

There was no sense in getting out of the bed until he had to. An hour later a prisoner came by with cereal and coffee, but Peroff was determined to eat as little as possible. He had no intention of sitting on the toilet bowl, if he could help it.

Soon his cellmate returned, wearing a dishwasher's outfit and high rubber boots. "I'm boss of the cellblock," the young man said. He was carrying about eight boxes of cereal and four loaves of bread, plus some milk cartons filled with presweetened coffee which could be heated later. "I got all you want to eat," he said. "And listen, I run things in here, so there's no sweat. Anything you want, I'll take care of it."

"I ain't worried," Peroff said from the top bunk. "I don't plan to be here that long."

At last the guards began calling out names of prisoners who were scheduled for court. *"Peroff!"* came a loud voice, so he jumped off the bed and started dressing. Men were walking out of the cells on each floor of the prison. Peroff joined them and they were brought back down to the reception center, where they entered temporary cells. Their names were called again, so they lined up in another chain-gang formation and moved through the corridors to the bullpen outside the courtroom.

After a few hours of waiting, a young legal aide wearing spectacles approached the bullpen cell and said, "Mr. Peroff? I'm representing you." Standing outside the bars, the legal aide went on with the usual questions. "First I need your age, place of residence, the circumstances of these warrants—"

"Hey," Peroff interrupted, "just do me a favor. Cut the crap. This isn't a very clear thing here. I want you to call somebody for me. His name is Roy Gibson. Just call him."

"Hunh? Why?"

"Call him. And tell him that you're representing me here. And don't be surprised at whatever he says."

The legal aide smirked. "I'm not going to call him. Come on, Mr. Peroff, what are you trying to pull?"

Instead the legal aide petitioned for bail and was denied. He went over to Supreme Court but arrived too late for his client to be scheduled on the following day's calendar. Peroff was remanded to the House of Detention again, his hearing set for Wednesday morning at ten o'clock.

So there were at least two more nights to spend in the prison, unless Roy Gibson could do something.

Gibson had called Ruth that Monday morning and had told her to take a cab down to see her husband. Not realizing that the visiting hours began at six o'clock, Ruth arrived at two thirty in the afternoon and waited for the next three and a half hours.

Peroff, meanwhile, had returned to his cell on the fourth floor of the jailhouse. By the time they met in the visitors' room at six in the evening, Ruth was crying. They sat in a booth, talking on a phone while they looked at each other through the window.

"See if you can get me some clothes," he told her. "Don't worry, I'll be out of here on Wednesday."

There was still no word of what, if anything, the DEA might do to help.

The next morning, Gibson showed up at the Hilton Inn. Ruth

gave him a bag of clothes and some cigarettes to take to the prison. Before he left, Gibson said, "When we see him tonight, tell him he has to do exactly as I say. Otherwise I can't help him."

"What do you want him to do?"

"Look, Ruth, if he doesn't behave—if he wants to do things his own way, that's up to him. He'll get all kinds of bad publicity down in Florida. If he wants our help in getting him out, he's got to do what we tell him, period."

"Roy," she said, on the verge of tears again, "on the record or *off* the record, is there a deal or not? Do *you* believe that the heroin deal is on?"

Gibson stared at her for a moment, then whispered, "Yes."

"Then why don't you *do* it?"

"First things first," Gibson said. "I'll talk to you later."

At about four o'clock that afternoon, Ruth called the DEA headquarters and got Gibson and Mike Reilly on their extensions. "He put himself into this," Reilly said. "It's *his* fault, not ours. *He's* the one who made those calls to the White House. It set off bells with the Secret Service."

"Look, Mr. Reilly," she said. "Say what you want, but *you're* the one who told Frank to go down to Costa Rica commercially." There was silence at the other end. "And the time factor is critical," she went on. "You both know it! Roy, *you* know that Frank's supposed to be on his *way* to Costa Rica!"

"Well," Gibson said, "the first thing is to get him out of there. You've got to make him behave, Ruth! It's a tough job, to spring him without problems."

Gibson came by the hotel and picked her up at about nine o'clock that night. As they drove through Queens, she noticed that he still had the bag of clothing. "Why didn't you go over there today?" she asked.

But Gibson mumbled something, avoiding the question. They parked near the courthouse and entered a special room below the cellblocks. It was not the same as the visitors' room, although Ruth would still have to speak to Peroff by phone. She and Gibson were in a small section while the prisoner would have to use a booth on the opposite side of a tiny window.

When Peroff appeared behind the glass, he looked horrible. He hadn't shaved since Sunday morning, and his bright yellow shirt had turned gray from the sweat. Ruth began weeping and went to the window while Gibson, nervous, paced the floor behind her.

"Frank," she cried, "you have to do—you have to do whatever they want. Otherwise," Ruth sobbed, "it's going to be bad! They said—"

"Ruth, please . . ."

"No, Frank, listen! You'll have the bad publicity, and they won't be able to help us—and Frank, please do what they say!"

She was on the brink of hysteria. Peroff watched her through the window and, for the first time, felt he knew what was happening to him. They've brainwashed her, he thought. They've put *me* away so they could get to *her*. They've been using my wife! He felt the rage build up inside him and shouted to Gibson, "Come here, you bastard! Come here!"

"Hi, Frank," said Gibson, who seemed to be going through a silent agony of his own.

"You dirty fuck! You used my wife! When are you gonna be a man!"

"Frank, it's the truth. If you bond out on your own, it's gonna make every newspaper in Florida. But if *we* take you out, it'll be kept quiet. But we're *not* gonna do it, unless you agree to do things our way."

Peroff gripped the phone with one hand and banged on the table with the other. He felt as if he were going mad, wanting to smash through the window and choke him.

"You have to agree," Gibson went on, "to continue this case *exactly* as we tell you. No ifs, ands or buts."

"*Blackmail again?*"

"Are you gonna do what we say or not?"

"Do what?"

"All right—the first thing, if we get you out of here, you have to go back up to Canada. Right away."

Before you go to Costa, Bouchard had said, *don't come here.*

"Wait a minute," Peroff sighed, trying to keep control of himself. "For God's sake, Roy, Bouchard is expecting me to *call* him, to say when I'm leaving for Costa Rica! Roy, listen to me—Bouchard emphatically ordered me *not* to go up to Montreal!"

"Those are your orders," Gibson said. "If you don't agree, I can't help you."

"I don't understand, Roy! I don't understand! Why?"

"The only thing I know, at this point, is that you gotta go up to Montreal. Don't *ask* me why, Frank. You *can't* ask me why. *You can't question!*"

Peroff started banging on the desk again, shouting through the phone at Gibson's face in the window, and he realized that Ruth was still crying—My God, he thought, she's never been like this! What have they done to her?

"Roy," he pleaded, "don't you *believe* in this deal?"

"Yeah, Frank, I do! All I want is an answer—yes or no! I'm not gonna listen any more!"

"Come back here!"

One of the guards, aware that Gibson was a federal agent, came over and shouted, "Keep it down!" But then he leaned down and said to Peroff in a confidential tone of voice, "Look, you don't have to stay here and take this. You can go back upstairs."

"No," Peroff said. "I'll be all right."

"Well, keep it down."

The guard walked away. Ruth was sobbing while Roy Gibson stood off to one side, almost out of his vision. At last Peroff broke down at the sight of his wife's emotions.

"All right!" he yelled. "Get me outa here! I agree!"

"Do you mean it?" Gibson asked.

Peroff slammed down the phone and walked away, forgetting to say good-bye to Ruth as he wiped the tears from his own face.

"Don't worry, Ruth, we'll fix everything."

She was in the front seat of the car with Roy Gibson, riding back to the Hilton Inn on that Tuesday night. She felt as if she might have betrayed her husband, having become so upset, but what other choice had they given her?

"Why," she asked, "are you sending him back to Canada?"

"It's not for us to question, Ruth."

"I don't understand."

"Well, we do what we have to do."

"But why can't you let *another* agency know what's going on? Don't beat around the bush, Roy. Just give me a straight answer!"

Gibson shook his head, trying to maintain his normal poise and lack of emotion. "We'll talk about it tomorrow," he said.

"Roy, you *know* the facts of this case! Just send him down to Costa Rica! And then you'll know *everything*, one way or another! If there's no money waiting for him, *then* it's all over. But why stop it now?"

Gibson forced a laugh. "Ah," he said, *"you're* the brains behind this family, eh?"

If it was meant as patronizing humor, Ruth Peroff was not in the mood to appreciate it.

Word had traveled upstairs, through the prison grapevine, that Peroff had been shouting and cursing at "the feds" for the past hour. By the time he reached his cell, all the other prisoners were convinced that he was an important Mafioso who could help them.

"I hear," his cellmate said, "that you really blasted 'em down there."

"Yeah, well . . ."

"They're crazy, those feds. They've been bugging me for years."

Peroff ignored the conversation. Ruth had managed to give him clean underwear and a new shirt, so he went to take his first shower in three days.

It's a bitch, Peroff thought as he lay on his bed after dark. No control. How could Ruth let them do that to her? Well, they worked on my soft spot. They used her to break me. I've been a pawn again. And Ruth, too. What's going on out there? What are the kids doing in the hotel? Why am I going to Canada? Oh, shit . . .

Later in the night, he lay awake realizing that he was dirty, tired, hot, exhausted—but in some way, a lucky man. Half the prisoners in here were facing murder charges. Compared to them, he thought, I don't have it so bad.

It was almost a pleasant surprise to think that he was getting through this ordeal in prison without any trouble. The worst part was the lack of privacy. And the regimentation. And the fear that other prisoners might try to kill you. Some were unstable; there had been several recent suicides; and, of course, the racial tension was just below the surface.

In the darkness, some of the prisoners began making animal calls, the way young boys do. It was too hot to sleep. Suddenly a girl's voice could be heard on the outside, calling up, *"Jimmy! Jimmy, it's me!"*

"Yeah!" came a chorus of male voices from the cellblocks. *"Here I am! Right here, sweetheart!"*

Peroff laughed so hard that he shook the entire double bunk. When it was quiet, he heard prisoners masturbating, groaning, waking up with nightmares, snoring, wheezing. At least, he thought, I'm getting out. The question is, should I become the *original* Frank Peroff again? I could get myself a jet plane and go down to Costa Rica anyway. Get the money and take off. Pull a big scam on Vesco, Bouchard, Cotroni, the Government—all of them.

The most painful thing was what they had done to Ruth. It was unforgivable. Well, he thought, I'm going to *force* those bastards to finish their own case. We've put too much into it; we've gone too far in this direction. I'll do what they ask, but they'll have to explain their behavior to someone. If they mess it up, I'll scream so loud that they'll have to kill me to shut my mouth.

But maybe, just maybe, there was some hidden strategy or purpose which had eluded his mind. Maybe Roy Gibson and Mike Reilly knew things that he did not. Maybe the upcoming trip to Montreal was, in fact, logical. But why, he wondered, aren't they explaining it to me?

I'm not the enemy, am I?

In the morning, Wednesday, he went to shave for his appearance in State Supreme Court. He arrived upstairs on another tier of the prison, where a room was set up with a barber's chair and a sink. Peroff waited on line for the special razor which was impossible to open without a key. By the time he reached the sink, eight other prisoners had used the razor before him. He leaned over, applying regular soap as shaving cream and using a glossy metal sheet for a mirror. When he was finished, his face was completely raw and most of the beard still remained, but he felt much better.

By ten o'clock he was on his way to court in another line of handcuffed prisoners. He was placed in a large cell with about fifteen men facing felony charges, most involving murder and rape. There was a long wait before he was able to enter the huge, beautiful Supreme Court. He looked around for Roy Gibson, but the DEA agent was not in the courtroom. But the young legal aide now approached with a pile of his own law books (apparently having done research), and they went before the judge and petitioned him for bail. "I don't know," the judge said, scratching his head. "This involves Florida—am I allowed to grant bail?"

"Yes, Your Honor," said the legal aide, now flipping through his books and citing passages to make his case. The wrangling and arguing continued while Peroff stood there nonchalantly, wondering when someone from the DEA would appear. The legal aide had begun by requesting that his client go free without bond, while the State prosecutor had asked that Peroff remain in jail and not be granted bail at all. By now the issue had narrowed to how much bail would be required, but suddenly a D.A. came bursting through the main door of the courtroom. The D.A. walked up to the judge, almost out of breath.

"Your Honor," he said, "excuse me, but we'd like a postponement in this case until two o'clock. We've just gotten a phone call that involves this very situation, here."

"Well," the judge replied, "that's good, because I really didn't know what to do here."

"Thank you, Your Honor."

"Okay. Recess until two o'clock."

Peroff left his bewildered defense counsel and was taken back downstairs to a cell where he was offered some lunch. He took the meal and gave it to other prisoners, drinking several glasses of Kool-Aid instead. By two thirty he was upstairs again in the cell near the courtroom.

A few moments later he saw his counsel talking to the jailer. Peroff was taken out and placed in a private cell across the way, so the legal aide could speak to him alone. The young man was excited, pacing around and shaking his head. "What the hell's going on?" he asked. "I mean, who are you? The Justice Department has interceded! On your behalf!"

"Lower your voice, will ya? Calm down."

"Listen, the Queens D.A. was in the judge's chamber, with this federal agent named Roy Gibson, and—"

"I *told* you to make that phone call, didn't I?"

"Holy shit," the young man whispered. "I didn't realize—I mean, it's all very secret stuff, hush-hush, and—who *are* you?"

"Look, I—"

"Never mind!" the legal aide said. "Don't tell me! I don't think I want to know. Listen, you don't have to go *along* with anything, if you don't want to."

"Hey," Peroff said. "Cut it out, will ya? Just tell me what you want to tell me, okay?"

"Well, they're gonna rig up a phony bail! Either fifty or twenty-five grand! But you don't have to put up a nickel! All you do is sign a piece of paper."

"Then what?" Peroff asked.

"Well, as soon as you're released, the agent wants you to meet him across the street from the courthouse. In the Part One restaurant. Got it?"

"Yeah," Peroff said, smiling at the young man's confusion.

"Jeez," the legal aide whispered. "This is the weirdest case I've ever handled."

"I'll call you someday when I'm *really* in trouble."

"Good luck," the legal aide said.

It was about four o'clock in the afternoon when Peroff stood before the judge to be released on $25,000 bail. He signed the slip of paper, paid nothing and walked out of the courthouse carrying his paper bag of extra clothing. He went down the steps and started across a parking lot, looking for the Part One restaurant, but then he saw Roy Gibson at the far end. The DEA agent removed his sunglasses briefly and stood there watching him approach. His only sign of greeting was a slight smile that grew into a broad grin.

"You look terrific," Gibson joked.

Peroff reached up and touched the patches of beard on his face. He had spent three nights in the prison.

"We're going to a meeting," Gibson added as they walked, in utter silence from then on, back into the courthouse building and upstairs to the office of Michael Armstrong, the Queens District Attorney, whose staff had helped the federal agents to gain Peroff's release. Several men were waiting around a large conference table. Peroff was introduced to Armstrong's assistant, Carl Born-stein, plus a deputy inspector from the Police Department and an official in charge of organized crime. Bornstein made a short speech to confirm, for the record, that the DEA had requested his help.

"What do you think of our jail?" he asked.

"Well," Peroff quipped, "actually you can take it and shove it up your ass. Why don't *you* go up there and try it out?"

"Is it that bad?"

"It was no fun, but it could've been worse. I *thought* it was going to be worse."

"We'd like you to do us a favor. If the DEA—the Department of Justice, that is—will agree to it."

"Not now," Gibson broke in. "Maybe in the future, though."

The meeting was short but pleasant. Peroff felt exhausted as he rode in silence with Gibson toward the Hilton Inn. When they went up to the adjoining rooms, he greeted Ruth with a hug and went to his children, who had no idea where he had been. Ruth had told them only that their father was attending a long meeting and that he'd been staying in another hotel.

Roy Gibson settled into a chair and they ordered some drinks up to the room. Peroff sipped a bourbon and Coke, which acted as a kind of tonic, reviving him somewhat. "There's no question in my mind," he told Gibson. "You guys put me in the can. I don't know why, but you did."

"No, no," Gibson said. "I swear to God, Frank, we had nothing to *do* with it."

"Yeah? Who did, then?"

"The Secret Service!"

"Oh, come on," Peroff said, listening as Gibson continued to insist that the DEA had taken no part in his arrest. The calls to the White House, according to Gibson, had set off an alarm within the Secret Service's protection detail, which initiated a check of his background and discovered the Florida warrants. Agents of the Service called the Florida authorities, Gibson said, and those officials then made contact with the New York City Police Department.

But the explanation made no sense. First of all, Peroff had given the White House his special code number. He had explained his circumstances thoroughly. Was it logical to believe that the Secret Service had *not checked* with DEA officials? No, the sheer timing of Peroff's arrest was too suspicious. Here was an undercover agent making calls to the White House and charging that the DEA was trying to sabotage its own case. At that critical moment, this same undercover agent is thrown in jail and told that his release is contingent upon whether he agrees to follow any instructions that the DEA gives him!

Peroff unloaded all his feelings, but Gibson held fast to his version of the recent events. "Some day," Peroff told him, "the truth about this will come out. I promise you, Roy."

"Listen," Gibson said, ignoring the remark, "I'll talk to you in the morning. I'm not sure when you'll be leaving, but it should be soon."

"By the way," Peroff asked, "what the hell am I supposed to *do* when I go to Montreal? Because I've told you already, Roy, *I'm not supposed to be there!* I should be on my way to Costa Rica!"

"No questions," Gibson said. "That's our bargain, and you'd better keep it. And listen—no more calls. Not to Bouchard, not to the White House or John Wing, nobody. Just stay here and do nothing, till you hear from me."

During that night and all day Thursday, Peroff took at least ten showers to rid himself of the prison smell. Gibson called to say that there was a "slight problem" in Canada, but he added that the trip was tentatively scheduled for the following morning. Plans were being coordinated with the Mounties and with Hal Roberts, who was still in Montreal but now as a DEA agent. Roberts was also receiving orders from Mike Reilly.

It was Friday, the twenty-seventh of July, exactly one week since Peroff had spoken with Bouchard and received his final orders from Costa Rica. First Gibson called and said, "The Mounties will be in touch, to correlate what time you'll get up there." The DEA agent added, to Peroff's surprise, "And you'd better help me with details of how to lease a new plane."

Maybe, Peroff thought, I've been wrong! We're getting another Learjet? Fantastic! He eagerly offered his advice, emphasizing that the lease should be in his own name, predated to coincide with what he had been telling Bouchard.

Later he spoke by phone with the Mounted Police, agreeing to be on an evening flight out of Kennedy Airport to Montreal. The only question was, what would he say to Bouchard when he arrived? What excuse could he give for disobeying those explicit instructions not to go there?

Hal Roberts was at the Montreal Airport to greet him but the agent's entire manner had become formal and cold. They walked together through the crowd to a phone booth, where Roberts made some calls to be certain that Peroff's room was set up at the Martinique Hotel. Once again there would be a complete bugging operation conducted by the Mounties.

Roberts said, "I guess you can ring Connie when you get there."

"No, I have to wait for Roy to call. I need details of the new airplane lease. Bouchard is bound to ask about it."

"By the way, Frank, you have to get $10,000 from him. Otherwise, the deal is off."

"Say that again?"

"Tell Bouchard that you need ten grand, for the plane, or you'll refuse to go ahead."

The order was astonishing, incomprehensible. Peroff stood there with a rueful smile, shaking his head in exasperation and defeat. He was no longer capable of raising his voice to argue. "Well," he said, "just by me being here, I think this deal will be off. But there's no way that Connie can come up with ten grand. He's pouring everything into his trials, his defense."

"Look, Frank, I don't know from nothing."

"I know, Hal, you're an asshole like the rest of 'em. Here I'm supposed to be taking *twenty* grand off the top, down in Costa Rica—for the plane! And now you ask me to come up here and blackmail Connie! I don't even feel like asking why."

"I don't have the answer," Roberts said. "Just do as I say."

But Peroff was not listening any more. He felt his insides harden as a wave of cold bitterness seemed to envelop him. Was he being used to bring about an end to the heroin deal? By his own hand? He took a cab by himself to the Martinique Hotel, where Pierre Boudreau, the Mounties' electronics man, was on duty in the room adjoining his. Peroff spent the night alone with his swirling, hate-filled thoughts.

In the morning, Saturday, the Mountie came to Peroff's room and placed a call to Roy Gibson in New York, taking details about the airplane lease. Through it all, Peroff waited and watched and kept all his feelings inside. Pierre Boudreau wrote down that the new Learjet had been leased from a firm in Washington, D. C., called Jet America, secured under the name of one of Peroff's old corporations. The lease option was backdated to April.

When he was finished taking notes, the Mountie looked up and said, "You want to speak to him?"

"No," Peroff replied.

He took the slip of paper and went back to his own room. He sat by the phone for a few minutes, agonizing over the thought that he was about to sabotage the case by himself, but then dialed Bouchard's number. He waited for the inevitable reaction, and it came as he heard Bouchard's angry voice in his ear: *"Why the hell are you here! What are you doing here? I'm coming right over! What the fuck is the matter with you?"*

When Peroff hung up he lay down on the bed staring at the ceiling. Nobody would believe this, he thought. Even I don't believe it.

Conrad Bouchard's eyes were glazed, as if his fury had momentarily blinded him and turned him into a wild animal. He was pacing around the hotel room, screaming, while his bodyguard, Victor Fauci, sat in a chair to watch the battle. At least, Peroff thought, this whole conversation is being taped. It'll be on the record.

"Why," Bouchard demanded, *"why are you here?"*

"Connie, I ain't got any money to take the plane!"

"God damn it! Why didn't you tell me that before? On the phone?"

"Look, I—"

"Frank! They expected you down there a week ago!"

"Connie, I've been doing everything I can to raise the money on my own! But I can't do it! I'm in trouble, and that's that! Look, it's a minor problem, but—"

Bouchard cut him off again, screaming at him with a torrent of abuse. He mentioned Vesco's name once but focused his argument around Norman LeBlanc, the French Canadian who was with Vesco in Costa Rica. "This is a big guy!" Bouchard yelled, referring to LeBlanc. "If there's any kind of wrinkles at all, this deal is gonna blow! Even *I* don't know what the hell's gonna happen!"

"Well, I gotta have the money!"

"Pepe's people are mad," Bouchard said. "There's gonna be a *war*, Frank, and *you put me into this situation!* They're furious! They're all saying to forget the whole thing! I warn you—you're fooling around with something that's over your head! You don't know what you're playing with!"

"What am I supposed to do?" Peroff replied. *"You* give me an answer, Connie! I ain't got the money to take the plane, so how am I gonna do it? What d'ya want me to do, go down there *commercial?"*

The question had come out almost by accident. Peroff wished that Mike Reilly could be present to see Bouchard laugh at the suggestion with scorn, as if he considered it a bad joke. That, Peroff thought, is just how far I'd have gotten with Reilly's instruction! Here's the proof!

Calming down, Bouchard asked, "Well, how much do you need?"

"I gotta have at least ten grand. Whatever you can get."

Bouchard cursed under his breath. He went to the phone and made several calls, speaking in French. At one point he said to Peroff, "There's a guy coming in with seven kees, from Europe. He owes me a favor. Maybe I could take some of it and give him a good profit. But it would take a week." He made more calls and, at last, lay down on Peroff's bed for a nap. "They'll call me back," he said, now referring to some loan sharks with whom he'd been talking.

Peroff and Victor Fauci watched a baseball game on TV while Bouchard slept for at least an hour. In the afternoon they ordered sandwiches up to the room and Bouchard received three phone calls. He made appointments to see two of the loan sharks and, glaring at Peroff, he said he would be in touch as soon as he could. He and Victor Fauci left at about five thirty.

That night, Bouchard called a few times and reported that he was still working on the money problem. On Sunday morning he called again and announced, "I got a meeting this afternoon. Very important. Listen, I want you to talk to a guy, here, who might be giving us a loan."

The next thing Peroff knew, he was on the phone with a stranger who had dozens of questions about the plane. Where is it located? What color is it? What are the serial numbers on it? How has the financing been arranged? As Peroff answered in detail, he had the suspicion that he was talking, not to a loan shark, but to Pepe Cotroni's younger brother, Frank. He had met the third Cotroni brother a few years ago, here in Montreal, while making stock deals with Bouchard. The voice sounded familiar.

There was a long wait after that, but in the evening the phone rang again and Bouchard was on the line with a new tone of satisfaction in his voice, as if the crisis had passed. "I didn't get the ten," he reported, "but I've got five. Three for sure, but probably five. We'll get together at about noon tomorrow. Stay there. I'll bring over the bread."

Peroff was stunned. He lay down on the bed again, allowing himself to savor what had just happened. He had thought that the whole deal would die for sure. The Government *sent* me here to make it die! But Connie's coming up with the money!

If the DEA had hoped to kill its own case by forcing an impossible demand upon Bouchard, the underworld leader unwittingly had just overturned that decision by himself. The last conversation had been taped in the adjoining room, as all the others had been, so that by now the information would be well known.

The phone rang.

"Frank," came Roy Gibson's voice. "What's up?"

"You've already heard the news, Roy. I don't need to tell you."

"Give it to me again."

"Connie'll be here around noon tomorrow. With three to five grand."

"Mmmmm."

Peroff hung up. For the first time in a long while, he started to laugh.

At nine the next morning he ordered breakfast up to the room, deciding not to bother getting dressed for a while. Bouchard was to show up in three hours, with up to $5,000 in cash. It would constitute irrefutable proof that the heroin plan was serious and real.

Any amount of money given to him by Bouchard would prove it beyond a doubt. Despite themselves, the federal agents would have a bona fide case on their hands.

It was ten o'clock when Peroff heard a knock on his door. He went to answer it and found himself staring at Pierre Boudreau, the Mountie from the next room. "Hello," Peroff said, letting him in. "Well, Pierre, it's really something, ain't it?"

"What do you mean?"

"You heard it. Connie is coming here in a few hours, with the bread. Ain't that a twist? The U. S. Government is gonna have its biggest case in history, whether it wants to or not!"

"Frank, you'd better get dressed."

Peroff laughed. "What, are you playing my mother now?"

"Look," Boudreau said, "you gotta leave. Right now."

"Why? What do you mean?"

"These are my orders. Go ask Roy Gibson."

Peroff was about to protest, to scream at him, but instead he took a deep breath and told himself, I should have known. "At least," he said, "let me call Bouchard."

"No, no. You're not calling anybody. Those are my orders. Now hurry and get dressed."

For a long time Peroff stared at him, searching his face for answers, but it was no use. If he had refused to believe it before, now he knew, beyond the last lingering hope, that the Government was determined to kill its own case by any means possible. One way or the other. All doubt, all suspicion, was gone. Peroff went into the bathroom to dress, trying to show as little emotion as possible.

When he came out, he saw that Boudreau was throwing his things into the suitcase. "We have to hurry," the Mountie said.

"Why?" Peroff whispered. "Do *you* know why?"

"I'll say only one thing, Frank. I know what you're going through. But our viewpoint up here is different."

"You don't believe the case is real?"

"I didn't *say* that. What I mean is, well, Vesco is an American. Right? And we've got other cases—uh, this isn't the *only* case we have to work with the Americans. So we're keeping our hands off. We do what they ask."

"*Why* are they killing it, though?"

"I told you—ask Roy Gibson. Ask your own people."

Peroff went downstairs with his bag and checked out of the hotel. He wanted to get to a phone, to call Bouchard with some excuse for leaving, but the Mountie whisked him into an unmarked police car. At the Montreal airport, Peroff was taken into a special room and quarantined until it was time for takeoff. There was no chance to reach Bouchard. On the plane bound for New York, he sat back and tried to stifle the screams of protest in his mind.

Roy Gibson was smiling. He was leaning against the wall in a section of Kennedy Airport, his head tilted backward, chewing gum and flashing the grin which had become so familiar.

Peroff approached him with great weariness. "Roy," he said, "you guys are something else. A real scam—this whole thing."

"Why? What's the matter, Frank?"

"Oh, stop. Just stop jerking me around. *Stop* it already."

"Hunh?"

"Please. Just come out and say it to me!"

"Say what?"

"Be honest, man! Why are we going through all the exercises?"

"What d'ya mean?"

Peroff stood in front of him, squinting through his dark glasses, and he realized that Gibson, too, was in agony. The entire attitude of the man was only a big act—and a bad one, at that. If he was white, Peroff thought, he'd be red in the face.

"You're a son of a bitch, Roy. And you know it, too. You make me go up there, you make me ask the guy for bread. Right? *And he was coming up with the money!* So why, Roy? Why didn't you let me stay there and get it from him? Go ahead, chew your damn gum and smile, but I see right through it, man. You wouldn't even let me call Connie! I mean—"

"You want to call him now? Go *call* him, Frank. I won't stop you. Matter of fact, you can use my Government credit card. Here," Gibson said, handing him the card. "Go ahead."

Peroff grabbed the credit card and went to the nearest pay phone. He called Bouchard's home number in Montreal, but it was busy. He waited a few minutes and tried again. Still busy. Determined, he stood there for half an hour, trying every ten minutes, but the result was the same.

He rode back to the Hilton Inn with Gibson, certain now that everything was over. Despondent, he spent several hours that night trying to reach Bouchard, always getting a busy signal, but around midnight he managed to reach Maurice Dufrenne. The bodyguard reported that Bouchard's phone was broken.

So now it made sense. Of course—the Government had jammed up Bouchard's telephone precisely so Frank Peroff could not reach him. The question was, at this point, how much did Connie suspect? Or even if he had no suspicions, how *angry* was he?

The next morning, Tuesday, Roy Gibson called and said, "Don't try to reach Bouchard until I get there."

When Gibson arrived at the Hilton Inn, he brought a tape recorder with him. He set it up to record and monitor the call, while Peroff and his wife watched in silence.

"Okay," Gibson said. "Go to it."

Peroff gave the long-distance operator the number for Bouchard's home and, for the first time, there was no busy signal. After a few rings the French Canadian answered.

"Connie?"

"Where are you?"

"Connie, I had to fly down to Atlanta, to take care of the plane. It was down there, in trouble, and—"

"Fuck it, Frank! Forget it! The deal is off! I've talked to the other people and it's over."

"Connie, it couldn't be helped. Listen, calm down, I—"

"Forget it, Frank! It's over!"

After Peroff and Bouchard screamed back and forth for half an hour, Roy Gibson scribbled a note and passed it over: "Tell him the plane was repossessed."

Peroff held the slip of paper, staring at its message in utter confusion and fury.

"Connie? Listen," he said into the phone, taking a deep breath. "They took the plane away," he added, his face burning. "The guy I was leasing it from—he wanted his bread, you know? And it was too late, so the guy repossessed it."

Bouchard was quiet at the other end for a moment. "Ah, well," he replied at last. "It don't matter, anyway. The deal is off. And Frank—if you were in Montreal right now, you'd be dead."

239

There was a click on the line. "Well," Gibson said, unhooking his recorder, "you heard him, Frank. You, too, Ruth. He says there's no deal. It's over, so do like he says—forget it."

They stared at him in silence. This is killing him, too, Peroff thought. He's one helluva cop; he'd put his body between me and a bullet to save my life; but he's lying, pretending, and it's eating him up inside.

"Just remember," Gibson said. "You may not believe it, neither of you—but I'm your friend."

They watched as he went to the door by himself, visibly sickened, and took his leave. Peroff and his wife sat there thinking, listening to the children's voices in the other room, letting it sink in that after more than six months of this nightmare they had been left alone in a hotel near Kennedy Airport, with nothing.

IX

The case was over, a complete shambles, to be forgotten by everyone. And who, in this summer of the televised Watergate hearings, would have either the time or patience to listen to the confusing, complex details of still another scandal in high places? The proper word for it, in Frank Peroff's vocabulary, was not scandal but scam. A scam was any illegal act, idea, plot or swindle carried out by the power of one's brains instead of guns or violence. From Peroff's viewpoint, the Government itself had turned out to be the scammer in this case, using him as its victim or pigeon.

But they've underestimated me, he thought. They haven't stopped to figure out what I might do. Their manual, so to speak, says that I'll just disappear. Chapter Seven, Section Four, Paragraph Nineteen, must read, "Subject will hereby collapse and slink off, tail between legs."

In many respects, Peroff reasoned, the federal agents were probably right. Most men who are used as so-called informants are too afraid, justifiably so, to fight back. There was no profit in such a move. It could only bring down more heat. But Peroff saw himself as no ordinary informant. He was, rather, a con man who had been conned. He'd been blackmailed into doing undercover work and promised huge rewards, then forced to ruin the very case he had developed at such personal cost.

There at the Hilton Inn, with his wife and family, Frank Peroff set off on a single-minded course to put together the pieces of the puzzle, to seek revenge and justice. They don't expect me to do anything, he thought. They've put me in jail—so they think I'm afraid that they'll do it again. But this is worse than jail. Nobody's

241

ever pulled a scam on me like this and gotten away with it. And besides, what more can I lose? That's the key; that's their mistake. They've pushed me too far and don't realize that I have no other choice but to fight back.

It was awesome to realize who the enemy might be. The Secret Service. The Bureau of Customs. The Drug Enforcement Agency of the Justice Department. The White House. The U. S. Attorney's Office in Manhattan as well? Who knows? The problem is, who in hell can I really trust?

He narrowed his choices to the office of Archibald Cox, the special Watergate prosecutor, and the Senate Rackets Committee under Senator Henry Jackson. These two bodies seemed to be the only ones with the kind of independent power needed to help him. Still, he wondered, how could they take my word over all the others? Out of hundreds of tape recordings, Peroff had managed to hold onto several cassettes, in only two of which Bouchard spoke about Vesco and LeBlanc and the $300,000 in Costa Rica. The remaining tapes contained conversations between himself and Mike Reilly, Roy Gibson and various other agents or Mounties. The two "Vesco tapes" were crucial ones, but were they enough, by themselves, to make people understand their importance?

Peroff had declared war, but as yet he could not determine where to begin waging even his first battle.

He and his family spent the rest of that week in the Hilton Inn. Roy Gibson called once just to say hello, but the conversation was brief. Gibson sounded in low spirits, even somewhat nervous when he asked Peroff what his plans were. In return, Peroff was bitter and curt on the phone, saying only that he was planning to move into the Shelburne Apartment Hotel on East Thirty-seventh Street in Manhattan. The family did make the move over that weekend, August fourth and fifth.

Gibson called again on Monday, almost as if he could not bring himself to sever the relationship yet. His excuse was to relay a message from the Queens District Attorney's Office. "I promised them that I'd bring you to a meeting," Gibson explained.

"Yeah," Peroff said. "You're taking the place of Bouchard."

"Hunh?"

"Well," Peroff went on, half joking, "you volunteered my services, just like he did."

It was true, however, that Peroff still had to appear in Queens court on the Florida charges, so it was in his best interest to maintain a friendship with the District Attorney. Beyond that, he had liked Carl Bornstein, the assistant D.A. whom he had met briefly after being released from jail. Borenstein was a young man, in his early thirties, and appeared to be both intelligent and honest.

So Peroff went with Gibson to a second meeting in Queens. Once the introductions were made again, the DEA agent left him on his own and Bornstein took charge. Peroff's first task, if he agreed, was to investigate a private flying school near La Guardia Airport, to determine if the owner was using his planes for smuggling or any other illegal activities. He spent several days checking out the school, going out there as if he were a special detective and using all his powers as a con man to elicit information. At last he reported back to Bornstein that the flying school was, in his opinion, entirely legitimate, used strictly for lessons and sightseeing trips.

A few days later Roy Gibson again called to say that the Armstrong-Bornstein office wanted to use his services in connection with recent gold robberies in New York City. Would there be any way for Peroff to find out if the gold was still around?

"Maybe," Peroff said. "But I'm tired of all this."

"By the way, Frank, do you mind if I come over?"

"What for?"

"Just as a friend."

"Sure," Peroff said. "I don't care."

It was a strange relationship that had evolved between Frank Peroff, the Jewish con man, and Roy Gibson, the black federal agent. On the one hand, Peroff hated him and blamed him for much of what had happened to the case; yet he could not bring himself to summon up any real anger at him on a personal, man-to-man basis. Peroff was almost certain that Gibson had only been taking orders, doing as instructed, being the "company man" who was proud of his position and afraid to lose it; and he was sure that despite Gibson's cool facade, the agent was going through a crisis of conscience.

When Gibson came to the Shelburne he settled into a chair with a drink, staring morosely at the glass in his hand while Peroff and his wife waited for him to speak. "Well," he said at last, "what are you gonna do, Frank?"

"I'm not sure," Peroff said. "But maybe you can help me decide."

"I'm taking a leave," Gibson volunteered.

"You are? How long?"

"A few weeks."

His mind is bad, Peroff thought. Now's the time to get him to open up, when his resistance is down. "Listen, Roy—I want you to play a little game, here. Okay? Just imagine, now, that you're not an agent. You're a farmer or a businessman. Or a senator, even. Anybody but a cop. And imagine that you picked up a newspaper or a report of some kind, whatever, and it listed what I'm about to read to you, in this order. I want to know what you think, okay?"

Gibson nodded, staring now at the tips of his shoes. Peroff took a spiral notebook and a pen and began to write his list as he spoke. "Number one," he said. "Funds were cut off. *My* funds—right?"

"Yeah."

"Okay," Peroff said. "Number two. Was ordered by Mike Reilly not to speak to any other federal agency. True?"

"True."

"Three. Was told by Roy Gibson that my life wouldn't be worth two cents if I spoke to the Senate. You remember that, Roy?"

"Uh-hunh," Gibson muttered.

"Number four. Was asked to go to Costa Rica commercial. Completely contrary to my role. For pickup of three hundred grand. Okay," Peroff went on, pausing while he finished jotting it down. "Five—case was killed when I arrived in New York from Puerto Rico. No communication from control agent. Meaning you. Fair enough?"

"Mmmm."

Peroff thought for a few minutes. The sixth point on his list would have something to do with the Americans versus the Canadians. At some time during the case, Gibson had mentioned that the Canadians had expressed reservations. Yet the Mounties had always passed the buck back to the United States. "Had conversations with Canadians," Peroff said, writing, "and was told that the DEA *lied* in stating that the Mounties wanted to kill case."

Gibson glanced up, about to say something, but he held back. Ruth went to freshen his drink.

"Okay," Peroff continued. "Number seven. Had long conversations with the White House. Eight. Had conversations with U. S. Attorney John Wing. Nine. Was arrested by direction of Secret Service—at least, that's the explanation so far. Ten. Was released when I agreed to do exactly as told in relation to case. Eleven. Went to Canada—was told *not* to by Bouchard—at direction of DEA. Twelve. Obstacles and harassment were caused by me, at direction of DEA and RCMP, which caused, uh, great pressure. How am I doing?"

Gibson said, "Go on," stretching his legs out and staring up at the ceiling.

"And number thirteen—I told Bouchard that the plane was repossessed."

On that last note, Gibson visibly bristled as if his insides were knotting up.

"Okay," Peroff said. "Now, Roy, the key to this thing is the series of events. You have to read it in order, the way I've written it down. You could pick out each item and try to explain it. But not when they're all together, Roy. It can't be done. Now, if you were an average citizen, what would *your* opinion be?"

Gibson stood up and went to the window of the apartment. He walked around a bit, stopped, and said in a low voice, "Conspiracy."

For a moment, Peroff thought the agent might have been joking. But Gibson was rubbing the back of his neck, obviously uncomfortable and wishing he were somewhere else.

"Roy, you've just told me what I'm going to do. You just made up my mind for me."

Gibson merely stared at him, saying nothing. He forced a thin smile, nodded slightly and left the apartment.

The word "conspiracy" seemed almost absurd. It would mean that some huge, coordinated effort to suppress the heroin case had been carried out by many of the people with whom Peroff had worked. It would have taken a powerful guiding hand to throw all the gears into reverse. First the Government had used every means at its disposal to force Frank Peroff into his role, to develop the case; then, once Robert Vesco was mentioned as the financier, the Government had to marshal even more energy to hold back what it had put into motion.

That night, Peroff lay awake hearing voices out of the recent past.

Just as long as it's in the house, Vernon Acree had said.

How's the machine? Bouchard had asked.

We want you to take a commercial flight, Reilly had said.

I'll get back to you, John Wing had said.

This is a go situation, the man in Costa Rica had said.

Sit tight, the White House had said.

You're under arrest, the detective had said.

You can't question, Gibson had said.

Tell Bouchard that you need ten grand, Roberts had said.

Vesco is an American, the Mountie had said.

Tell him the plane was repossessed, Gibson had said.

I don't know from nothing, Roberts had said.

Your life wouldn't be worth two cents, Gibson had said.

You're a walking dead man, Reilly had said.

If any sort of conspiracy existed, there had to be a strong motive behind it. To suppress the largest narcotics case in history, the orders had to come from very high up in the Government. The White House itself? The President? Why would Richard Nixon, the law-and-order politician, have any such motive? To keep Robert Vesco from being brought back to the United States? Why?

From Peroff's random reading of the newspapers, he could construct a motive based on sheer speculation. The essence of it was that Vesco, if extradited to the States, could unload all kinds of information about corruption within the Nixon Administration, in exchange for immunity from prosecution.

For one thing, Vesco provided one more link between Nixon and the Bahamas. He was another wealthy contributor to the President's political campaigns, a backer such as Howard Hughes, Charles (Bebe) Rebozo and Robert Abplanalp, all of whom had connections in the Bahamas, where Vesco's financial operations were centered. The controversial fugitive's fortune was tied into the Bahamas Commonwealth Bank, which he controlled through Norman LeBlanc.

Three months ago, back in May, LeBlanc had held a news

conference at a hotel in Costa Rica, contending that he and Vesco had a "missing link" to Watergate with facts that would "startle the world" if they were released. He told reporters that Vesco's $200,000 contribution to the Nixon campaign had been made as the result of "extortion" and said they would come to the States with their information only if given immunity.

What could they unload about Nixon and his associates? The President's younger brother, Edward, had been mentioned by the press in connection with Vesco's dealings, and his other brother Donald as well. Also, the President's nephew was actually on the Vesco payroll, working in some minor capacity. There were other links—between Vesco and John Mitchell and also John Ehrlichman, the former domestic advisor to the White House.

Vesco and LeBlanc had led the plundering of Investors Overseas Services, the Geneva-based mutual fund built by playboy Bernard Cornfeld. It was a complex, brilliant series of sales and transfers of IOS assets into banks and holding companies controlled by Vesco and LeBlanc and other associates. The Securities and Exchange Commission accused them of bilking IOS funds of more than $224 million, but the United States was basing its extradition bid on a $50,000 fraud case. Now Vesco was wanted, not only for the Mitchell-Stans trial, but as a supplier of information for the Senate Watergate Committee and the special Watergate prosecutor, not to mention the Internal Revenue Service.

In March, Vesco had announced that he was taking up permanent residence in Costa Rica, where he already had invested a large chunk of his fortune. It was possible that if too many obstacles had been placed between Vesco and his holdings, he might well have gone along with a narcotics deal for a quick profit of more than a million dollars in cash. In a world such as the one in which Vesco operated, cash was essential to maintain and wield power. And this particular investment had been guaranteed by the Montreal mob against any loss by the financier.

But whether or not it was true that Vesco had agreed to underwrite a narcotics deal, what excuse did the Government have for not pursuing it? There had been only one way for the truth to be found, conclusively, and that had been to send Peroff down there to Costa Rica, to the San José airport where Vesco himself parked his private jet, in order to see if the $300,000 would be waiting. And who had the authority, the power, the motive, to call a halt to that crucial step? The Nixon White House?

For Frank Peroff, the questions became too far-reaching, making him feel even smaller and more alone than before.

During the remainder of August, he made daily trips by cab from the apartment-hotel in Manhattan to the District Attorney's Office in Queens, consulting with officials about the stolen gold. In return for his services, the D. A. was paying him a good part of his living expenses.

The investigation seemed to be progressing, although a jurisdictional dispute had developed. At the Queens D.A.'s office, the Bureau of Customs had begun arguing with the Secret Service over which agency was controlling the case. Eventually it ended in a draw and Peroff was asked to go see some gold traders to set up a buy. On one occasion he met with a mob figure inside a Broadway movie house, where *Cops and Robbers* was playing, and the mobster referred him to a fence in the jewelry district.

From various sources, Peroff learned that there was, in fact, stolen gold being offered for sale. If some of this "hot metal" could be purchased, perhaps tests would link it up to the recent robberies. Peroff was wired by the agents and, three separate times, he negotiated with underworld traders only to have the Government force him to stall.

After having to turn down three gold deals in a row, the entire operation folded. The bickering and indecision among rival agencies had made Peroff's role almost impossible, since he was unable to keep making up excuses for the dealers.

The experience, however, had gained him a personal relationship with Carl Bornstein, the assistant district attorney. One evening, Peroff met with Bornstein and his boss, Michael Armstrong, up in a conference room at the D.A.'s Office. They sat munching on apples while Peroff played his two remaining tapes in which Bouchard mentioned Vesco and LeBlanc. He went through his entire story from the beginning, from Rome to London to Paris to Manhattan to Washington, D.C. to Montreal—five separate trips —and back here to New York City. He outlined his troubles after Vesco's name had been mentioned, including Reilly's threat that he would be "a walking dead man" if he ran to the Senate for help.

D. A. Armstrong had been quiet for a while. He looked up now and said, "Well, in my opinion this stinks. It really smells rotten."

For the first time in weeks, Peroff's hopes began to rise. He listened while Armstrong and Bornstein discussed the case, realizing that they were posing the same questions which he'd been asking himself. Who ordered the DEA to sabotage its own operation? Was Vesco the reason? Had the White House acted to protect John Mitchell and Maurice Stans by keeping Vesco from returning? By now the Mitchell-Stans-Vesco case in New York had been postponed, so that the timing was still important. With these two tapes, plus the right testimony from Peroff and the federal agents, wouldn't it still be possible to try for Vesco's extradition? Even at this late hour?

Armstrong's suggestion was to approach Paul Curran, the U. S. Attorney in Manhattan whose office was prosecuting the Vesco case. Peroff reminded Armstrong that he had never heard back from John Wing, one of Curran's assistants, the very man who was scheduled to handle the case in court.

"Well," Armstrong said, "I have no doubt that Curran would like to have Vesco back here. It could make the whole difference in whether he's successful in that case."

"But it's dangerous," Peroff replied. "I don't want the DEA to find out, you know? They might come after my ass and retaliate."

"Curran's a good friend of mine," Armstrong went on. "We could approach him on a confidential basis, man to man."

"Just as long as he won't blow me out of the water. I mean, that guy Reilly has already threatened my life."

"Don't worry, Frank."

"All right—I'm the layman in this thing. You're the expert, so do what you think is best."

A few days later, Peroff received word from Bornstein that an actual investigation of the case would be conducted by Curran's office. Bornstein came and took the two Vesco cassettes to a meeting with Curran, but that night he reported, "They didn't listen to the tapes. Not yet, anyway. We discussed everything, and John Wing came in. He admits your phone call to him, by the way."

"But why didn't they listen to the tapes?"

"I don't know, but Jacob Tyler, an assistant, has taken charge. He'll meet with you tomorrow at the U.S. Attorney's Office. Come pick up the tapes and bring them when you go there."

The next day, Peroff retrieved his tapes and brought them to Tyler's office in Foley Square. He put the cassettes on a table and said, "Here they are. You want to listen?"

"Wait a minute," Tyler said. "You're making serious charges against federal agents, do you realize that?"

"You're damn right I do."

"Well, I suggest that maybe you shouldn't be talking to me. You might prefer to get a lawyer, and I'll talk to him instead."

"Are you going to do something? Make an investigation?"

"It's really not your business, what I'll do."

"Wait a minute, now. I'd like to know what your plans are. I can't have you going to the DEA on this. I mean—"

"But that's *exactly* what I will do," Tyler said. "*I'm* investigating, so it's necessary to get statements."

"Yeah, but from which people?"

"From the DEA, who else? I'm having Roy Gibson brought in —to get *their* side of the story."

"Hey," Peroff shouted, "that's not the agreement! Armstrong went to your boss, to Curran, on a confidential basis! He had an understanding that you wouldn't tip off those agents!"

"Mr. Peroff, I don't know about that."

"If you're gonna blow me out of the water with those agents, I want protection from you!"

"Protection?"

"From the *agents,* man! From the DEA! I'm making accusations against them, like you said!"

"Well, *I* can't give you protection, Mr. Peroff. If you want to call me in a week, I'll let you know what's going on."

"And you don't want to hear these tapes?"

"No."

Peroff put them back in his pocket and left in a state of extreme anxiety. Bewildered, he returned to the Shelburne and called Bornstein, who was incredulous when he heard what had taken place.

"I don't get it," Bornstein said.

"Neither do I. He told me to get a lawyer! It was as if he didn't want to know anything, like I was some sort of disease! Carl, is this actually happening?"

It was Thursday night, the twenty-seventh of September. Three days later, that Sunday, Peroff and his wife took the children up to the Bronx Zoo. They left the Shelburne and piled into two taxicabs. They spent the afternoon wandering around the zoo, trying to behave like normal parents for a change and to forget everything for a couple of hours. But Peroff was plagued by the thought that by going to Curran's office he had walked right into a setup. Armstrong was deceived, he thought. The guy actually trusted Curran. But they wouldn't hear the tapes, on two separate occasions. Not Curran, not Wing, not Tyler. They don't want to hear a thing! And now Tyler says he'll tip off the DEA! But why, unless they're both on the same side? Now I'll be in danger from the agents, because I have the tapes—the evidence!

When they returned from the zoo to their hotel-apartment, Peroff stayed in the living room for a while to watch the end of a World Series playoff game on television. When it was over, he started to walk into the bedroom. He got just inside the doorway when he saw that his briefcase, visible inside the open closet, had been moved. He walked over and bent down. The briefcase was unlocked! The combination lock had been tampered with by someone who must have been a professional. He opened the case and saw that some papers had been removed from its pouch. Also missing were six tape cassettes filled with Peroff's conversations.

X

During the same month of September, the Permanent Subcommittee on Investigations for the U. S. Senate was finishing up its hearings into stolen securities and white-collar fraud. This was the so-called Rackets Committee which had pursued organized crime under Senator John McClellan, earning a reputation as the most powerful investigative body in the Senate. For three years, the committee had been delving into what McClellan had called "the role of organized crime in the thefts of millions of dollars' worth of stocks, bonds and other negotiable instruments from brokerage houses and banks and from the U. S. mails." Now headed by Senator Henry Jackson, the committee had shifted its focus to the actual disposal of hot securities by swindlers and scammers. One such "paper man" on the committee's list, who had eluded its grasp, was Frank Peroff.

On the eighteenth of September, the committee heard public testimony from its chief investigator, Philip Manuel, a solidly built man in his late thirties who had become known for his qualities of fairness and toughness. Manuel told the Senators that he and his staff had established "that there is, and has been developing for some time, a burgeoning group of professional confidence men and international swindlers who are, to a great degree, closely knit and interlocking."

"They cooperate rather openly," Manuel went on, "each promoting the fraudulent schemes of the other." The group, he said, "has applied sophisticated corporate principles to the age-old art of swindling. Their forte is that they know 'how to use bad paper' and in so doing, are limited only by their own ingenuity."

Manuel pointed out that the swindlers formed a "natural alliance" with the mob. (A good example would have been Peroff's relationship with Conrad Bouchard, whose access to stolen paper made him a major supplier. The Bouchards of the world needed the services of the Peroffs and vice versa, although Peroff himself had developed other sources as well.) Making an "educated guess," Manuel said the trend had begun to snowball in the late 1960s. He estimated that as much as $50 billion in lost or stolen securities was now being used by paper men.

Nearly every witness brought before the Jackson Committee had come into contact with the elusive Frank Peroff. Most of the swindlers operated in Florida and the Bahamas, the same territory, and Peroff's name had been mentioned many times during the staff's investigations. Phil Manuel and his principal assistant, Bill Gallinaro, knew only that Peroff was a "manipulator" who could "move paper" and who, somewhat mysteriously, had a reputation as a pilot and owner of airplanes. They had tried, without success, to locate him.

On the second of October, a Tuesday, Manuel and Gallinaro had completed their securities hearings. The last thing they expected was to have Peroff reach out to them, as if from nowhere, on his own.

At his desk in the Old Senate Office Building in Washington, D.C., Phil Manuel took the call. "Can I help you?" he asked.

"This is Frank Peroff."

"Uh-hunh."

"I want to know if my name is gonna pop up in those hearings you're having."

"Well," Manuel said, "if you're the same Frank Peroff that we've been looking for, it's very possible. We've been trying to *find* that same Frank Peroff for a helluva long time."

"Maybe I'll get lucky and I *won't* be the same Frank Peroff."

"Maybe so," Manuel replied, trying to keep a slight edge. "But we'd like to talk to you."

"Under what conditions?"

"Well, I can give you my word that nothing happens, good or bad, until we sit down and talk."

"All right. I'm in New York. . . ."

A meeting was set up for that Friday, the fifth of October, at the Senate investigators' field office in Foley Square. Both Manuel and Gallinaro decided to make the trip. They were curious about Peroff, wondering what new light he could shed on the subject of stock fraud and related topics, but they also wanted to know the real reason he had called. Was it merely out of fear that he would be subpoenaed as a Senate witness? If so, he was mistaken. Not only had the two investigators been unable to track him down; they also held not even a shred of evidence to link him with any specific crime. Whatever his motive for wanting to meet them, maybe it would result in a lucky break.

They arrived in New York on Friday morning and went to their private office high up in the Federal Courthouse. At the appointed hour, there was a knock on the door and in another moment they were shaking hands with Peroff. The large man took a seat at the table, appearing somewhat nervous. For the first several minutes the conversation was strained, as if Peroff was experiencing second thoughts about the meeting.

He was being cautious, playing a kind of cat-and-mouse game. It was nothing new for a subject to behave this way. The remedy was to be patient and slowly try to gain his confidence. They asked him about the whole Florida scene, but while Peroff was nodding and giving unspecific answers his mind seemed to be somewhere else.

"Look," he said at last, interrupting one of their questions. "We've got to talk a deal."

Manuel shook his head. "We can't make deals, Frank."

"I can give you something that I think is hot. I mean, it's about as hot as anything could be."

"No guarantees," Manuel said.

"All right," Peroff replied. "I don't think I've got much choice, anyway. Actually I was warned against talking to you guys. I was threatened, but—"

"Who threatened you?" Gallinaro asked.

"Well, it was a federal agent. A boss in the DEA, as a matter of fact."

"What?"

"Look, uh, let me give it to you. I don't think you'll believe it, but here goes. At the beginning of this year, I was living in Europe.

In January, I was forced into becoming an undercover agent. It started in Rome. . . ."

Manuel and Gallinaro were staring at him. They were stunned, dazed, incredulous. Peroff had been talking for nearly five hours. He was nearing the end of his wild story, telling about how he had met with Jacob Tyler, the assistant U. S. Attorney in Paul Curran's office, eight days ago.

"I put the tapes right down on his desk," Peroff said, "but he absolutely had no interest in them. He didn't even want to *see* them, as if they were poison. See, Armstrong really believed in Curran. But I got sold out. I think Tyler went right ahead and called up Reilly at the DEA. He gave me up and I went flying down the river!"

"Anything else?" Manuel asked.

"Look, all I want is personal justice. I want the truth."

"What about the tapes?"

"Oh, yeah," Peroff said. "Three days after I met with Tyler, my apartment was burglarized. I'm sure it was the DEA that did it."

The two investigators listened as Peroff described an event that was too coincidental for comfort. When he was finished describing the theft, Gallinaro groaned and said, "So they got the tapes?"

"They *thought* they did," Peroff said. "The six tapes that they got weren't very important. The two Vesco tapes were in Ruth's purse. For some reason, maybe an act of God, she'd taken them with her to the zoo."

"So you still *have* 'em?" Manuel asked.

Peroff nodded, adding that the burglary had made him almost frantic. His first thought had been to find a safe place to hide the tapes. But how? Where? To buy time, he had put them in a manila envelope and mailed them to his own address at the Shelburne. Then, while the tapes were en route back to him, he grabbed a book from the shelf and began cutting into it with a razor blade. It was a thick hardbound volume of science-fiction stories entitled *Again, Dangerous Visions*. His choice of that particular volume had been made without intentional irony. Peroff cut two rectangular-shaped openings in the center of the book and, when the tapes arrived in the mail, he immediately put them into their new hiding place.

So the two important tapes were safe. The disturbing aspect was the timing, though. Once before when he had reached out for help, to the White House and to John Wing, he had been arrested. And having reached out this time, to Curran's office again, his apartment had been burglarized!

"I'm sure it was the DEA," he repeated. "First they put me in jail to keep me quiet. Then they tried to steal my evidence. What's more, I think that Curran's office tipped them off. And that's why nobody wanted to hear the tapes. See? Because if they were stolen, then Tyler and the others could deny that they even knew about the *existence* of the tapes. And by the way, I called Tyler just yesterday and he says that his so-called investigation is over. The matter is closed, he says, and I should forget about the whole thing."

Manuel and Gallinaro sat back, glancing at each other and shaking their heads. It was almost too much to digest all at once. "You know," Gallinaro said, "if this is true, *if* it's true, then it's the biggest bomb we've ever had."

"I told you it was far-out," Peroff said. "Especially if you hear it cold like this, for the first time."

"It wasn't what we'd expected," Manuel laughed. "Actually it's incredible. I don't know what the hell to say, Frank."

"Phil's going back to Washington right away," Gallinaro said. "But I could stay in town overnight and get the tapes from you."

Peroff shook his head. "At this point I *know* how important those tapes are. Maybe I didn't realize it *before,* but I sure as hell do now. And I don't trust anyone, not even you guys. Why should I trust you any more than I do Curran's office? So I'm not about to surrender 'em. You want to *hear* 'em, fine."

"Can we make copies?"

"Nope. Nobody's getting a thing until I know what you're gonna do."

The next morning, Gallinaro dropped by the Shelburne and heard the two taped conversations of July sixth and eighth, when Peroff had spoken to Bouchard from Puerto Rico. The first one mentioned Vesco and LeBlanc by name; the second referred to the $300,000 in Costa Rica.

"That's Bouchard all right," Gallinaro said. Again he pressed for the tapes, but Peroff was adamant. These two cassettes were his

256

only remaining link to the truth; they were proof that he hadn't just imagined everything.

"Well," Gallinaro went on, "it's one helluva thing, Frank. We'll do some checking on our own. Believe me, if your basic story holds up, the Senate will get involved. The way I figure it, we've got nothing to lose."

"At this point," Peroff replied, "neither do I."

XI

There was no assurance that the Senate investigators would pursue the truth to its full extent. Judging from previous experience, Peroff had every reason to believe the exact opposite. In a sense he was at their mercy, living at the Shelburne with his family and waiting for something to happen; and at the same time he was forced to make plans for the future in case, as he expected, the investigators decided to drop him. He kept in daily phone contact with Bill Gallinaro, who was making "discreet inquiries" and preparing an initial report for Phil Manuel. Both investigators came to New York again and Manuel heard the tapes for the first time, but they refused to make any promises on behalf of the Senate committee. Peroff, in turn, remained firm in refusing to give up his cassettes.

As the weeks of October dragged by, he started reaching back into his former life. He made contact with friends in Florida and even held phone conversations with Conrad Bouchard again, discussing the possibility of making some paper deals. Needing money, Peroff resorted to the occupation he knew best.

"I may have to start my own action again," he told Ruth, adding that he planned to build up his cash reserves and, ultimately, return to Europe.

Yet that was not what he really wanted. The truth was, he had come to despise Bouchard and wished that the heroin case had been successful, if only for the satisfaction of helping to put the French Canadian behind bars. And he knew, more clearly than ever, that his life in crime had never been worth it. What real wealth and security had he obtained? What did it add up to, after all the effort and worry that he'd expended to pull off so many deals which had fallen through? More often than not, he had walked away from adventures because they were too risky. True, he had traveled more than most people and had seen a lot of the world, but the work had been hard, filled with constant pressure. Most of the deals had begun with excited talk about the millions of dollars which could be made; but most of the time, after he became involved, it turned out that too many other crooks were getting slices of the pie. And beyond that, what sort of real friendships had he made? Most of the people he called "friends" were con men like himself and not to be trusted; there was always the threat of being double-crossed, stabbed in the back. It seemed strange, but he was only now beginning to realize how unhappy he had been during so much of his life. It made him wish for a different kind of existence, one that was uncomplicated and more stable.

What he really wanted was to make a clean break with the past. But first, he hoped the Government could be forced to explain its actions. Otherwise, he would become just what the federal agents had tried to make him: a lowly informer who was used and then discarded as if he were not even human. The agents had lied, they had failed to keep their commitments, they had made him dependent upon them for financial survival; and then they had simply walked away, leaving him to crawl back into the world of crime, where they could grab him and use him all over again if they wanted.

No, he thought, I won't let them. I did my best for them, but they killed the case. Now it's *my* case, not theirs, and the way to beat them is to play the game the way *they* do. But to strike back at the DEA, and therefore the Justice Department as well, was a frightening prospect. He needed other allies, in case the Senate decided against pursuing an investigation. There was no point in remaining absolutely alone.

So one evening toward the end of October, he placed a call to *The New York Times*. When an editor came on the line, Peroff spoke to him in the language to which he was accustomed: "Look, I've got some information you might want. It has to do with Robert Vesco. I don't want to discuss it over the phone, but maybe we can set up a meeting and work out a deal. . . ."

* * *

Wednesday, the thirty-first of October, became a crucial day in Frank Peroff's struggle to make the correct moves. The Florida warrants case against him in Queens had been dismissed, so his relationship with Armstrong and Bornstein had virtually ended. Besides, the two district attorneys had unwittingly led him into the hands of the enemy, if his assessment of Curran's office was correct. But there had been new developments, and he was waiting for the arrival of two parties on the same day: the Mounties, who were requesting a favor, and a representative from the *Times*.

While he waited, there was an unexpected phone call from Jacob Tyler. The assistant U. S. Attorney made the surprising announcement that he, on behalf of Curran's office, had decided to pursue the investigation after all! Peroff listened, thinking, And I know why, too! By now they know that the Senate is on their trail. They don't want to be caught in the conspiracy—with egg on their faces, for having done nothing.

"I'd like to hear those tapes," Tyler said.

Peroff could not help being sarcastic. "I'm not hiding," he said. "You already *had* two chances to hear them. Why do you want to hear 'em *now?* What's making you change your mind? Is Phil Manuel breathing down your neck? Come on—what's the matter, are you afraid you're gonna get caught with your pants down?"

Tyler was incensed. "Are you refusing to bring those tapes to my office?"

"No. But at this moment they're not in my possession," Peroff said. It was true, in a technical sense. They were still inside *Again, Dangerous Visions,* and the book was in Ruth's possession.

When he got off the phone, Peroff sat there wishing that the Senate would hurry up and decide its course of action. If the Rackets Committee were to make him a witness, he would fall under its protection, with U. S. marshals to guard him. As of now, however, he was still on his own. I'll bet, he thought, that the DEA and Curran's office were furious when they discovered that the wrong tapes had been stolen. Now they're getting frantic.

Meanwhile there was the impending visit from the Mounties. A few days ago, Jean Sourbier of the RCMP had called the Shelburne to say that Connie Bouchard had hired a public-relations man to help influence his narcotics case, which still hadn't gone to trial.

The underworld leader was creating favorable press coverage for himself in Montreal, and would Peroff agree to come up there "one more time" to try to sink him? But Sourbier had added that the U. S. Government—the DEA!—was requesting Peroff's services as well.

"The DEA wants you to help us with it," Sourbier had said. "They know that you're pissed off at them, so they asked me to ask you."

If anything looked like a setup, a trap, this was it. Isn't that something, Peroff thought. The DEA knows I've gone to the Senate, they know I'm making accusations against them—yet now they want my help on another case? But they *also* know that the Senate hasn't committed itself yet. So there's still time to get rid of me. . . .

Sourbier arrived at the Shelburne apartment that afternoon. He was accompanied by another Mountie, Pierre Boudreau, the electronics man who had whisked Peroff out of Canada on the previous trip. And with them was a DEA agent whom Peroff had never met. *A setup*, he thought. *The Mounties may or may not be in on it, but that's what it is.*

"This is extremely important for us," Sourbier said. "As you know, Bouchard's case is built on circumstantial evidence. No eyewitnesses, no solid evidence—except we know the bum is guilty. What we need is another case to get him off the streets."

The Mounties mentioned that Bouchard had access to $400,000 worth of counterfeit Canadian hundred-dollar bills.

"I know about that," Peroff said. "Bouchard offered it to me at least a dozen times, but I told him it was crap. I mean, it's more difficult to work a deal with Canadian stuff."

"It's still there, Frank. Bouchard is trying to peddle it. And listen, nobody can deal with that counterfeit the way you can. We need your help."

"Look," Peroff said, "I don't want to go on with this shit any more. I really don't."

"Please think it over," Sourbier went on, adding that Peroff would be paid a minimum of $25,000 to go back up to Montreal as an undercover man. "And fifty grand," he said, "if your cover is blown and we need you in court. Plus all the protection you might need."

The offer was tempting, from both the standpoint of the money and of the satisfaction it would bring to put Bouchard in prison. But Peroff wavered, remembering his fears of a setup.

Now the DEA agent in the room said, "Mr. Tyler wants you to call him, Frank."

"What the hell for?"

"I don't know."

Peroff tried calling the U. S. Attorney's Office, but Tyler was unavailable. He told Sourbier that he would have to think about the proposition and let him know his decision in a few days. When the two Mounties and the DEA agent left, Peroff reached Curran's office again and this time Tyler came on the line.

"Did you agree?" Tyler asked him.

"Agree to what?"

"To what they want you to do?"

"So you know all about this?"

"Yes, I've been informed. Did you agree?"

"Not yet," Peroff said, thinking, They're sure eager as hell to have me put my life on the line again.

That night, as expected, the reporter from *The New York Times* showed up at the Shelburne. He was Wallace Turner, who had flown into Manhattan from San Francisco. Apparently the *Times'* editors had assigned him to the story. Peroff had never heard of him, but Turner had won the Pulitzer Prize for his journalism and was widely respected in his field. He was a tall man, perhaps six-one, and Peroff judged that he was in his midfifties. He had graying hair and wore a conservative gray suit with an old-fashioned thin tie, looking just the way newspapermen did in the late-show movies on television. Turner came inside holding a notepad and, almost as soon as they said hello, he began taking notes, continuing all through his visit.

"Wait a minute," Peroff said. "First we gotta have a deal. Everything I tell you remains confidential, until I say otherwise."

"I *can* give you my word," Turner said, "to hold back the article until you say to print it."

"Good, because I may be going up to Canada on something very dangerous. I have to make up my mind on that first."

For the next few hours, Peroff outlined his tale while Turner took furious notes. It was difficult for the reporter to absorb everything so quickly, and equally hard for him to know whether to believe Peroff or not. He kept shaking his head, asking questions, scribbling and murmuring over what he was hearing.

When he was ready to leave, Turner said, "You let me know when you're ready. I'll be back in San Francisco, but if you need me just give a call to the *Times* and I'll come across the country. I'll be back, Frank."

There was a great deal for Peroff to think about later that night. Should he go up to Canada to sink Bouchard? Should he have called the *Times* and spilled so much to Turner? If a story hit the papers, he would have every mob in the country after him, not to mention the federal drug agents.

It was Thursday, the first of November—nine months since his ordeal had begun. Peroff called the Senate committee for advice on whether he should go to Canada. Phil Manuel said, "I'm not going to advise you either way, Frank. But if you can help by going up there, I don't see anything wrong with it. I'm just not going to tell you to do it or not to do it."

"*Don't* do it," came Bill Gallinaro's voice on another extension. "Frank, I think it's a setup. You'd be an ass to do it! I mean, if they didn't believe you about Vesco before, why are they sending you up to Canada now? Something's wrong, Frank. I think it stinks."

After that call, Peroff sat for a long while trying to come to a decision. The thing was, he hated to give up the chance to put Bouchard in jail. As much as he hated the DEA and distrusted the Mounties, it would be worth it if the operation succeeded. I *know* I can lure Connie into a deal, he thought. Man, that would give me some satisfaction. Because Bouchard started this thing! And how many people has he caused to be shot? How many guys has he ruined? I could use the money, but seeing that bastard put away means twenty times more.

As a test, he put in a call to Bouchard in Montreal. He referred to the $400,000 in phony Canadian bills and said, "Is it still there?"

"Yah," Bouchard replied.

"Well, I think I've got somebody that's bent. I'm trying to work on it, Connie, but I'm not sure yet."

"Who is it?" Bouchard asked.

"It's a banker here in New York, with the Chase Manhattan. I'm trying to bend him. Maybe we can do something with that paper. I'm trying to convince him to take the stuff—you know, put it in the bank as collateral, like a time deposit, and then make a loan against it."

Bouchard sounded eager. "You think he'll do it?"

"I'm *working* on him. This guy—he's a loan officer with the bank. His *mind* is bent, but *he* isn't yet. I'll know in the next day or two. So if I show up there, don't be surprised."

"Okay, good! I'll be glad to see you."

Peroff hung up and mulled it over some more. The mission might be easy to accomplish. Later in the day, Sourbier called from Canada to say that the FBI would be involved in the case.

"Really?"

"Yeah, they'll take part in it."

"How come? What do they have to do with counterfeit? That's the Secret Service—you sure it's the FBI?"

"I'm sure."

The FBI was one of the few federal agencies Peroff still trusted. The Secret Service, the Customs Bureau, the DEA—they had dealt with him unfairly, but never the FBI. In Peroff's judgment, the FBI was far superior to any other law-enforcement bureau in the country.

"I might do it," he told Sourbier. "I've already told Bouchard that I've got a bent banker from Chase Manhattan."

"Great. The FBI will send a man to pose as the banker."

"As long as I call the shots," Peroff said.

XII

It was his sixth trip to Montreal this year. When Peroff got off the plane, he saw Jean Sourbier of the Mounties waiting for him near the Customs counter. They nodded to each other and walked quickly out of the terminal building to Sourbier's car. By now on this Friday night it was past eight o'clock; but as they rode into downtown Montreal, Sourbier indicated that they would go straight to a meeting.

They went to the Mounties' headquarters, Peroff hurrying quickly through a back entrance. Sourbier led him downstairs into a large clubroom called the Sergeants' Mess. There were a bar and some card tables, and Sourbier fixed some drinks. Pierre Boudreau joined them, plus a corporal with the Mounties who was in charge of counterfeiting investigations. Also joining them, much to Peroff's discomfort, was a representative from the Drug Enforcement Administration.

The venture was to be carried out jointly by the Americans and the Canadians, but Peroff would have control over the operation itself. His task was to lure Bouchard into a transaction with the counterfeit money, using an FBI man who would pose as a crooked banker. If necessary, Peroff would introduce Bouchard to the "banker" and, in turn, the "banker" would attempt to buy the bogus paper for use in a deal of his own. Once Bouchard delivered the counterfeit bills, he would be arrested.

When the FBI agents arrived, Peroff conferred with them at one of the card tables. Concerned about his own protection, he told them, "If we sink Bouchard, then I want to be arrested along with

265

him. That's number one. You can get me out of the can later, but I don't want my cover blown."

"That's the plan," one of the agents said. "We arrest you, too."

"The second thing," Peroff went on, "is what happens if I *do* become hot. I mean, what if I'm really burned, you know?"

"There's a plan for that," they told him. "Arrangements have been made—if you get hot, everything will be taken care of. Don't worry."

"What kind of arrangements?"

"We don't know just what exactly, but we know there's a plan."

"That's right," the second agent said. "Trust us, Frank."

Discussion then turned to the operation at hand. Peroff was told to choose one of the FBI agents as his accomplice. He picked out the agent named Dominic Germano, who was tall and wore a mustache and, somehow, seemed to fit the part of a banker.

"First of all," he told Germano, "I'd like you to explain something to me. Why would the U. S. Government send FBI agents to help in a counterfeit investigation? That's handled by the Secret Service, right?"

"Yeah, but this is a special case. It's different."

"Well, I think you're bullshitting me. You're with the Service."

"No," Germano insisted. "Why do you think that?"

"Because everybody knows my feelings about the Service. They double-crossed me in the first place, you know. I think it's well-known that I don't trust you guys."

"Look, Frank, we're FBI!"

"Yeah? Let's see your IDs."

"We left them in the States. After all, Frank, this is an undercover job."

Peroff felt that the agent was lying, but there was no way to prove it. They discussed the operation some more and he concluded, "When I call Connie, I'll know if we have a deal. If we do, it'll happen very fast."

There in the Mounties' headquarters, he placed a call to Bouchard but got Victor Fauci on the line instead. "Conrad is here," Fauci reported, "but he can't come to the phone."

"Why not?"

"Well, he had too much to drink. There was a bad article about him in the paper today. He just got through vomiting in his own face."

Peroff took a room that night in the Martinique Hotel. Pierre Boudreau, the electronics man, had already set up his eavesdropping and wiretapping equipment next door. And Germano, the FBI agent, was in another room on a separate floor. In the morning, Peroff made phone contact with Bouchard and announced that he and his "banker friend from New York" were there in Montreal.

"I think I've got him hooked," Peroff said. "The guy is eager, you know?"

"Good, good."

"But he won't be here too long, Connie. He's nervous," Peroff added, going on to explain how the banker intended to use the counterfeit bills if he decided to buy them. He would give the $400,000 in phony Canadian hundreds to one of the bank's clients— "a guy who's bent, but with good standing and credit at the bank" —and this customer would come in and offer the bad Canadian currency as collateral against a loan of good American money. The crooked banker, of course, would oversee and direct the transaction.

"Okay," said Bouchard. "I'll be there in a few hours."

"You'll bring samples?"

"Yeah, yeah, yeah."

"Just *bring* the shit, Connie."

When Bouchard arrived, he called from a house phone in the lobby. "Is the guy up there?" he asked.

"Yeah, he's in his own room. You want to see him?"

"No, not now. Come down here alone."

Peroff went downstairs, but the lobby of the Martinique was empty. He looked through the glass doors and saw that a dark blue Buick was parked at the curb. Bouchard was seated in front with the driver, his face showing no expression. When Peroff approached, Bouchard quickly stepped from the car and told him to climb into the back seat. It was a two-door model, so that Peroff suddenly found himself a virtual prisoner.

"This is the printer," Bouchard said, nodding to the middle-aged man behind the wheel. "He can't understand English, so I'll have to translate."

"Let's see the stuff," Peroff said.

Bouchard conversed in French with the printer for a few minutes. The man appeared nervous and upset, glaring over his shoulder at Peroff and gesturing to Bouchard, who turned to the back seat again. He smiled slightly and said, "Frank, the guy thinks you're a cop. He smells a rat."

Peroff laughed uneasily, cursing aloud but wondering just how serious his situation was. "Fuck him," he said. "Didn't you tell him about you and me? About all the deals we've worked together?"

Now Bouchard spoke in French again, to the printer, who abruptly reached into his pocket and pulled out an old wrinkled bill. It was a Canadian hundred.

"What's this?" Peroff said as he took the bill.

"That's a real one," Bouchard said.

"So?"

But now the printer opened the glove compartment. He took out a small pad of lined, yellow paper and, from inside the pad, he pulled another Canadian hundred. This one was brand new and crisp, without a wrinkle.

"This is the sample," Bouchard said as the printer handed Peroff the second bill.

"Well," Peroff replied, "it's beautiful. But there's no way I can compare it with the old one. It's just impossible."

"It's a good job, eh?"

"Connie, it's almost too good to be true. I'll need time to examine it upstairs. My man up there will want to see it, too."

"Yah, Frank, go ahead. We'll ride around the block a while," Bouchard declared, letting him out of the car. Peroff kept both bills.

"Come back here in about twenty-five minutes," Peroff said.

"Fine."

As he walked through the lobby and into an elevator, Peroff could tell just by feeling the "bogus" bill that it was actually a real one. Unlike Bouchard's previous counterfeit money, this "sample" was engraved rather than the product of an offset machine. It was an old trick that counterfeiters used. They would show the buyer a real bill as a sample, to demonstrate the quality of their merchandise, and the buyer would pay a deposit on that basis. Then the actual counterfeit money, having nowhere near the same quality, would be delivered.

Peroff walked into Germano's room and told the agent, "Well, here's the sample. They're trying to pull some shit, though, because it's real. Connie's people just don't turn out counterfeit stuff this good. No way. This thing is made from plates. It's perfect, really a beautiful goddamn bill. But it ain't counterfeit. I knew it the minute I put my hands on it. I mean, money is money, and it's *impossible* to make a bill this good."

"Are you sure?" Germano asked.

"I'm positive. I don't know why, but it's a real bill."

"I'm not familiar with Canadian money, Frank. We'd better get the corporal in here," Germano added, turning to the wall and shouting, "Uh, come on over! We got the sample!"

The Mounties' counterfeiting expert, who had been waiting next door, now joined them in Germano's room. He looked at the hundred-dollar bill and said, "Hey, this is real!"

"Yeah," Peroff replied. "That's my opinion, too. I can't figure out why they did it, because Connie should know me better."

"Maybe they suspect you," the RCMP corporal said. "It could be a trap."

"It's possible," Peroff said, "but I don't think so. This kind of shit is pulled all the time."

"Well," the corporal went on, "let's forget the whole thing. Pack up, Frank. It's a dead issue."

"Wait a minute," Peroff told him. For the first time, he felt a real panic grow inside him, but not for the usual reasons. He was determined to have Bouchard put away, and the thought of simply calling off the operation was unbearable. "I'm not gonna pack up yet," he said. "Let me go down there again. I'm gonna go have a fight with him and play with his head. I know how Connie's mind works. He's so desperate for money, you have to realize—and, well, I just know I can pull this off."

"All right," the Mountie said. "But be careful."

Bouchard and his printer were parked across the street from the hotel. When they saw Peroff step outside, the printer started the engine of the Buick and turned into the driveway. Peroff got in the back seat again and they began riding around the streets of downtown Montreal.

"Well?" Bouchard said.

"You son of a bitch," Peroff replied.

"What?" said Bouchard, who was already laughing.

"Jesus, Connie, you know what! Look, you can't even keep a straight face!"

"What, what?"

"Come on, Connie, this bill here is real!"

"It is?"

"Connie, you of all the people in the *world* should know better! What the hell are you trying to pull? This banker up there is a guy that I'm gonna do a *lot* of business with, you know? He's waiting with real bread, man, and I gotta tell him the truth! And you turn around and make a jackass out of me! I had to *tell* him what you did here. He's upstairs in the hotel, Connie, and he's saying to forget the whole deal! He don't *want* to do business with you now. He don't trust you any more, and I think it's dead!"

While Peroff continued to scream, the printer drove around one block after another, bewildered by the argument, asking Bouchard in French what the trouble was. At last Bouchard said, "Look, Frank, *I* didn't know it was a good bill. *This* guy did it, not me! *He* pulled the fast one."

"Why?"

"Well, probably because the stuff is stashed so far away," Bouchard said, explaining that the counterfeit money was hidden in a house somewhere in the countryside outside Montreal. "He probably didn't have time to go get a sample, Frank! I don't know what the hell he gave you."

"Bullshit," Peroff shouted, and now he began tearing the hundred dollar bill, to show why he knew it wasn't counterfeit. The printer's eyebrows went up and he began shouting in French, realizing that Peroff was ruining his perfectly good money. "If this bill is bad," Peroff laughed, "then why's he getting so upset?"

Bouchard joined the laughter. "I don't know," he said. "Listen, what the hell do you want? How can we work this out?"

"Well, Connie, even to save it at this point, I'm gonna have to go back up there and literally kiss that guy. But I want, *right away,* at least two bills with the same serial number. That's the only way he'll believe it, this time." It was a good ploy, because the Mounties would want proof as well.

"It can't be right away," Bouchard said. "It's going to take at least three or four hours," he added, referring to the fact that the printer would have to drive out of town to get the counterfeit money and come all the way back again.

"Well, okay. I'll try to keep my man here. But I'm warning you —he's very upset."

"Tell him the samples are coming," Bouchard pleaded.

"All right. Listen, call me in a while."

They rode back to the Martinique Hotel and Peroff got out. The operation was still on.

As the car drove off, Peroff made a mental note of the number on the license plate. He went back up to his room and gave it to the Mounties, who ran an immediate check and identified the printer's name and address. They brought in some photographs and Peroff easily picked out the printer's face. The man was a known counterfeiter, so at least Bouchard was telling the truth about that aspect of the deal.

Bouchard called again that Saturday afternoon to say that the printer had gone "up to the mountains" to get the bogus bills. "It's a long drive," the French Canadian added. The waiting continued, with more phone calls from Bouchard well into the evening and, finally, past midnight.

From his end, Peroff tried to keep Bouchard filled with anxiety. "I don't even know where my banker is," he said.

"What do you mean?"

"Well, he went out. I thought he went to dinner, but he's not back yet."

"Jesus, Frank, this deal is on! The printer will be here tomorrow!"

At two in the morning, Bouchard made his final call and asked, "Is the guy back yet?"

"Nope. I don't know where he is, Connie. I don't think he's checked out of the hotel, but he's not back."

On Sunday morning the phone conversations resumed. Peroff decided to throw even more apprehension into Bouchard by telling him that the banker was *still* not in his hotel room.

"Maybe he found a broad," Bouchard said.

"Well, I don't know. Where's the samples?"

"There's just a little problem, Frank, but I'm trying to straighten it out."

"Hurry up, will ya?"

A while later Bouchard called back and, this time, Peroff told him that the banker had returned to the hotel. "But he's getting ready to check out, Connie. *Where's the stuff?*"

"It's here! It's here! But listen, Frank, there's still this problem."

"Goddamn it, what's the matter?"

"Well, look—*I'm* not controlling the deal," Bouchard said. "This printer and *his* people are in charge, you know? And they said that the only way they'll go ahead is if I can take you as hostage."

"What?"

"The deal is on, but they want Victor Fauci to take you up to the mountains. The printer will deal with your banker direct. But if anything goes wrong, we still got you. *I* didn't suggest it, Frank. They just want to be sure they get paid. They're worried about their bread, that's all."

Peroff said nothing for a moment, trying to imagine himself somewhere in the countryside, with Victor Fauci holding him hostage at gunpoint. It was unthinkable, of course, but he decided to call Bouchard's bluff. "Okay," he said. "Sure I'll go. I know the guy here has the money, so I'm not worried."

"Good," said Bouchard, who sounded somewhat surprised. If he had any suspicions about Peroff at all, now they seemed to have been wiped away.

"So when do we get the samples?" Peroff pressed him.

"They're on the way, Frank. For real. The stuff will be there in fifteen minutes. Wait out in front of your hotel. We'll send it over in a taxicab."

As promised, a cab pulled up outside the Martinique Hotel in less than twenty minutes. Peroff took an envelope from the driver and began walking away, but the cabbie said, "Hey! Nobody paid the fare!"

That's Connie for you, Peroff thought, reaching into his pocket and handing over some change. He walked back inside the hotel and opened the envelope on his way upstairs. There were two offset-printed Canadian hundreds, with no resemblance in quality to the brand-new real one. These bills were definitely counterfeit.

Back in his room, Peroff got on the phone and began bona fide negotiations with Bouchard, who demanded that the banker put 3 percent of the $400,000 figure—or $12,000 in cash—up front. This would be an advance against the full price, which was 7 percent or $28,000.

"Not on your life," Peroff said. "We're not putting up a dime in front, Connie."

"Look, it don't *belong* to me. I'm the, uh—how do you say? The middleman! I am just in the middle, here. And they won't give it up without some cash in advance, you know?"

"Damn it, Connie, you know me better than that," Peroff said, once again behaving the way he would if he were actually bargaining as a criminal. "It's not the way I do business, and that's that. Let's forget it and talk about it some other time."

The negotiations continued through the end of Sunday afternoon, but neither man would budge. Bouchard finally asked if he could come over and meet the banker. "Maybe I can persuade him," he said.

"I don't know. Connie. The guy's pissed off. He's so mad that he's already packing. He's gonna check out right now. I think he's in the lobby at this very moment."

"Stop him!" Bouchard screamed. "I'm coming over! I'll be right there! Hold him!"

Peroff and Germano went downstairs to meet Bouchard in the bar off the lobby. "Keep up the act," Peroff said. "Tell Connie that as far as you're concerned, the deal is off. Make him get down on his knees and beg."

In the bar the three men sat together at a table in the semi-darkness and Germano, playing his part as the banker, indicated that he was backing out of the counterfeit deal and leaving momentarily for New York.

Trying to convince Germano of his honesty and trustworthiness, Bouchard referred to his relationship with Peroff, going overboard and exaggerating here and there for effect. "We've known each other years and years," he said. "Me and Frank, here, we've *trusted* each other. We've done tens of millions of dollars' worth of business together. And there was never a problem. Nobody ever got beat.

So there's nothing to worry about, if you put some bread up front. I *guarantee* it."

"Nope," Germano said. "When we see the stuff, when we have it in our hands, then we'll pay for it."

On the actual sale of the counterfeit bills to Germano, Bouchard would get 2 percent based on the $400,000 worth of bad bills, or a mere $8,000. Peroff got an equal guarantee, but both men would receive their money from the "crooked banker" only *after* the loan was made in New York City. The printer alone wanted money up front.

"Well," Bouchard said, "let's do it in two lumps. I'm going to try to arrange for my people to come up with a small part of it, without *any* cash in advance from you. How's that?"

"Sounds fair," Germano said.

"I'll see if he can send about eighty grand of the stuff over here," Bouchard continued.

The meeting in the hotel bar broke up with handshakes all around. A short while later, Bouchard called Peroff's hotel room and said, "Okay, the stuff's on the way. Eighty-two grand. All hundreds. It'll come in a taxicab again. The driver will wait until your guy has a chance to check it out. No cash, until he's satisfied. If he is, then give the driver two percent of the delivery, and the cabbie'll bring the cash back to us."

The Canadian Mounties took over the Martinique Hotel as if an ambush of major proportions was about to take place. What did happen was the arrival, once again, of a taxicab. It was exactly seven o'clock on this Sunday evening, the fourth of November, when Peroff greeted the driver in the lobby.

"I'm Peroff," he said.

"This is for you," the cabbie replied, handing him a plastic shopping bag.

"Okay. I'll be back in a few minutes with an envelope for you."

He took the shopping bag and nervously stepped inside an elevator without pressing the button for his floor. He quickly reached into the bag and ripped through the paper wrappings and saw the counterfeit Canadian hundreds. There was no time to count all eight hundred and twenty bills, but the size of the load seemed right.

"This is it," he said to Dominic Germano, who was standing

right there. "All yours," he added, throwing the shopping bag to him. "I'm going upstairs."

(As soon as Peroff pressed the elevator button, at least twenty Mounties got ready to descend upon the unsuspecting cab driver, who was seated there waiting. There was utter confusion, however, because for some reason the Mounties thought that the driver had escaped. For fifteen minutes the plainclothesmen ran around as if they were in a Mack Sennett comedy, looking for a man who was right under their noses. Apparently they *saw* the driver but were unsure that he was their suspect. At last they approached the man, who had been watching them all the time, and placed him under arrest. Warrants were issued immediately for Bouchard's capture, on charges that he had arranged to pass the bogus bills.)

Upstairs, Peroff found that the door to his hotel room was locked. He had misplaced his key, so he went next door, where another group of Mounties was already celebrating. One of the Horsemen had broken out a bottle and drinks were being passed all around. Peroff lay down on the bed, on his back, watching them and trying to imagine what it was going to be like when he went to the Montreal jail. Maybe I'll get to confront Connie right there in the cell, he thought. That would be best—I can accuse *him* of the whole mess. Yeah, you were too hot, Connie, and you brought all of your fucking heat down on me, too! You bastard, Connie, look what you've done to me! Right, he thought, that way he'll never suspect me and then I'll be released because of some bullshit about the Americans wanting me on other charges or whatever. Beautiful, beautiful . . .

The partying went on and on, with Peroff as a kind of honored guest in the room. It was mentioned that the cab driver would be held for a while, although he was probably not involved at all. The cabbie would be kept in jail at least until the bail hearing. Word also came later that Bouchard had been caught trying to sneak into his house through a side door. No doubt he had become worried and upset when the cab driver had not returned.

At one point, Peroff overheard Dominic Germano say something and, if he wasn't mistaken, it had to do with the Secret Service. So I was right, Peroff thought. He's *not* an FBI agent.

Jean Sourbier, the Mountie in charge, came over and said, "Well, Frank, you did it. You sank Connie Bouchard."

"Do I get to confront him in the can?"

"No, no, no."

"Well," Peroff said, "when do I get arrested? And booked?"

"You don't, Frank. There's no need."

"What? I'm supposed to be busted!"

"It can't work that way," Sourbier said.

"Wait a minute," Peroff shouted, now off the bed and standing face-to-face with the Mountie. "What about my cover? Why not work it to throw me in the can and then squeeze me out? Otherwise you'll be blowing me sky high! I'll be burnt!"

"Nah, Frank, don't worry. Get your stuff, because I'm taking you to the airport right away. You'll be back in New York tonight. We'll just say that you escaped. You got away, that's all."

"How the fuck did I escape, when the hotel was crawling with you bastards? Who's gonna believe that story?"

There were no answers. Protesting all the way, feeling as if he might became a raving maniac, Peroff packed his bag and followed Sourbier into an unmarked police car. They sped to the Montreal airport in time for one of the last remaining flights to La Guardia. In the terminal building, Sourbier left him at the top of a stairway. As Peroff walked down toward his plane, the Mountie called to him, joking, "Listen, don't come back to Canada—I may have to arrest you!"

Peroff had no appreciation for the humor. He was glad that Bouchard was in custody, but his own situation was precarious. Once again, he thought, I'll have to explain how I escaped! Like in Paris! It's no good—why didn't they bust me like they said they would? Was this the setup? The trap? Or maybe I *won't* be hot. After all, Connie would never be able to *prove* I was under-cover. . . .

He kept walking toward the gate for his plane, refusing to turn his head and acknowledge the Mountie's last remark. During the flight, he tried to keep his thoughts on the positive side, reasoning that the Mounties would give him some sort of cover story about his having escaped arrest. The phrase "cover story" dredged up all of the old emotions from the year's events. He suddenly remembered the pledge by Tom Glazer of the Secret Service to give him a fake press release about the original counterfeit money. He hoped this experience would turn out on a different note.

Two DEA agents were waiting for him at the airport in New

York. Neither of them had any specific information about his situation, nor did they know exactly why or how long they would be protecting him and his family. It was confirmation, however, of the fact that the operation had been run jointly by the Mounties and the DEA, with the FBI supposedly supplying Germano as an undercover agent to help him.

"We're assigned to you," one of the DEA guards said. "We have orders to stay in your apartment."

Maybe it wasn't a setup after all, he thought. The Mounties and the DEA asked me to go up and sink Bouchard and I did it. Now maybe I'll get some of that bread they promised and get out of here, and why should I give a damn if the Senate does anything or not on the Vesco deal? At least I got Bouchard.

Three other DEA agents were in the Shelburne apartment when he arrived. Peroff greeted his wife (the children were sleeping by now) and ignored his protectors. On Monday morning he decided that he could not resist calling Roy Gibson, his former control agent. When he reached him he shouted, "Hey, did you hear what happened?"

"No, what?"

"We sunk Bouchard!"

"Yeah? On junk?"

"No, man, on a counterfeit deal! Didn't Reilly tell you?"

"Nope. I'm back at Customs, now."

"You left the DEA?"

"Yes, I—"

"How come?"

"Well," Gibson said, hesitating, "I just think I can work better with Customs."

"Are you sure it wasn't Reilly?" Peroff asked, trying to get the real answer.

But Gibson avoided the topic. "That's great news about Bouchard," he said, sounding as if he truly meant it.

Peroff was certain that Gibson's transfer had been motivated by the Vesco experience, even though Gibson himself was too "professional" to admit it. Later Peroff got on the phone with Jean Sourbier in Montreal to hear the latest news. Bouchard was being held without bail until a hearing on Wednesday.

"What about the papers?" Peroff asked.

The Mountie hesitated, then said, "Yeah, there was a story."

"What'd it say?"

"It gave news of the arrest," Sourbier replied.

"Yeah, but what about *me?* Did it say that I escaped?"

"No, Frank, it didn't. Somehow, the paper says you're a Government agent."

The fear, for his family and himself, was like nothing Peroff had ever experienced. It was as if a white flash of lightning had blasted through his insides, making him perspire until his clothes were soaked and giving him a sensation that he was falling down some huge, dark abyss. Was this the result of his having gone to the Senate with charges against the DEA? Now they've blown my cover, he thought. They've made me hot and turned me into a wanted man. Why? Why? Sourbier says that "what's done is done" and it "just worked out that way"—but why? Bouchard's people and every bad guy in the world will know that I was a rat—and how many of 'em know that I'm here at the Shelburne? Plenty. How many contracts will they put on me? Does the DEA expect me to run? Is that it? They think I'll be forced into hiding? And I'll forget the Senate thing? Is that what they're hoping?

As far as Peroff was concerned, he had as much to fear from the drug agents as he had from the mob. And the enemy was literally sitting in his own living room. How long the DEA agents would stay to protect him was unknown. But maybe, he thought, they're just here to see what I'll do! In fact, the DEA guards were answering all his calls for him and, without question, they were listening in on his conversations. Twice on Monday afternoon, however, there had been mob members on the line, trying to reach him. So it was important to have the agents' protection. It was essential for his family's safety, whether the agents were with the enemy or not. Ruth and the children had been instructed to stay inside the apartment at all times. Peroff remained in one of the bedrooms, refusing to speak to the agents.

He spoke on the phone that night with Phil Manuel and Bill Gallinaro, the Senate investigators, urging them to press the Rackets Committee into a decision. Then he could be transferred from the protection of the DEA to that of the U. S. marshals, under direct orders by Senator Jackson. Meanwhile he was at the mercy of the

DEA agents, needing their protection while, at the same time, fearing that they had put his life in danger in the first place.

"Just don't talk to anyone," Manuel said. "Not without one of us present. We've advised the U. S. Attorney's Office that your case is under investigation. If they want to talk to you at all, have 'em reach me first. That's an order."

Peroff was resting on his bed at ten-thirty the next morning, Tuesday, when four new DEA agents unexpectedly came into the apartment. Two of them walked into the bedroom where Peroff was still lounging in his pajamas. The agents stood on either side of the bed, staring down at him; and Peroff lay there watching them, bewildered.

"I'm here to serve a subpoena," one of the agents said, using a formal tone of voice as if he were making a speech. "I'm instructed to read it to you."

"Okay," Peroff said, not moving. "Go ahead."

The agent held up his long white document and proceeded to read: "Grand jury subpoena . . . United States District Court, Southern District of New York . . . To Frank Peroff . . . Greeting: We command you that all business and excuses being laid aside, you appear and attend before the grand inquest of the body of the people of the United States of America . . . to be held at Room 1401 in the U. S. Courthouse, Foley Square . . . on the sixth day of November, 1973, at 12:30 o'clock in the afternoon, to testify and give evidence . . . and that you produce at the time and place aforesaid the following: ALL TAPES AND/OR CASSETTES OF CONVERSATIONS BETWEEN FRANK PEROFF AND CONRAD BOUCHARD . . . And for failure to attend and produce the said documents you will be deemed guilty of contempt of Court and liable to penalties of the law . . . Signed, Paul J. Curran, United States Attorney for the Southern District of New York . . . Assistant, Jacob M. Tyler. . . ."

The agent read the entire subpoena down to its fine print. Peroff lay there staring up at the ceiling, not hearing much of it at all. The only part he had heard, clearly, was that he was being summoned to testify in court before a grand jury and that he should bring his Vesco tapes.

There was a silence when the DEA agent had finished. "Thank you," Peroff said.

"Well?" the agent replied.

"Well?"

"We have to go."

"What?"

"We're here to take you to the courthouse. I just read it to you."

"When? The grand jury is today?"

"Yeah, the sixth. At twelve thirty. Weren't you listening?"

"Nope."

"Well, you'd better get dressed."

"Mind if I do it in private?"

"Yes," the agent said.

So Peroff proceeded to put on some clothes while the two agents stood there in the bedroom watching him. "What is this," he grumbled, "Hitler time?"

The DEA agents drove him down to Foley Square and accompanied him up to Jacob Tyler's office. They waited with him just outside the door. The assistant U. S. Attorney came out and announced that he was pursuing his own investigation of Peroff's accusations that the DEA had sabotaged the heroin case. But it was clear to Peroff that Tyler had only started his own inquiry after he had heard about the Senate's possible involvement. And if, as Peroff suspected, Curran's office was on the same side as the DEA, then all they really wanted was to take the tapes away so his evidence would be gone. No way, he thought, is this guy really conducting an investigation. And this protection provided by the DEA is probably just until they can get their hands on the cassettes.

"You heard the subpoena?" Tyler asked.

"Yeah."

"So give me the tapes."

"What tapes?"

"Come on, Mr. Peroff! You want an investigation? Well, I'm conducting one!"

"I don't have the tapes," Peroff said. In fact, they were still lodged inside his copy of *Again, Dangerous Visions*, technically in Ruth's possession.

"Where are they?"

"I don't know. I'll do my best to find 'em."

Tyler turned and walked into his office. He came out again in a moment and said, "I'm having my secretary type up another subpoena. I'm serving you for this Friday, and you'd better have those tapes at that time."

"A funny thing," Peroff said. "I mean, those tapes were here twice before. Remember? And you didn't want to hear 'em, even."

"Are you trying to be a wise guy to me?"

"No, I'm really interested to know the answer. Why do you want them now, when you could have had them before?"

Before Tyler could answer, the secretary came with the new subpoena for Friday, when Peroff would go before a grand jury with his tapes. It was, he thought, a desperate attempt to get them before the Senate did.

In the afternoon, Bill Gallinaro of the Senate Committee spoke to Frank Peroff by phone and learned about the subpoena. The only answer, he urged, was for him to fly up to New York and get the tapes that night. "I'll come back down here to Washington and make some copies," he said. "That way, we'll have 'em no matter what. I'll get them back up to you before Friday, so you can still honor the subpoena and bring the original tapes to the grand jury."

Gallinaro immediately boarded a shuttle flight to La Guardia Airport. He took a cab to the Shelburne, arriving in the evening. He flashed his credentials at the DEA security guards, who had no idea that the tapes were still right there inside the apartment.

In the bedroom, he spoke with Peroff and his wife and looked in on the children in the adjoining room. They were just kids, the oldest only thirteen, and they were living in a situation that was almost intolerable.

"Okay, Frank," said Gallinaro. "We're gonna do this without you in the room. So if you have to say that you don't know where the tapes are, it won't be perjury."

When Peroff had left the bedroom, Gallinaro took the 760-page edition of *Again, Dangerous Visions*, with the cassettes inside, and dropped it into his attaché case. Then he walked through the living room, past the unsuspecting DEA guards, and out of the apartment.

Gallinaro arrived at La Guardia Airport just in time to catch the last shuttle flight back to Washington, D. C. He could feel a slight nervousness, an undercurrent of excitement, knowing that he was carrying evidence that could mean all the difference in Peroff's case, one way or the other. He stopped for the airport security man, placing his leather attaché case on the checking counter. The official unzipped it, took out the book, flipped through the pages and suddenly stopped, staring at the two cassettes which were imbedded inside.

"What is this?" the official said.

Saying nothing, Gallinaro took out his wallet and removed his credentials, which showed him to be a special investigator for the United States Senate and which also carried a photograph of the White House.

"Oh, Jesus!" the official whispered. "These are the tapes!"

The man was referring, Gallinaro knew, to President Nixon's "missing tapes" in the Watergate scandal. A policeman came over and grabbed the book to see for himself.

"Holy shit," the cop said. "All right, don't let anybody see you, let's go, come on!"

Gallinaro put the book back into his attaché case and followed the policeman, who was in a state of utter panic. The cop gave him full VIP treatment at the gate, nearly saluting as the Senate investigator boarded the plane with his valuable tapes. Gallinaro could hardly stop laughing during the flight home.

Peroff was beginning to feel the full impact of what had happened to him. If the whole mission to Canada was part of a continued conspiracy, first to stop the Vesco heroin case and now to keep him silent, then it had been not only a setup but an attempt to have him killed. The first time it had happened was when Mike Reilly had asked him to take a commercial flight down to Costa Rica. Now it was even more serious, with underworld figures right here in New York probably trying to come after him.

The safety of his family outweighed any other concern at the moment. If the Mounties made good on their promise of money, perhaps he could take it and make an escape, go somewhere else in the world and hide. Nothing was clear or certain as to which way he should move.

On Wednesday morning, however, the Mounties called to say that the Crown Prosecutor wanted a meeting with him. It required a brief return to Canada, under DEA guard. Peroff made the trip that morning and went under heavy protection to the DEA office at the U. S. Consulate in Montreal, where the Crown Prosecutor unexpectedly asked him to go into court for the hearing, to testify against Bouchard. Peroff wavered; he wasn't ready for such a confrontation and, besides, he was not about to volunteer himself as an open target for a bullet.

"What are you," the prosecutor demanded, "a coward?"

"You son of a bitch! Do you think you'd have the balls to do what I did?"

"Well," the prosecutor admitted, "I agree that you couldn't be any hotter than you are—so why not testify?"

"I'm not ready to go into that courtroom, period."

One of the DEA agents suddenly interjected, "Hey, Frank, what'd you tell the Senate down there?"

The question was a surprise, but it demonstrated the DEA's concern. "None of your business," Peroff replied.

He finally agreed to a compromise with the prosecutor, sitting down and giving him a twenty-page affidavit which could be brought into court on the counterfeit case.

At the same time that Peroff was flying back to New York City, the bail hearing went on as scheduled. The taxi driver was granted $5,000 personal bail and Bouchard, who was still being held as a prisoner, faced a postponement of five days. Dominic Germano testified during the hearing, however, and admitted that he was, in fact, a Secret Service agent. And Peroff's role as an undercover man was further exposed to the point where he would remain a hunted man forever.

The Montreal *Star* on the following day referred to Peroff as a "police informer" and added that a Mounted Police constable had testified in court "that he saw Bouchard, Peroff and four other men alight from a private jet at Windsor, Ontario" back in March. The others had been Maurice Dufrenne, Victor Fauci and the two pilots. The *Gazette* reported that the constable had "exhibited photographs taken of the group" and had "said he followed four of the men into downtown Windsor, then back to the airport." The photos were proof that Bouchard had disobeyed his bail instructions.

In other words, now it would be clear to Bouchard and to the Cotronis that Peroff had been an undercover man for at least several months. The Doctor's underworld group would know that Peroff had been responsible for the arrests of Savotok, Spellman and Handel in Paris. They would know that the story of the Chile money had been false. The mobs in Montreal, Detroit and New York would realize that Peroff had been working for the Government all during the hundred-fifty kilo case. The Florida mob would realize that they, too, had been dealing with an undercover agent. And the gold traders as well. not to mention underworld figures with whom Peroff had been in touch during that brief escapade. All of it was overwhelming to comprehend, not to mention Peroff's growing fear that the DEA also wanted him eliminated, for its own reasons. If he continued to fight back, to make accusations that the agents had sabotaged the heroin case, how fiercely would they retaliate? And what might Vesco's people do?

The turning point in Peroff's mind came on Thursday, the ninth of November, when Jean Sourbier of the Mounted Police called to say that the Canadian Government was offering him a reward of $100,000 if he would take his family to Australia and settle down with a land grant of 850 acres there. So now we have the kicker, he thought. They want to get rid of me, so first they make me hot as hell, hotter than any undercover agent ever has to be. Then they come up with the bread, but only if I'll go to Australia! They still think that I won't stand up to them. They think I'm just a two-bit informer who'll take their money and go hide wherever they tell me. They don't think I'll be able to resist it! They figure they know my mind, according to their rulebook again. *But they've tried to kill me twice!* The DEA has put the Mounties up to this offer, thinking I'll just take it. Then there won't be any investigation. They'll never pay for what they've done. They'll just go on, business as usual, because without me there's nobody to bring them down to their knees. And besides, if I *did* go to Australia, that would be the last that the world would ever hear of us. It's the equivalent of another trip to Costa Rica to get my head blown off. This time, somewhere in the bush country. What do they think I am, a total fool? They still don't believe I'm a man? That I have any principles? Why don't they know any better?

"I'll think it over," he told Sourbier, but his decision was already made.

Bill Gallinaro returned to New York that night with the tapes. Having made copies at his Senate office, he returned the originals to Ruth Peroff with a receipt for her to sign.

The investigator stayed for a while to chat with them, saying that his "discreet inquiries" were proceeding favorably and that he, too, believed that something much larger was behind the events which Peroff had experienced. "There was just no good reason to make you hot like that," he said. Still, there was no decision yet by Senator Jackson and his committee.

In the morning, Friday, Peroff prepared to bring the tapes with him to go before a grand jury. The same group of DEA agents joined the security guards in the living room and, shortly after, he went with them down to the courthouse again. He entered Jacob Tyler's office and saw that the assistant U. S. Attorney had two new agents with him. They were "internal security" men from the DEA and Customs, in charge of investigating any wrongdoing within their own agencies.

"Did you bring the tapes?" Tyler asked.

Peroff nodded. The two cassettes were in a pocket of his sports jacket.

"Will you give them to me?"

"No," Peroff replied. "But I'll give 'em to a grand jury. I'd *love* to testify and give the evidence."

Tyler gestured to the two agents, explaining that they were conducting an official investigation of the charges, but it occurred to Peroff that no grand jury was being contemplated at all. Had the subpoena been issued on false pretenses? Solely in order to get the tapes? Was it just a charade?

"Look," he said, "this subpoena says that I'm supposed to testify before a grand jury. Now, unless this is a miniature grand jury in this room, here, I think you've misused your powers."

"Mr. Peroff, we are here to listen to your statements and get your evidence! What more do you want?"

"I'm not supposed to talk to anyone without Phil Manuel."

Enraged, Tyler placed a call to the Senate committee and began a verbal battle with Manuel that lasted more than an hour. Eventually Peroff took the phone and Manuel told him, "You do what you want, Frank. I'll withdraw my instruction to you for *this* meeting only. You do what you want."

So Peroff made some statements to the agents from DEA and Customs, and he gave over his tapes. "But I want them back," he said. "You listen to them and—"

"No, no, we're not giving 'em back to you."

"Then I want copies for my possession. I don't trust any of you," he added, neglecting to mention that the Senate investigators also had copies. But the DEA agent made new copies and gave them to Peroff before he left the office.

Now that they have the tapes, he thought, I wonder how long they'll continue the protection. Will they try to force me into taking the land grant in Australia?

That night, Peroff had a new visitor. The DEA guards were in the living room, as usual, when one of their colleagues showed up with an envelope for Peroff. It contained five hundred dollars. To get this meager sum, he had to move himself and his family to another location—where, it didn't matter—as soon as possible. His protection was going to be removed in less than a week.

On the phone later that night, with Jean Sourbier of the RCMP in Montreal, Peroff made a frantic, desperate plea for assistance. When the Mountie asked if he was recording the call, Peroff denied it although, in fact, he was. He held the conversation from the bedroom of his apartment in the Shelburne. What follows is an edited version of what was recorded:

PEROFF: They're gonna take away the protection! And I don't understand, Jean, I don't understand! I can't *believe* that you're *agreeing* to all this shit.

SOURBIER: Agreeing to what?

PEROFF: To all that's *happening* to me. I'm here, I can't pay my rent, I don't have *food* money any more—and I'm hot as a pistol, you know? Before I went up to Canada last week I was *not* hot. Now all of a sudden my life is ten times worse than it was a week ago! It ain't *right*, Jean! I tried to do what was right!

SOURBIER: Yeah, but listen—do you think the DEA is really responsible for your protection?

PEROFF: You want to know why? Let me tell you why. Because when I went up there, everybody said there was a whole plan arranged if I became hot. I was told not to worry. And *you* said to me, Jean, that if I got hot that everything would be taken care of. *Trust* you, you kept telling me. *Trust* you. Now I don't undertsand why, *now*, all of a sudden there's a problem! Is it because the DEA *wants* it to be a problem?

286

SOURBIER: *You* are creating the problem, right now.

PEROFF: What am I supposed to do, take a gun and blow my brains out? Jean, Jean—you can't leave me without protection! I got three kids, babe! You can't *do* that to me. And a wife! The minute they see the DEA take off, I'm a dead guy!

SOURBIER: You think so?

PEROFF: I *know* it, Jean! They call every day! They called *today,* even.

SOURBIER: Who called today?

PEROFF: That's a good question. The DEA's answering my phone calls. Jean, I can understand problems about money. But I *can't* understand you taking the protection away. That's *ten times* more important to me than the money.

SOURBIER: Ten times more important?

PEROFF: Absolutely. I mean, it's my *life.* And it's my *family.*

SOURBIER: Yeah. Okay—how much money do you think you would require, at this time, to move out to a new hotel? A new location?

PEROFF: But if I do that, the DEA said they're gonna leave!

SOURBIER: Well, I'll get back to you.

PEROFF: Jean, listen—I'm not trying to give you heartaches. I'm just asking you one thing. Live up to the part about the *protection.* Because I'm *scared,* man.

An hour or so later, past midnight, the phone rang and Peroff quickly picked it up in the bedroom. He was certain that the DEA guards in the other room were listening, but it made no difference. He switched on his recorder again.

SOURBIER: What are you doing?

PEROFF: Thinking.

SOURBIER: Thinking what?

PEROFF: How much trouble I'm in.

SOURBIER: Well, I'll tell you the only thing I can come up with. They're gonna give you eight hundred dollars. Right now. And you're gonna take it and relocate yourself. I just can't help, this time, with the DEA. Because they have to move out. They have to drop you.

PEROFF: They're gonna leave me cold?

SOURBIER: That's between you and DEA, this thing.

PEROFF: But *you* promised me protection!

SOURBIER: Well, what am I supposed to do if the DEA wants to drop you? How can I convince them to stay with you?

PEROFF:	It's a real setup, isn't it? A real setup. The DEA wants me hit, don't they? This whole thing was a plan, wasn't it? Nobody intended to get me bread, or—
SOURBIER:	I tell you—I'm working hard to get you money. It still hasn't come. As soon as I—
PEROFF:	Just tell me one thing—which guy in the DEA was calling the shots? Was it Reilly?
SOURBIER:	I haven't talked to Reilly in the past three days.
PEROFF:	This is the second time Reilly's tried to set me up for a hit. Don't you understand what the hell is happening? They want me hit, Jean!
SOURBIER:	No, I wouldn't say so.
PEROFF:	Jean, they want me to get shot.
SOURBIER:	I think you're turning into a big sissy right now.
PEROFF:	You're damn right, because I got three kids!
SOURBIER:	Jesus Christ, three kids—I'll give you eight hundred dollars. You move out of the hotel. Once you've relocated, give me a call. I'll talk to you then.
PEROFF:	What you're saying, in other words, is to go fuck myself.
SOURBIER:	No, I'm doing my best to get you the bread.
PEROFF:	I don't *want* the bread! I told you—keep the bread and give me the protection! What happened to all the promises?
SOURBIER:	The protection you did get this week.
PEROFF:	Oh, so that's it—my life is worth a week.

Conrad Bouchard remained in confinement over the weekend. When he appeared at his court hearing on Monday, he was denied bail and sent back to prison. The prosecutor mentioned that Bouchard had four previous cases before the courts and that his official record covered "about every possible crime except murder." The history of his heroin-smuggling travels was outlined, including a review of his still-pending narcotics case which had involved ten million dollars' worth of powder. Once again, Frank Peroff was mentioned as a "police informer" who had worked with the Mounties and the U. S. Secret Service on the counterfeiting case.

The Canadian judge came down hard on Bouchard. "The best way to keep an eye on the accused," he said, "is to keep him within prison walls."

Peroff, who had remained under DEA protection at the Shelburne over the weekend, was informed that the guards would leave in less than twenty-four hours, at noon on Tuesday. One of the DEA agents also gave him eight hundred dollars on behalf of the Mounties and told him he had better relocate fast. The protection would be gone by noon tomorrow, no matter what he did.

The reality of exposing his family to the wrath of the underworld was almost too much for him. Once again he reached out and pleaded for help, this time to Jacob Tyler at the U. S. Attorney's Office. For the moment, he was unconcerned about his fight for the truth. "I can't be any hotter," he told Tyler. "They're getting off me by tomorrow noon—but I've received over a dozen phone calls this past week, since this thing happened. From bad guys, wanting to know where I am. I'm calling you now at the suggestion of Phil Manuel, because he feels that it's your responsibility."

It was true. Manuel had also advised him that the Senate committee still had not decided, officially, to take on his case. As long as he was not yet a witness, no protection from the U. S. marshals could be gotten for him.

While Peroff's tape recorder was running, Tyler informed him that he had "absolutely no control" over the DEA.

"Well," Peroff said, "you're the U. S. Attorney and I'm saying to you that if they pull these guys off me, I need protection."

"Why don't you call Mr. Manuel?" Tyler replied. "Maybe he can offer it."

"This is the second time that Mike Reilly has tried to set me up."

"Mr. Peroff, I must say I can't do anything insofar as your immediate problem is concerned."

"Well, every phone call that's come in here from the bad guys, it's been emphasized that there are cops here. And that's the only reason I haven't had any trouble. But if word gets out that I'm not protected, I'm going to be a dead man. I'm making a plea to you, Mr. Tyler. I'm calling because I'm scared. I'm not asking for any goddamn money. They can keep it. I'm looking for my neck protected. All I've tried to do from the time this thing started was to help the Government. And I've done them good. It hasn't been a dry run. They asked me to go up there and finally beat Bouchard. And I got him. And it was the *United States* that first got me involved. And they turned around and took that heroin case and shoved it down the drain. But they came back and they wanted Bouchard put away and I went up there and I did it. So now they're gonna just expose me? They made me *twice* as hot as I had to be.

Do you know what they're using in court, right now, to keep Bouchard in the can? Pictures of him and me in the Learjet in Windsor! They're absolutely showing Bouchard that there's no question that I've been in this thing from the very beginning. And they even put in the paper that I'm an undercover guy. What a crazy thing—they didn't have to do that. I think it was just another setup. And I think that this, what's going on right now, is one *more* phase in the whole goddamn plot. . . ."

Tyler responded to the plea by saying that he would get guidance from his superiors. When Peroff asked who had the power to summon help, Tyler replied, "It would seem to me that the man in charge of each of those agencies is the one who controls them. The ultimate, of course, is the President."

"I tried that once," Peroff said.

The protection went off, as expected, at noon. The DEA agents, who had been guarding the Peroff family at the Shelburne around the clock, walked away from the apartment and left them alone. Peroff locked the door and told everybody not to answer the phone if it rang. His life had been reduced to the singular task of personal survival. The U. S. Attorney's Office under Paul Curran and his assistant, Jacob Tyler, had come up with no help whatsoever. The Mounties were promising money, and the land grant in Australia was still available; but it would only take, Peroff thought, a fleeting moment for a bullet to shatter everything.

His first call was to the Senate committee, to Bill Gallinaro, who said he was trying to force a decision to make him a witness. Peroff then reached Wallace Turner of *The New York Times,* telling him all that had taken place and adding, "The DEA is off me, now, because they know I've gone to the Senate. They'd rather expose me and have me killed."

Turner, in San Francisco, said he would fly in right away. "Hold on," he said. "I'll try to help you, Frank."

"It's a different set of rules," Peroff said. "All I want from you is two things, if you can. First I want you to help me get the hell out of here. And then I want to get somewhere close to the Senate. Down in Washington."

While Turner was on his way to New York, Peroff called the office of Senator Henry Jackson, chairman of the Investigations Committee, begging for U. S. marshals' protection. Neither Jackson nor the committee's chief counsel would get on the line with him. An assistant took the phone and told him to try Phil Manuel, the chief investigator, but Manuel had gone on a trip to Florida.

"Meanwhile," Peroff screamed, "I'm gonna get a bullet in my head! What are you gonna *do* about it?"

"The Committee has to hold an executive session, before your protection can be authorized."

"Yeah," Peroff said, "but while you're all doing that, I'm sitting in a place where every bad guy in the world knows where I'm at. What good's your executive session if I'm dead?"

Wally Turner arrived in New York the next day and came up to the apartment. He took copious notes, as usual, and went outside again to arrange help. A few days later, one evening, the Peroff family—Frank and Ruth and the three children, with the thirty pieces of luggage and the French poodle—sneaked out of the Shelburne and climbed into a station wagon which Turner had arranged to drive. The car sped out of Manhattan, heading south, into an unknown future.

The Investigation

He was registered at the old, inconspicuous Jefferson Hotel in down-town Washington, D. C., under the name of Mr. James Gray. The Peroff family was in seclusion, in two adjoining suites on the fourth floor, waiting for official protection at the request of Senator Henry Jackson. The hotel rooms had been secured by Wallace Turner prior to their clandestine trip down from Manhattan.

Peroff had little money to live on until he could become an offi-cial Senate witness. Jean Sourbier and another Mountie did come with some funds for him, however. They flew down to Washington and waited at the Statler Hilton Hotel, just a couple of blocks from the Jefferson. Peroff arrived by cab, to give the impression that he was staying somewhere much farther away. As far as he was con-cerned, the Mounties could not be trusted any more than the federal agents. The Canadians may well have been used, he thought, to have him set up, or they might have done it with full knowledge.

Sourbier gave him $8,000 from the RCMP, all in cash, for his services. It was less than the huge amounts Peroff had been prom-ised, but he was in no position to turn it down. Then Sourbier reiterated his offer of more money if Peroff would only accept an Australian land grant.

"No thanks," Peroff told him. "I'm sure the DEA would love to see me run to Australia. But they're in for a full-scale war. They haven't seen the end of this. The Senate will get to the truth."

For Phil Manuel and Bill Gallinaro and other staff members of the Jackson Committee (Senate Permanent Subcommittee on In-vestigations), getting to the "truth" would prove to be an arduous, frustrating task. They faced a long series of unanswered questions, all under the heading of possible sabotage by the U. S. Government itself. Was there a deliberate act, by the Government, to kill its own heroin case? If so, who gave the orders? And why?

Up to July 6, 1973, the case had been building slowly but persistently. A 150-kilo heroin deal was being put together by the Montreal underworld and its contacts in France. The transportation from Europe to North America would be supplied by the Government's own undercover agent, Frank Peroff. The narcotics would be concealed aboard his private Learjet.

But then came word, while Peroff was still in Puerto Rico, that Robert Vesco would supply the money to buy the drugs. Peroff received orders from Conrad Bouchard to fly the jet first down to Costa Rica, to pick up $300,000 in cash.

The case still would have gone smoothly, at least to the point where Peroff would have arrived in Costa Rica to meet the financiers. But Mike Reilly of the DEA, speaking by phone from New York, suddenly suggested to Peroff that he fly *commercially* instead. Why?

As Senate investigators studied the case, there was no logical explanation for Reilly's suggestion. The staff noted, "If Peroff was to be of any use whatsoever in a heroin conspiracy, it was to provide an executive jet. Without the executive jet, he was just another person to share in the profit, a person Conrad Bouchard and others could easily do without."

Was the suggestion to fly commercially to Costa Rica the result of mere stupidity? Or was it the beginning of the sabotage? Was it a deliberate attempt to stop the heroin case by forcing Peroff himself to back out of it?

The Senate investigators posed dozens more questions which were only logical when viewed as part of continuing sabotage by the Government. Once Peroff had been made to balk, it was easy to pin all blame on him for the case coming to a stop. Why wouldn't Reilly permit another agency such as the FBI to get involved? Was that plea on Peroff's part too much to ask? And why, when Peroff mentioned that he might seek help from the Senate, did Reilly suggest that he'd be "a walking dead man"? Why such fear of a third party's objective eyes?

293

And why was there an argument over Peroff's bringing his family with him from Puerto Rico to New York? In the first place, there had been agreement on that point; and Agent Luis Cruz of the DEA had helped the Peroffs move, on orders from his superiors. The Senate investigators made the following observation as well: "Spokesmen from DEA acknowledge that Peroff was owed more than $1,000 at a time when his rent was due in Puerto Rico, when he had no other apparent means of support, when he was still reporting to DEA agents on his contacts with Bouchard. Again, his payments were delayed. There was, under these circumstances, considerable logic to Peroff's bringing his family to New York, in that they had no place to stay in Puerto Rico." Was Reilly's anger a means to further aggravate the situation and justify his foiling of the heroin case?

And why, when the Peroffs landed at Kennedy Airport, did Roy Gibson and the other DEA agent simply walk away and abandon them? Investigators for the Subcommittee were incensed over that part of the story. "Against the backdrop of a man certain that his life was in danger," they wrote, "it took an exceptionally unfeeling and hateful decision to leave Peroff standing alone with his family July 17 in the lobby of Kennedy Airport. It was a fact that Peroff had been on the phone planning a major narcotics deal with Bouchard, and it was a fact that Bouchard did believe Peroff had a Learjet, and it was a fact that Peroff did owe some sort of a logical explanation to Bouchard when plans changed. The Government had put Peroff up to entering into his talks with Bouchard. The Government was obliged, the staff finds, to help Peroff out of his relationship with Bouchard."

The real possibility was that Peroff could have been murdered if he had made a false move with Bouchard. "It is difficult to understand," the investigators said, "how Reilly could have allowed his subordinate, Roy Gibson, to abandon the Peroffs at that point. Professionalism, coupled with a sense of decency, should have compelled federal drug agents to take steps to help Peroff explain to Bouchard in a persuasive way why he, Peroff, was dropping out. But no such steps were taken."

One fact established quickly by the Senate staff was that Peroff had made the calls to the White House, as he claimed. Records from the Hilton Inn near Kennedy Airport showed that he had placed at least ten calls to the White House, the conversations lasting from ten minutes to an hour. Yet the investigators could not obtain cooperation from the White House to verify or disprove Peroff's claim that he had received half a dozen calls in return. Why? How could the Executive Branch simply avoid examination by representatives of the public? And on so simple a matter as telephone-call records?

Furthermore it turned out that the men with whom Peroff had spoken were Secret Service agents at the White House, not aides of J. Fred Buzhardt, as they had identified themselves. Why? And why, upon request, did Buzhardt refuse to confirm or deny that he himself had conversed with Peroff twice? Why didn't John Wing of the U. S. Attorney's Office call Peroff back, as he had promised? Why didn't someone from the Government wish to monitor Peroff's call from Costa Rica at the International Hotel? And why was Peroff arrested, when it was obvious that the Secret Service had checked his identity with federal drug agents? Besides, the arrest was for Florida warrants which had been well known to authorities for months. And to top it off, the warrants turned out to have been false, without any basis, from the beginning. What sense did any of it make?

The questions continued. Why did Roy Gibson order Peroff, as a condition of his release from jail, to go up to Montreal? What was the purpose, when he was supposed to be in Costa Rica? Why, at that point, was Gibson still going through the motions of getting details of how to lease a new Learjet? And in Montreal, why did Hal Roberts of the DEA tell Peroff to ask Bouchard for money for the plane lease? Why so, when Bouchard had agreed to let Peroff "take $20,000 off the top" from the cash he would receive in Costa Rica? Was all this activity an attempt by the DEA to make the heroin deal die, this time, by *Bouchard's* hands?

There seemed no other way to explain the events that soon followed. Why, when Bouchard was on his way to Peroff's hotel in Montreal with some money, did the Mounties—at the request of the Americans—suddenly whisk Peroff out of Montreal? Why wasn't he allowed to call Bouchard with an explanation? Did the authorities cut off Bouchard's phone so that Peroff couldn't reach him? And a day later, why did Roy Gibson instruct Peroff to tell Bouchard that "the plane was repossessed"? At that point, the sabotage was complete.

A second overall question then developed. After the deal had died, Peroff began to fight back by seeking an independent investigation. Did a massive "coverup" of the sabotage then begin, in response? Was the U. S. Attorney's Office part of it?

When Jacob Tyler of that office was put in charge of following up Peroff's allegations, why didn't he want to listen to the crucial tapes with Vesco's and LeBlanc's names? Why did Tyler insist on making those charges known to the DEA, the very agency under suspicion? Who broke into Peroff's hotel-apartment room in New York and stole all but those two tapes, which had been in Ruth Peroff's purse? Why did Tyler drop his "investigation" so quickly? And why, after it became known that Peroff had made contact with the Senate committee, did Tyler suddenly "reopen" his inquiry? Why, with equal abruptness, was he now so eager to hear the tapes? Had Tyler been forced to put on a greater show of concern?

During that period, Peroff was asked to go to Montreal again, this time to entrap Bouchard on a new counterfeit-money scheme. Why was he told that he would be working with the FBI when it was, in fact, the Secret Service? Why was the DEA involved? Why, when Bouchard was arrested, didn't the Mounties also take Peroff as a prisoner in order to conceal his undercover role?

Why was the DEA suddenly in charge of "protecting" Peroff and his family in New York? Why did Dominic Germano of the Secret Service stand up at Bouchard's bail hearing and identify Peroff as the informant? Why deliberately make him a marked man?

Meanwhile, Jacob Tyler was summoning Peroff to a grand jury. When Peroff arrived at the U. S. Attorney's Office, he was told to hand over his tapes. Wasn't that a misuse of a grand-jury subpoena? And why did Tyler proceed to interview Peroff in the presence of two agents from the DEA and Customs? Both agents were, in fact, trying to defend their own agencies against Peroff's allegations!

Why did the DEA remove its "protection" of the Peroff family so quickly, leaving them in desperate financial straits and in fear for their lives again? Was it hoped that Peroff would accept the $100,000 and run to Australia? Was it all part of a conspiracy—by the DEA,

Customs, the Secret Service, the White House, and the Justice Department—to cover up the sabotage and prevent Peroff from making his charges public?

In late November, 1973, while Peroff and his family were still at the Jefferson Hotel in Washington, Wallace Turner broke the story first in *The New York Times*. The next day, *The Washington Post* printed a longer article which stated that so far Peroff's claims had "withstood intense checking" by the Senate committee. Turner then followed his own effort on page one of the *Times* and, by then, the story had broken wide open.

Senate investigators had to wonder if the Government's coverup was now continuing in the press. For the first time, the DEA was being required to respond publicly—with the advantage, however, of being able to fool the public by relying on the complexity of the case.

The opening shot of the battle, from the DEA, came from a spokesman named George Brosan, who came up with the startling explanation that Conrad Bouchard had been lying to Frank Peroff all along! Why? Because Bouchard "really wanted to have Mr. Peroff's airplane available, so he could escape from Canada if his trial on the earlier narcotics charge went against him."

Peroff was flabbergasted by the statement. In a formal reply for the benefit of the Senate committee's staff, he argued, "If Bouchard's intention was to use me to escape from Canada, why would he have instructed me to go *directly* to Costa Rica to pick up the $300,000 from Vesco or LeBlanc? Certainly, if acting on instructions from Bouchard I proceeded directly to Costa Rica, one of two things would have happened: Either I would have picked up the money as directed or I would not. If I had, the case would have been made. If I didn't pick up the money, Bouchard would never leave Canada through me."

Besides, Peroff went on, there *was* an escape plan for Bouchard. He knew about it and so did the federal agents. All Bouchard had to do was *ask* to be flown out of Canada, but he did not. Instead he told Peroff to fly down to Costa Rica by himself.

And if, in fact, Bouchard was lying, why didn't Mike Reilly just say so? Why go through the whole charade that followed?

Well, Brosan was only "hazarding a guess" that Bouchard

had been lying. He "really had no hard evidence" for the guess.

Wallace Turner reported that there was "no indication that the DEA or Customs had tried to explore the chain of their underworld contacts, to determine whether Mr. Vesco actually was involved in the heroin scheme."

Brosan told reporters, "Peroff's story about Vesco was a little wild, as far as we were concerned, but we told him to go to Montreal and try to get more of a line on the plot." What Brosan forgot to mention was that, before going to Montreal, Peroff had reached out to the White House and then had been thrown in jail. By the time he was sent back to Montreal, he was being ordered to blackmail Bouchard by asking for advance money.

Another statement by the DEA was that the Mounties had reported that Bouchard had *not* been meeting with Pepe Cotroni at all, during the critical month of July. But Peroff pointed out to Senate investigators that the Mounties "repeatedly told me during that period that Bouchard was definitely meeting with Cotroni on a daily basis."

So the DEA had put up its first public defense by stating that, in its opinion, there had never been any real heroin scheme. Its second defense was that, in any event, Peroff had been "too hard to handle" as an informant. He had demanded money, he had made accusations, and so forth. The Senate committee staff reacted with a vengeance against that excuse:

> Evidence shows that Peroff was after money. But it is also apparent that Peroff, if nothing else, was a reliable informant. In Paris, Rome, New York, Montreal, and Windsor, Ontario, and in Puerto Rico, Peroff did his job and he did it well. If it was distasteful to have to work with Peroff which, for some agents, it apparently was, that may be reason enough to dislike and disrespect and even hate him. But it is no basis to assert that Peroff was not giving the government its money's worth. The staff finds that Peroff did carry out the duties that federal agents asked of him.

> Accordingly it is the view of the staff that Peroff had every right to expect a reward for working as an undercover agent. Twice, and perhaps more than that, the government did not pay Peroff what was his due. A factor in his constant complaints about not being paid what he was worth was the fact that on two occasions he was not paid at all, when he deserved to be.

The staff finds that Peroff was motivated by factors in addition to money, particularly as his involvement in the case grew deeper. As 1973 wore on, as spring gave way to summer, Peroff became more and more convinced that he and his family's lives were in danger, and that they needed some form of protection.

To be sure, Peroff lived fast and high and demanded money all the time. But to say that his only desire in his informant work was money is only partly true. It is the staff's view that until he could be assured of relocation assistance from the government, he had no choice but to remain on as an informant. At least then he had some semblance of protection.

The staff acknowledges that Frank Peroff—manipulator, swindler, confidence man, individual of devious means—may have an extraordinary ability to inspire anger in others. But professional drug-enforcement officers, particularly those who function at group-supervisor levels, perform best when they do not allow their personal feelings toward others to influence their judgment. Federal heroin investigations should be ended, not in the terminals of major airports, and not in fits of pique, but objectively, privately, professionally, and according to established procedures and regulations.

The staff went on to say that the Peroff case "demonstrates in detail an aspect of government operations little-known to the Congress or the American people." That aspect was the manner in which federal agents use their underworld sources. By nature, the Peroffs of the world are of questionable moral fiber, but who else normally comes upon information about heroin smuggling? The relationship between the Government and its informants is tenuous at best, ironically built on trust while informants *by definition* are untrustworthy.

"They are selling out trusted associates for a price. Agents know this and must act accordingly. . . . Informants perform a service, but have no avenue of appeal if they feel they have been wronged. They have no recourse but to accept whatever payment for their services federal agencies decide to give them."

Peroff, for example, had been promised $250,000 if he uncovered a heroin lab. But after he was deeply involved, the agents changed the direction of the case and withdrew their promise. Beyond that, "Peroff was, in a sense, being employed by the government. He was given expense money, he was given directions by officials, he was met at airports by government agents, he was given tape-recording equipment by agents, and they paid his hotel and phone bills. Since he had no other job he became almost a ward of the government. The question is, why was it so difficult for him to receive the money that was owed him?"

As for Peroff's accusations, it is conceivable that an informant may be the only "outside" person to know that a case was bungled or killed, for whatever reason. But "because there is no accountability" required of the agents, "they have the unique capability to cover up their own failures, their own shortcomings, their own jealousies and arrogance."

The DEA's contention that the heroin deal had never existed, plus its depiction of Peroff as unruly and unreliable, was followed by denials and reactions from elsewhere. Robert Vesco himself issued a statement claiming that the whole story was a "foul and sneaking lie." He denied everything. And the White House stated "categorically" that there was no high-level involvement in the matter.

Even Conrad Bouchard got into the act. Perhaps taking his cue from the DEA statement that he'd been lying, Bouchard claimed that yes, he had misled Frank Peroff from almost the beginning, at least since May. While Bouchard remained in a Montreal prison, a legal associate told reporters that the underworld figure had led Peroff "down the garden path."

"Bouchard knew in May that Peroff was working for the U. S. authorities. Peroff was baiting Bouchard, attempting to get him involved in some criminal activity, so Bouchard decided to turn the tables on him. Bouchard felt certain the conversations were being taped or that Peroff was keeping police informed, so he invented the Vesco story. It just happened that Vesco's name was appearing in newspapers at the time. Bouchard could have used any old name. Once he realized that Peroff was an undercover agent, he started running him crazy. Bouchard sent him on a wild goose chase around the world."

It was an absurd contention on its face, reconstructed with the benefit of the current newspaper stories. If Bouchard had known

300

everything since May, why had he allowed *himself* to be duped on a counterfeit deal with Frank Peroff? Why had Bouchard dealt with someone whom he "knew" to be an informant?

At first glance, Bouchard's statement seemed to fall in line with the DEA's explanation of the case. But at second glance, it was a total contradiction. What happened to the theory that Bouchard had been stringing Peroff along, hoping to use his plane for an escape? How could he think of escaping with an undercover agent?

And at third glance, the Bouchard statement could be shattered completely. If Bouchard felt that Peroff was working for the Government, how could he "turn the tables" on him? To what end? Why endanger his own situation, which was precarious enough? Why be willing to come up with money for the Learjet? Why make phone calls from Peroff's hotel rooms in Montreal, if agents were listening? Why mention Pepe Cotroni's name on the phone? Why play such a frivolous game when the stakes, for Bouchard himself, were so high? Why, when he faced trials of his own, would Bouchard jeopardize his chance for freedom? To send Peroff on a "wild goose chase" around the world? What goose chase? Peroff was going nowhere from Costa Rica until he picked up the money!

The fact was, Bouchard had gone to prison, where he now sat, because he had maintained his trust in Frank Peroff. And he was making statements of innocence in order to avoid disaster in his upcoming trials.

The burst of publicity served to push the Jackson Subcommittee into more speedy action. Before Christmas, 1973, Peroff was made an official witness of the Senate and, at Jackson's request, the Justice Department dispatched its marshals to maintain around-the-clock protection. (The irony of his situation was not lost on Peroff. The DEA was *also* under the wing of the Justice Department, so that he could not be blamed for a certain lack of enthusiasm for the protection offered.)

From the fifteenth of December onward, two marshals were always on duty at the Jefferson Hotel, each pair working twelve-hour shifts. Under terms stipulated by the Witness Protection Act, the Peroff family began receiving monthly payments of $1,080 from the office of the Attorney General. And by Christmas they were

relocated to a house in Maryland, again accompanied by the marshals wherever they went.

The "inquiries" into Peroff's allegations had been completed by
the U. S. Attorney's Office in New York and by the DEA along
with Customs. Assistant U. S. Attorney Jacob Tyler found that
there had been no possibility of resurrecting the Vesco lead in
time to do anything about it; and, second, he found that there had
been "no effort" by the DEA to protect Vesco by sabotaging the
heroin case. Then the joint Customs-DEA inquiry was written up
in a report which exonerated all federal agents of dereliction of
duty. The report said that if anyone had failed to live up to what
was expected of him, it was Frank Peroff.

Was the DEA-Customs report another in its efforts to continue
a coverup? The report concluded that the reason why the Vesco
lead had never been pursued properly was that "Frank Peroff
refused to fly to Costa Rica."

The Senate committee staff saw that statement as "foremost
among the untruths" which it had uncovered so far. The conclusion was "simple-minded at best. It ignores the facts of the case,
facts which comprehensive investigation would have revealed. The
manner in which Peroff was to fly to Costa Rica was the crucial
factor in his unwillingness to go. Yet the DEA-Customs conclusion
neglects to mention that aspect of the Costa Rica trip."

> In a word, the conclusion of the DEA-Customs inquiry that Peroff
> undercut the Vesco-LeBlanc lead is incorrect. The conclusion
> misses the essential point of the dispute concerning the Costa Rica
> trip. Peroff wanted to fly into the Central American nation in a
> private jet. For reasons not altogether apparent, Mike Reilly of
> the DEA decided that Peroff must travel commercially. For the
> DEA and Customs to arrive at its conclusion without mentioning
> the dispute over the plane indicates that either the officials who
> wrote the conclusion did not fully understand the case, or they
> were determined to exonerate federal agents and put the blame on
> Peroff, no matter what.
>
> That conclusion is typical of the tone of the entire DEA-Customs
> investigation. It was structured so as not to arrive at any informa-
> tion that might demonstrate shortcomings on the part of federal
> personnel. No one person or federal agency is perfect. Surely an

objective assessment of the Peroff controversy would have concluded that some of the problems that emerged in the heroin case were not the sole responsibility of Frank Peroff. Instead the DEA-Customs inquiry completely exonerates all federal personnel of any mistakes. The inquiry would have the Subcommittee believe that everything that went wrong was Frank Peroff's fault.

The sweeping exoneration of all government wrongdoing or incompetence is a practice federal agencies have used in the past. "Deny everything" is a tactic federal bureaus have deployed before Congress before. Of late, the tactic has come to be known by the generic term "stonewalling." By whatever name, the device is not a credit to public service and the public servants who use it.

The Senate investigators saved their biggest blast against the DEA-Customs report until the end. It was "an effort to cover up bureaucratic and investigatory blunders" and, therefore, a new inquiry should be made by those who would be "less defensive about the agencies they work for and more determined to get to the truth."

Into the new year of 1974, Senate investigators grew more deeply involved in the arduous task of developing Peroff's full story in detail, trying to verify facts on their own through documents and corroboration. Each day, Peroff was brought by the marshals into downtown Washington, D.C., to the subcommittee headquarters in the Old Senate Office Building. From morning until night he would go over and over his version of the events from January of the previous year. Slowly, painstakingly, the investigators began to believe that he was telling the full and complete truth, from his vantage point.

"If we catch you in just one tiny lie," Manuel had warned him, "you're finished. We'll turn it against you."

In early February, the Canadian courts found Conrad Bouchard guilty of his previous heroin charges. The Sessions judge declared that "the proven facts indicate that the accused was the guiding hand in the heroin trafficking that occurred" more than two years beforehand. About three weeks later, Bouchard was sentenced to "two life terms" in prison.

"The importing and trafficking of heroin," the judge noted,

"are recognized as the worst forms of pollution, as they serve to destroy human beings."

Also noted by the judge was the fact that Bouchard had been arrested and placed again in prison back in November, "while he was at liberty pending these and other charges." So the counterfeit case caused by Peroff's undercover work, not to mention the publicity over the Vesco matter, had made it far easier for the judge to order such a severe punishment. Bouchard would never be a free man again.

According to the Montreal *Gazette,* the concurrent life sentences were handed down "in a courtroom packed with lawyers, police and Bouchard's friends and relatives." The decision had concluded "one of the major narcotics cases of recent years."

Bouchard had been surrounded by eight guards. He had stood impassively as the judge had read his thirteen-page decision. Then, Bouchard's wife burst out crying and rushed to embrace him. Later, outside the courtroom, one of Bouchard's sons (by a previous marriage) slammed his fist into the wall.

In late April, former Attorney General John Mitchell and former Commerce Secretary Maurice Stans were acquitted of federal charges of conspiracy, obstruction of justice, and perjury. Afterward, Prosecutor John Wing of Curran's office found himself surrounded by reporters who wanted to know if the case would have gone the other way had Vesco been extradited in time for the trial. Wing, who had listened to Frank Peroff eight months ago describing his information that Vesco was involved in heroin traffic, gave his reply: "If we could have gotten Vesco back, it would have been different."

Frank Peroff testified in secret before the Jackson Committee on the seventeenth of May, nearly eight months after he had made his initial call to Phil Manuel, the chief investigator. His statement was typed out on sixty pages, double-spaced, and he read aloud to the Senators during most of that Friday. He gulped water and puffed cigarettes and, on several occasions, sat back while supporting documents were introduced. Twice during his testimony, the key tapes were played in full. The Senators listened to Conrad Bouchard in Montreal speaking to Frank Peroff in San Juan,

Puerto Rico, discussing the large shipment of heroin, Robert Vesco, Norman LeBlanc, Costa Rica, the Learjet, the $300,000—all in cryptic yet unmistakable language.

Peroff admitted to the Senators that "over the years I have been involved in various forms of criminal activity, all of it prior to January of 1973." He described his wheeling and dealing as mainly involving "international fraud and traffic in stolen securities and counterfeit money." His background, he argued, was at the root of his ability to "penetrate international criminal groups"—such as the Montreal mob—in the first place. He added that his dealings with Bouchard "ran into the millions of dollars' worth of bad paper" and mentioned that his ability to use private planes was well-known and valued by Bouchard.

"I had a reputation," he said. "I could fly in and out of the United States, Canada and elsewhere, undetected. It was Bouchard's belief in that capability which enabled me to be effective as an undercover man."

Ruth also appeared at the Old Senate Office Building that day, issuing a sworn statement of eight pages without having to read it aloud. The entire ordeal had been a "nightmare," she recalled.

"We both felt that things started going wrong immediately after the name of Robert Vesco was brought into the case," she testified. "We felt that this fact and this alone was the reason for the death of the case."

And now that they both had had the chance to tell their story to the Senate, what would happen? Peroff, unable to believe that he really had cause for hope anymore, simply returned to his temporary home, under guard, and sat down to wait still further. What was he waiting for? The truth, he would say. The full truth, out in the open, from all sides. A man who had spent his entire life using the fine art of deceit had come to know truth as his only salvation.

Following Peroff into the hearing room, to testify secretly before Senators of the Jackson Committee, was a parade of witnesses from the Government. They included Customs Commissioner Acree, DEA Administrator John Bartels, U. S. Attorney Paul Curran and his assistant, John Wing. Also taking the oath were Mike Reilly, Roy Gibson and Hal Roberts of the DEA, plus Peter Grant of the

Secret Service and others in the drama, collectively giving more than fifty hours of sworn testimony.

In his statement to the Senators, Mike Reilly made the following assertions, among others:

1. That Peroff was an untested and ineffective informant, motivated purely by a desire to extract large amounts of money from federal agents and give nothing in return.

2. That from the very beginning, Reilly did not have any confidence in the July 6 tape in which Bouchard implicated Vesco.

3. That the reference to Vesco was a ploy by Bouchard to keep Peroff's Learjet available for an escape from Canada.

4. That he only mentioned the possibility of Peroff flying commercially to Costa Rica the day before Peroff left Puerto Rico for New York (a week after Peroff's recollection).

5. That he was outraged when he learned Peroff had called the White House.

6. That *he himself* had initiated action to have Peroff arrested, immediately after hearing about the warrants. He took the action because Peroff "was a fugitive, the warrants called for his arrest." He also initiated the action, he said, to coerce Peroff into being more cooperative.

7. That the heroin scheme was never real, that Cotroni was in no positon to involve himself in such a plan, and that Bouchard's reputation was so diminished by legal problems that no gangster of any consequence would do business with him.

Senate investigators, listening to Reilly on the sidelines, had Government documents showing that Peroff himself had met with Pepe Cotroni and that a major heroin operation had been, in fact, planned by Cotroni. The point was that the heroin scheme was either possible or it wasn't. "If it *was* possible," the committee staff wrote, "then Reilly's testimony and professional judgment were wrong. If it *wasn't* possible, then there was absolutely no justification for Peroff's continued use as an informant. In either case, the staff finds, the explanations offered Senators by Reilly and by other government witnesses are altogether unsatisfactory."

The staff also found Reilly's outrage over Peroff's complaints to the White House to mean that he "misunderstood the nature" of the informant with whom he was dealing:

It was typical of Peroff to try to go over the heads of government personnel with whom he disagreed. Had Reilly taken the time to read the file on Peroff, he would have know that. Had Reilly taken the time to learn the Bouchard heroin case that Peroff was working on, he would have known that Peroff, afraid for his life, resentful that money owed him had been delayed for so long, would probably do just what he did do.

The matter of Peroff's arrest also baffled and angered the investigators. Mike Reilly testified that he set in motion the events leading to Peroff's arrest *through his subordinate, Roy Gibson,* who got in touch with the interested authorities. Yet Gibson took the oath and swore that he had nothing to do with the arrest, directly or indirectly! Which man was telling the truth? The committee staff found it possible that neither man was being truthful.

> It is incredible—a kind of sordid, Keystone cop routine—to imagine the same federal government that went to such lengths to have Peroff put in jail [suddenly] working behind the scenes to get him out of jail. The staff finds that such performance by federal agents —men authorized to protect the American citizenry from criminals —to be an almost humorous but nonetheless tragic display of stupidity, incompetence, arrogance and unprofessional behavior. The only character in this tragicomedy who seemed to know what he was doing was Frank Peroff. He wanted to pursue the heroin case. What Mike Reilly, Roy Gibson and their colleagues wished to pursue is anybody's guess.

> Reilly's and Gibson's explanations of the jailing episode were inconclusive. If the DEA truly believed that Peroff could be of assistance in a heroin inquiry, the one action that reasonable DEA officials would not be expected to take at this time was to arrange for Peroff to be imprisoned. The staff finds Peroff's going to jail at this point to defy logic. But, once they had succeeded in jailing Peroff, to then have him released and *re-engage* him in the heroin inquiry is to defy logic again.

> These actions by DEA authorities raise questions about their frequent assertions that Peroff was uncooperative. At times, Mike Reilly and Roy Gibson and others seemed to be the uncooperative ones.

The Senate investigators were unhappy with most of the testimony because of its "inconclusiveness" on so many points. For example, various DEA agents differed on the reason why Peroff was sent to Montreal upon his release from jail, to the point where the staff found "a deliberate effort to confuse the hearing record."

And senior Justice Department officials were found to be too general in their answers concerning their dealings with Peroff and each other. Neither John Wing nor Jacob Tyler could even remember what month they first learned of the case. The "vague memory" of senior federal officers was again seen as deliberate, "another in a series of efforts" to spread confusion.

> For example, the poor memories of Wing and Tyler in connection with their first recollection of Peroff and his allegations are unexpected. Peroff was saying things that were substantive-enough-sounding to Wing that he stayed on the phone for about an hour with Peroff, to listen to what he had to say. Vesco's name came up, and Vesco was one of three men under indictment in a major case which Wing was prosecuting. The staff finds that it is incredible and altogether unlikely that Wing would testify before this Subcommittee that after one hour of talk with Peroff on this subject, Wing did not write a memorandum for the record on the substance of the call.

In fact, when Wing and Tyler made contact with the DEA, still nobody thought the matter worthy of a memorandum, according to their sworn statements. But these explanations were found by investigators to be "totally unsatisfactory and an effort to sidestep the truth."

The testimony of all Government officials was found to result "in the misleading and deceiving of Senators as to the heroin inquiry and how and why it failed." The testimony had "numerous inconsistencies" and "officials contradicted one another as well as themselves." Mike Reilly's "credibility was stretched" on several occasions, and on some points he "either did not make himself clear or he deliberately wished to convey a false impression to this Subcommittee." Peter Grant, the Secret Service agent from the White House, displayed a memory that was "vague and cloudy and very general and imprecise" on key issues.

Equally frustrating was that J. Fred Buzhardt, the White House lawyer with whom Peroff claimed he had spoken twice, refused to testify, claiming executive privilege. And the Royal Canadian

Mounted Police could not be made to come forth with their own memories and documents and tapes of the Peroff case.

Perhaps the most outrageous aspect of the hearings, in the view of Senate investigators, was the lack of adequate records provided by the DEA, the Secret Service and the U. S. Attorney's Office..

> Concerning several key aspects of the heroin inquiry, for example, officials said that no records were kept at all. As for the alleged role of Vesco and LeBlanc in the heroin scheme, not a single memorandum, report or communication was ever turned over to the Subcommittee about this development. Indeed, DEA officials testified that no such reports were ever written, an omission in violation of DEA's own regulations.

> The staff finds that the government was blatantly negligent in its responsibilities if, indeed, no records were kept on the Vesco-LeBlanc lead. In turn, the staff finds that a more reasonable explanation is that records were kept but that government officials have either destroyed them or deliberately withheld them from this Subcommittee.

Not only were reports missing but also the tapes which Peroff had given over to various DEA agents along the way. The only tapes available were the ones which he himself had kept until the end.

The Senate investigators wondered why no agent had been disciplined for failure to keep records of the Vesco development. They found it "unfair and difficult to believe" that the only agent to be punished had been Luis Cruz in Puerto Rico. His crime was that when Peroff was leaving for New York, he had paid fifty dollars for Peroff's television set!

Yet both Reilly and Gibson had been "negligent" in the more serious area of keeping reports:

> In this instance, agents were dealing with an allegation of some consequence: Robert Vesco, a major contributor to the Nixon reelection campaign, a world-famous financier, a fugitive from justice who was the target of extradition efforts, was allegedly involved in a heroin scheme. The staff finds it most unlikely that neither Gibson nor Reilly nor anyone else in government, who knew about the allegations, ever bothered to commit it to writing. Surely a reprimand is in order.

Sifting through their findings, Senate investigators concluded that the assertion that Bouchard had been lying to Peroff about Vesco and LeBlanc was "undocumented and unsubstantiated." At the same time, the staff was forced to focus not upon whether Vesco actually intended to sponsor the heroin deal but upon the behavior of the agents. It was found that the Vesco lead "should have been pursued in a more professional fashion, and this pursuit should have been carefully recorded and documented as the leads and crucial decisions were made." But once Vesco's and LeBlanc's names came into the picture, federal authorities had, "by their unprofessional behavior, foiled their own investigation."

With almost palpable disgust, the Committee staff admitted that "the whole truth in the investigation has not been found." There was glaring evidence of "incompetence" and "unprofessionalism" following the Vesco development, but no "hard" proof to show that the failure of the case had been deliberate and designed.

If a coverup had taken place, it had worked.

During the month of June, Frank Peroff often brooded up in his bedroom in the Maryland house while the ever-present marshals sat downstairs, reading and listening to a portable radio. Peroff wondered what to make of his future. His three children had been out of school for more than a year. Could they continue their education in the fall? Or should the family pick up and go elsewhere under a new name? With what sort of income? Peroff brooded and thought of a thousand schemes for making something—anything —happen to move his situation off center.

Almost every day he would call the Senate Committee's staff to ask if there might be some new development in their investigation. Most of the time, the answer was no. But then something dramatic took place, almost overnight. A reporter from California, David Harris of *Rolling Stone,* came to Phil Manuel's office asking if he might have an interview with Frank Peroff. Although Peroff declined, preferring to let the investigators proceed without interference, the reporter's visit produced an unexpected result.

Manuel and Gallinaro listened as Harris outlined some information he had obtained. Two former agents from the Bureau of Narcotics and Dangerous Drugs (BNDD) were claiming that they had been on Robert Vesco's payroll while they were working for the

U. S. Government! Their secret activities for Vesco had been carried out in the summer of 1972, fully a year before Peroff's narcotics case! If the information was true, then Vesco had infiltrated the same federal agency (now the DEA) at least a year prior to Peroff's accusations!

It seemed incredible. Until now Peroff had never believed, down deep, that there had been a true connection between Vesco and federal drug agents. All he had wanted was an explanation of what had happened. Yet now he was being told that his own allegations had led Senate investigators into completely new territory, and the advice to him was: "Hang on, Frank, be patient. This whole thing is bigger than we ever suspected!"

In mid-July, Senator Jackson himself issued a press release on the new development. He announced that a public hearing would be held "into information developed by Senate investigators that Federal agents were employed by a self-described 'friend' of Robert Vesco in June, 1972, to search Vesco's home and office for hidden bugging devices." The press handout might have added that the narcotics agents had done their work for Vesco *while he was under investigation by another federal agency,* the Securities and Exchange Commission. Such were the reaches of corruption in government; one hand trying to probe into Vesco's affairs and the other hand working to protect him!

The initial information provided by David Harris turned out to be true. The two former BNDD agents had flown secretly from Los Angeles to New Jersey, where Vesco then lived, and they electronically swept Vesco's home and office to see if his phone was tapped. The agents were paid by the "friend" of Vesco through their superior at the BNDD's Los Angeles office.

Two nights before the public hearing, a well-dressed man sneaked into the Old Senate Office Building and attempted to break into the Jackson Committee's offices. A secretary working alone, transcribing notes for the hearing, was all set to leave by eight o'clock when she heard a scratching at the door. Assuming it was one of the committee members trying to get in with a key, she opened the door. The well-dressed burglar was bent over, trying to pick the lock. The secretary screamed, and the burglar jumped into the air from fright and ran down the hall, escaping.

* * *

At the hearing, Vesco's friend testified that he had arranged for the drug agents to search Vesco's home for hidden bugging devices. He told Senators that Vesco had paid him $3,000 in gambling chips at a Bahamian casino. The agents, however, pleaded the Fifth Amendment.

Peroff read the news with increasing sense of wonder and loss of direction. How should he think of this development? The Senate committee was now "reopening" its investigation even before it had closed it out; the staff—Manuel and Gallinaro—was tracking down new leads all over the country and beyond; and what did it all mean, in terms of how long he would have to wait for some final verdict?

Toward the end of July, there were reports that Senate investigators had uncovered even more intriguing information about Vesco. The Associated Press sent out a story that "weapons and call girls" had been smuggled from the States to the fugitive financier's hideaway in Costa Rica. The weapons were described as "enough for a small army"—as many as two thousand machine guns, one source estimated—and they had been flown secretly to Vesco by the same "friend" who had arranged the electronic debugging.

One thing was becoming clear to the Senate investigators who were developing this new portrait of Vesco's activities: if their work led ultimately to the financier's extradition and prosecution, they could give a great deal of credit, indirectly, to Frank Peroff. Without his persistence in getting to them with his own story, none of these succeeding developments would have been taking place.

At the same time, the Justice Department was engaged in what Peroff regarded as an act of vengeance against him. As the publicity mounted, so did the Department's threats to remove its federal marshals from protecting him. At last, when the protection was definitely scheduled to end, Peroff filed suit in federal court to force Justice to keep the marshals on duty until it provided him and his family with a new identity and the necessary redocumentation papers. Senator Jackson helped by sending a personal letter

312

to Attorney General William Saxbe, requesting not only redocumentation but relocation for the Peroffs, who now feared for their lives all over again.

As if his uncertainties were not enough already, Peroff faced still another lonely ordeal when he was told by doctors in Maryland that he faced major surgery. Peroff sat down at a typewriter in his home and wrote lengthy separate letters to President Nixon; Attorney General Saxbe; William Lynch, chief of organized crime for the Justice Department; Special Prosecutor Leon Jaworski; and, last but perhaps more important than the others, U. S. Attorney John Wing. The letters were, literally, attempts by Peroff to make sure that his side of the story would be communicated even if he were to die in the near future.

To the President, he wrote that "while I am not an ardent supporter of yours, the events that occurred . . . were not politically motivated, especially on my part." He told Nixon that his "foremost desire" was for his family and himself to "soon begin to live a normal life."

"The Senate investigation," he wrote, "which is still progressing, has borne out my allegations; although the reasons for various acts and exactly who made the decisions are as yet unclear." As a result of his efforts, Peroff continued, "in trying to make those responsible for these acts accountable, certain officials in the Department of Justice have felt it necessary to engage in a vendetta against me and my family. They have finally decided to punish me, for a crime of trying to do the right thing, by forcing me and my family to live a life, which was endangered by their own hands, in a manner that is not only contrary to the normal protective procedures but in fact subjects me and my family to live not only in fear but in fact increases the chances for attempts on our lives tenfold. I know these men have the role as prosecutors, but I didn't know they were the executioners as well."

"My reasons for writing at this time," Peroff's letter to the President went on, "are that I am about to undergo major surgery and that I might not be around to help my wife and children stay alive."

Peroff continued: "Mr. President, I ask that you consider this letter as a plea that you might receive from a condemned man. . . .

I am not ashamed of what I have done, nor am I sorry. I am ready to go on fighting as long as I am able to do so. I feel that in time, all persons responsible for all the events that have taken place will be brought to an accounting."

Peroff's letter to Saxbe referred to the Attorney General's recent statement that "there will be no more dirty tricks" and suggested that "there is a whopper of a dirty trick going on right under your nose," meaning that the Justice Department was refusing to protect his family any longer.

His statement to Special Prosecutor Jaworski was far more specific. He referred to recent news of "absolute proof that Robert Vesco, immediately following his contribution to the President's [1972] campaign, had federal narcotics agents on his payroll for a variety of reasons. In addition, it appears that they in fact assisted him in criminal ventures. . . . It also appears that the trail left behind these actions could, indeed, lead to the White House."

At last came the letter to John Wing. "It has been a little more than a year since we spoke last," Peroff began with considerable irony. "As you know, quite a lot has happened since that time. . . . I spoke to you at the most crucial moment of the entire heroin case, a time when any positive action would have either proved or disproved whether Robert Vesco was indeed the money man. After I spoke to you, I believed that I had accomplished my objective, which was to force a sit-down of the parties concerned. Instead I never heard from you again—and you are aware of what has followed. There is no question, in my mind, that had I made the trip to Costa Rica, this case would have been successfully concluded; or, at the very least, we would have answered the question of whether Robert Vesco was involved. . . . In addition, when I spoke to you I made you aware of a telephone call which I was to receive from Costa Rica. Had law-enforcement officials monitored that call, possible identification of the caller might have established whether or not Mr. Vesco was behind the scenes."

"It's possible," Peroff wrote near the end of his letter, "that some day the whole story might come out. But whether it does or doesn't, I feel that I have done the right thing. In fact, I believe the only mistake I made was not going to the Senate while there was still a chance of saving the situation. I now believe that the case would have proceeded, had I done so."

Peroff ended his letter to Wing with a reference to the day they were supposedly going to meet, when the detectives abruptly came to the Hilton Inn and took him to jail.

"As far as you are concerned, Mr. Wing, I only wish we had kept our tentative Sunday meeting, instead of the one I did keep. I'm sure your office would have been more comfortable than the cell I was in. I will, however, admit it was one hell of an experience."

Recovery from his operation was fast. Frank Peroff's outlook on life had changed considerably; his will to make a new existence for himself and his family had gained in terms of hope; and his physical health returned so rapidly that he was able to go back home after only two weeks. Now the marshals were gone and the Peroffs had a new last name and documents for the identity change. Soon they moved out of the United States to try to put their lives back together.

In October, 1974, it was revealed that the new president of Costa Rica had accused the Nixon Administration of having been "less than sincere" in its efforts to return Vesco to the United States. President Daniel Oduber stated publicly that the efforts had "seemed aimed at the extradition failing, just as it did."

One incredible fact that came to light was that the lawyer who had represented the U. S. in its extradition effort, Cecil Wallace-Whitfield, was an associate of Robert Vesco and Norman LeBlanc.

One could only wonder whether Vesco's extremely delicate political relationship with the Nixon Administration had been the real reason for the foiling of Peroff's heroin case, which could have achieved extradition. When Oduber's comments were made public, Senator Henry Jackson asked aloud, "Did the U. S. Government wish to keep Vesco out of this country for some reason? Did he have some special information which he could supply to explain, in part, the national nightmare we have just lived through?" As one of the Senate investigators said, "More than any single person, Vesco has information which, if he talked, would make Watergate look like a picnic."

How else explain the personal nightmare of Frank Peroff?